Caritas Pirckheimer:
*A Journal of the Reformation Years
1524–1528*

Library of Medieval Women　　　　　　　　　**ISSN 1369–9652**

Series Editor: Jane Chance

The Library of Medieval Women aims to make available, in an English translation, significant works by, for, and about medieval women, from the age of the Church Fathers to the fifteenth century. The series encompasses many forms of writing, from poetry, visions, biography and autobiography, and letters to sermons, treatises and encyclopedias; the subject matter is equally diverse: theology and mysticism, classical mythology, medicine and science, history, hagiography, and instructions for anchoresses. Each text is presented with an introduction setting the material in context, a guide to further reading, and an interpretive essay.

We welcome suggestions for future titles in the series. Proposals or queries may be sent directly to the editor or publisher at the addresses given below; all submissions will receive prompt and informed consideration.

Professor Jane Chance, Department of English, MS 30, Rice University, PO Box 1892, Houston, TX 77251–1892, USA. E-mail: jchance@rice.edu

Boydell & Brewer Ltd, PO Box 9, Woodbridge, Suffolk, IP12 3DF, UK. E-mail: boydell@boydell.co.uk. Website: www.boydellandbrewer.com

Previously published titles in this series appear at the back of this book

Caritas Pirckheimer:
A Journal of the Reformation Years 1524–1528

Translated from the German
with Introduction, Notes and Interpretive Essay

† Paul A. MacKenzie

D.S. BREWER

First published 2006
D. S. Brewer, Cambridge

ISBN 1 84384 076 6

D. S. Brewer is an imprint of Boydell & Brewer Ltd
PO Box 9, Woodbridge, Suffolk IP12 3DF, UK
and of Boydell & Brewer Inc.
668 Mt Hope Avenue, Rochester, NY 14620, USA,
website: www.boydellandbrewer.com

A catalogue record for this book is available
from the British Library

This publication is printed on acid-free paper

Printed in Great Britain by
MPG Books Ltd, Bodmin, Cornwall

Contents

Acknowledgments

The journal of Caritas Pirckheimer is a text that deserves to be known more widely than it has been up to now. Thanks to Paul A. MacKenzie, that will now be possible. Unfortunately, he did not live long enough to shepherd his book through production. We are fortunate that his wife, Christine MacKenzie, who recognized the importance of Caritas's text, agreed to take Professor MacKenzie's place in ensuring that the manuscript would be prepared, proofs read, and an index compiled to facilitate its production.

Additionally, this project could not have been finished without the help of the secretary of the Language Department at Lycoming College, Lorri Amrom, whose dedication to the project and the typing of the manuscript resulted in the final text. Support from friends and colleagues in the Language Department – especially Garett Heysel for technical assistance, indexing and effort – enabled Christine MacKenzie to see the book to completion. Thanks also go to Lycoming College staff, especially Janet Hurlbert, for her aid in obtaining Interlibrary Loan materials.

Dedicated to his teaching and research, Paul A. MacKenzie always treasured the support of the entire college community as well as (and most especially) that of his family – Christine, his stepson Matthew, and his daughters Kate and Annah.

Christine MacKenzie is grateful to Jane Chance, the editor of the series, and Caroline Palmer, editor of the press, for their support, patience, and encouragement, both to Paul during the writing process and afterwards to her during manuscript preparation and the production of the book.

Jane Chance
Christine MacKenzie
August 2005

Introduction:
The Life and Times of Caritas Pirckheimer of Nürnberg

When Caritas Pirckheimer, abbess of the Nürnberg cloister of St. Clare's, died in 1532, her obituary in the cloister's *Totenbüchlein* included the simple words "a mirror of all piety and learning and a lover of all virtues."[1] The unique role that she played in defending her cloister and her faith during the period when the Reformation was formally accepted by the City Council of Nürnberg in 1525, however, remained largely unappreciated and unknown until the Bamberg archivist Constantin Höfler first published the manuscript of her personal account of that time in 1852, giving it the curious title of *Denkwürdigkeiten* (things worth thinking about).[2] There has never been a complete English translation of this important document.[3] The title *A Journal of the Reformation Years 1524–1528* seemed more appropriate and accurate than a literal translation of Höfler's vague and arcane title.

Barbara[4] Pirckheimer was born on 21 March 1467 in Eichstatt, Germany, the daughter of Dr. Hans Pirckheimer who, like his son and grandsons after him, studied in Italy, eventually earning a doctorate in Padua, Italy. Since Hans was in the service of the Archbishop of Eichstatt, the family lived in that city, although their ties to Nürnberg remained strong. The earliest mention of the family in Nürnberg dates from 1359. Barbara was the first of twelve children born into this

---

1 Staatsarchiv, Reichsstadt Nürnberg, Kloster St. Klara, Akten und Bände, Rep. 5a, no. 4, prod. 24, *Totenbüchlein Anna Ketzel*, fols. 13v–14r.
2 The complete title was *Der hochberühmten Charitas Pirckheimer, Äbtissin von S. Clara zu Nürnberg, Denkwürdigkeiten aus dem Reformationszeitalter*. Contrary to Höfler's assertion, however, Caritas Pirckheimer was far from being "famous" (*hochberühmt*). It was not until 1961, when Josef Pfanner's critical editions of her letters and the *Denkwürdigkeiten* appeared, that Caritas's importance began to be examined.
3 Francis Mannhardt's translation, *An Heroic Abbess of Reformation Days: The Memoirs of Mother Charitas Pirckheimer, Poor Clare, of Nuremberg* (St. Louis: Central Bureau, CCV of A, 1930) is incomplete and, in addition to its rather dated language, lacks any critical apparatus, which is necessary in order to explain the historical background and significance of the work.
4 Both her mother and paternal grandmother were also named Barbara. As was the custom, she received a new name, Caritas, when she joined St. Clare's.

well-to-do patrician family. Her brother Willibald (1470–1530) was born on 5 December 1470 and was to become the foremost representative of humanism in Germany, a leading figure in Nürnberg's Renaissance and Albrecht Dürer's best friend.[5] Two Pirckheimer children died young. Seven of Barbara's eight sisters were to follow her example and take the veil. Her other sister, Juliane, married Martin Geuder, a high-ranking civic official. Thus the Pirckheimer women followed the two most common "options" for females at that time, marriage and the Church.

Why did Caritas Pirckheimer become a nun? As a child she enjoyed a rather sheltered and care-free life. When Hans Pirckheimer accepted a position as councilor to Duke Albrecht IV of Bavaria, the family moved to Munich. Hans undertook the teaching of his son Willibald himself and, significantly, his daughter Barbara also was permitted to participate. When she was twelve, she was sent to St. Clare's in Nürnberg in order to further her education. In addition to her father's tutoring, she had received instruction in Latin from her aunt and was well-prepared for the convent school. The convent school had earned a reputation for excellence, and the cloister, which had undergone reform not many years earlier, practiced strict observance of the Rule.[6] Also, its library was outstanding, no small consideration for a family as dedicated to learning as the Pirckheimers. In short, it was the perfect "match" for the young woman. Unfortunately, we have no documentation to indicate why Caritas chose the life of a nun rather than marriage. The decision may not have been hers, but her father's. Each novice was expected to bring a "dowry" of sorts for the convent. Perhaps 10 gulden was the customary amount. This was probably less than the dowry a future husband might desire.

---

[5] Albrecht Dürer was Germany's greatest late-medieval artist. His painting, woodcuts, etchings, etc. enable us to visualize his era. Dürer's house in Nürnberg has been carefully restored.

[6] The "Rule" consisted of written by-laws, including religious duties, along with the timetable of when they were to be performed. In short, it listed the beliefs and customs of the order. In the fifteenth century there were many attempts to reform the monasteries. Many had become very lax in observing the stated rules and customs of their order. Many abuses of the oath to practice poverty, chastity and obedience were cited. Although some reforms were made, obviously enough abuses remained for the proponents of the "new faith," i.e., Lutheranism, to use them in their attacks on the "old faith" when the Reformation began. One of the most glaring abuses was the relationship between some nuns and priests (or monks).Wood cuts and printed broadsheets show them having sexual intercourse.

Much has been written about the piety of the population of Nürnberg in the late fifteenth and early sixteenth centuries.[7] This was demonstrated in a range of areas, from institutional reform, such as that of St. Clare's, to artistic patronage during the Franconian capital's golden age, for example of Veit Stoss's "Annunciation."[8] A list of the artists active in Nurnberg at this time reads like a veritable "Who's Who?" of fifteenth and sixteenth century German art.[9] The Pirckheimer family practiced this aspect of Nürnberg life. After his wife died in 1488, Hans Pirckheimer moved to Nürnberg. In his house opposite the Schöner Brunnen (Beautiful Fountain) he established a large library and, in his capacity as a lawyer, served the community with great dedication. Near the end of his life he entered the Franciscan monastery and died there on 3 May 1501. Thus, it is abundantly clear that Caritas Pirckheimer came from a very devout family in which the obligation to serve God and the community was felt most sincerely.

According to a ruling by the City Council, only daughters of patricians were allowed to enter St. Clare's. Because she was under age, Barbara Pirckheimer petitioned the Franciscan provincial authority for permission to enter the convent early. On account of her striking competency in Latin, her request was granted, and she joined the order at sixteen, receiving the name Caritas. After completing her novitiate, Caritas was assigned the position of head of the girls' school. This was the first step in her exemplary career, which was to culminate in her being unanimously elected abbess at Christmas time 1503, a position she held until her death in 1532.[10] Later Caritas's sister Clara also

7 Gerald Strauss notes, however, that according to the 1449 census Nürnberg counted only 446 clerics for a population of over 20,000. There were, nevertheless, several houses of worship. The two parish churches were St. Sebald and St. Lorenz. Other major churches included St. Aegidius, St. Jacob, Heilig Geist Spital, St. Martha, the Church of Our Lady (Frauenkirche), eight monasteries (Benedictines, Carthusians, Minorite friars, Dominicans, Carmelites, Augustinians, the Order of the Knights of St. John, and the Johannites). There were also two convents, St. Clare's and St. Catherine's. Gerald Strauss, *Nuremberg in the Sixteenth Century*, rev. ed. (Bloomington: Indiana University Press, 1976), pp. 155–158.

8 For a detailed account see Paul A. MacKenzie, "Piety and Patronage: Aspects of Nürnberg Cultural and Religious Life 1477–1526. Anton (II) Tucher and Veit Stoss," *Forum for Modern Language Studies* 49 (1993), 46–61.

9 An excellent source book for this period is Jeffrey Chipps Smith, *Nürnberg: A Renaissance City, 1500–1618* (Austin: University of Texas Press, 1983).

10 Electing their own abbess was an example of democracy within the cloister; however, one could search in vain for any signs of democracy in Nürenberg. The city was governed by the patrician class.

became abbess, as did her niece Catherine (Willibald's daughter), who was the very last abbess the cloister was to have.

It is interesting to note that when her brother Willibald learned that she had been elected abbess, he wrote to her (in Latin) saying that he was unsure whether he should congratulate or console her. He shows he is aware of the great burden on her shoulders as well as the dangers yet to come. He advises her to submit to higher authority and asks that God grant her wisdom and love, something which she gives ample evidence of in her journal. In addition, he urges her to be grateful for whatever befalls her. What began as an attempt at humor ends up as a very serious letter in which he evokes the example of Mary Magdalen, who chose to devote her life to serving the Lord. Ending with the motto "Sic itur ad astra" (In this way we reach the stars), Willibald's letter reflects the strong faith which both he and Caritas shared.[11]

Twenty-five years later the sisters of St. Clare's[12] celebrated Caritas's jubilee. Willibald's daughter Catherine, also a member of the convent, wrote to her father and described the celebration. He had supplied a barrel of wine along with his silverware. There was plenty of good food (including white bread and cake!) in addition to the wine, and even dancing.[13] This merry-making, however, made a sharp contrast with everyday life in the cloister. The *Journal* shows that in 1528 morale in the cloister was almost at its lowest ebb due to the changes brought about by the Reformation. The pressure from the City Council was unrelenting. Later Caritas's health began to fail. After another four years, on 19 August 1532, Caritas died. On 10 August 1959, her grave was discovered and later her remains and her tombstone were removed and placed in the floor of St. Clare's to the right of the front altar.[14]

Caritas attained a reputation as one of the most learned women of her time as a result of her study of the classics, the Church Fathers, the Bible and other works that often were made available to her by her brother Willibald, an avid bibliophile and translator with whom she carried on a life-long correspondence. Her letters (often in Latin) reflect the extent to which she devoted herself to the pursuit of knowledge, while at the same time performing her many duties as abbess of St. Clare's.

---

[11] Josef Pfanner, ed., *Caritas Pirckheimer, Quellensammlung, 3. Heft. Briefe 1499–1530* (Landshut: Solanus Druck, 1961), p. 36.

[12] At this time they numbered approximately sixty.

[13] Pfanner, p. 151.

[14] In November 1961 the Archbishop of Bamberg established a commission to resume the efforts first begun in 1932, but thwarted on account of World War II, to gather documentation for the purpose of her canonization.

Erasmus held her up as an example of Germany's most learned women, likening her to England's Margaret More Roper, the daughter of Thomas More. Caritas corresponded with her friend, the Nürnberg humanist Sixtus Tucher, for several years. Although it does not appear that she authored any original compositions or interpretations of works that she had read, one can see the depth of her interests and which classical works she read and loved. Her correspondence with Conrad Celtis, one of Germany's leading intellectuals, provides an excellent example of how she achieved her reputation for learning. Celtis, the Poet Laureate, may have been exaggerating when he called her the German Sappho,[15] but when he sent her a copy of his newly discovered works of Hrotswitha von Gandersheim,[16] it showed his respect for her intellect. Caritas, however, attempted to make it clear to Celtis that any literary activity on her part would only be in the service of God, with the Scriptures as a starting point. This was a limitation to which he did not really want to submit. He also dedicated his poem "Norembergia" to her, and again, in her letter of thanks, she attempts to persuade the poet that he would be better served by leaving secular subjects and turning his attention to the Scriptures. Later Celtis sent her a copy of his *Amores*, a work whose erotic subject matter, however, seems hardly appropriate for a nun.[17]

It is fascinating to note that Caritas often belittles her own scholarly gifts and tries to assume the role of a simple, ignorant woman. This is something she was to do later in her correspondence with the City Council and with Kaspar Nützel, but her quick intelligence almost always breaks out, and she does not hesitate to express her opinion. Such self-effacing behavior tended to be rather formulaic. Typically, the only way a woman could be considered "worthy" of engaging in an intellectual discussion (usually epistolary, especially in the case of nuns), was on account of her piety and chastity, which elevated her to the intellectual level of males for this purpose. If it were not for her reminding her reader of the limitations of her intelligence, it would be

15 Caritas does not seem to have written any poetry. If she did, none of it has survived.
16 Hrotswitha von Gandersheim (935 to after 1000), a nun in the cloister at Gandersheim, wrote several dramas in Latin. The rumor persists, however, that the plays were forgeries. In the series Library of Medieval Women, note the book by Katharina M. Wilson, *Hrotswitha von Gandersheim: A Florilegium of her Works* (Cambridge, UK: D. S. Brewer, 1998)
17 See Stephen L. Wailes, "The Literary Relationship of Conrad Celtis and Caritas Pirckheimer," *Daphnis* 17 (1988), 434–435.

extremely difficult to determine whether the writer was male or female. Needless to say, she proved to be more than equal to any male who attempted to persuade her to compromise any of the positions on which her faith was based. Neither Osiander, Wenzel Linck, nor Melanchthon, to name some of the most important preachers and theologians, was successful in his efforts to convince her to accept the "new teachings" of Lutheranism, renounce her vows and leave the convent.

Caritas and Christoph Scheurl, a well-known councilor and former Professor of Theology at Wittenberg, exchanged many letters. In 1506, he dedicated his work *Die Früchte der Messe* (The Fruits of the Mass) to her. Later, in 1515, he published the correspondence of his uncle Sixtus Tucher with Caritas and Apollonia Tucher between 1498 and 1506 as *Viertzig Sendbriefe* (Forty Letters). This was a "typical" humanistic discussion on matters of religious and moral concern.

As important as her correspondence with her contemporaries was in establishing her reputation as a learned woman, it pales in comparison to the significance of her journal, in which she paints a vivid picture of the very stressful times which befell St. Clare's. This document depicts the time when the Reformation was formally accepted by the City Council, as a result of which the pressure on the convent, its residents and especially its abbess increased almost daily. Caritas Pirckheimer refused to renounce her vows and leave the convent, despite considerable pressure from City Council to do so. Three nuns are forcibly removed by their mothers in one of the most dramatic parts of the *Journal*. Only one nun chose to leave of her own accord. Interestingly, the question arises as to why no fathers participated in "liberating" their daughters, especially since the Biblical principal "Honor thy father and mother" was frequently employed as a valid reason why a nun should leave the convent. One is forced to conclude that the fathers were "too busy," or that participation in such an activity was "below" their rank and unsuitable for a male.

Merry E. Wiesner, one of the foremost scholars of this period, has described women's responses to the Reformation as follows:

> Women were not simply passive recipients of the Reformation message, but left convents, refused to leave convents, preached, prophesied, discussed religion with friends and family, converted their husbands, left their husbands, wrote religious poems, hymns, and polemics, and were martyred on all sides of the religious controversy.[18]

---

[18] "Beyond Women and the Family: Towards a Gender Analysis of the Reformation," *The Sixteenth Century Journal* 18 (1987), 313–314.

Sister Jeanne de Jussie, a nun in the order of St. Clare from Geneva, Switzerland, offers a fascinating parallel to Caritas Pirckheimer in that, like Caritas, she defied the local authorities and left an account of her experiences as a loyal Catholic from 1526 to 1535. Unlike Caritas, however, she departed from Geneva and relocated in Annecy, France, where she later became abbess.[19]

Caritas was no Hildegard von Bingen and left no original works in which she celebrates her religious experience as beautifully as her fellow-nun from the Rhineland. Nor did she ever entertain the idea of becoming an activist like Argula von Grumbach, for example, and engage in a public theological debate. However, she was by no means a passive recipient of the Reformation. She refused to leave the convent, and yet she managed to defend her faith. The most vivid testament of that faith is without question her journal, a collection of commentaries and letters written by her and to her, and which she ordered be copied and collected as a historical record of the cloister's struggle to survive.

The *Journal* consists of 69 "chapters" which deal with the cloister's involvement with the Nürnberg City Council's efforts essentially to force it to accept the religious reforms of Lutheranism.[20] It details the "Religionsgespräch" (religious discussion) that had been held by the City Council from 3 to 14 March 1524, and the formal acceptance of the Reformation by the city fathers. Ostensibly, this gathering served the purpose of discussing or debating a dozen statements dealing with how one would achieve salvation. Representing the "new faith" were twelve highly respected Nürnbergers. The "old faith," however, had far less than twelve representatives. In truth, it was a big charade. The outcome was assured for the "new faith." The Catholic members of the group realized early that they would lose and stopped coming after a few sessions. Consequently, considerable pressure was brought to bear on all the monasteries, and the only monastery that remained was that of the Franciscans. All the others accepted the "new doctrine" and effectively closed.

After St. Catherine's followed the example of the other monasteries and was dissolved, only St. Clare's convent remained open. Those members of the monasteries who chose to remain were typically "pensioned off," while others either became Lutheran preachers or

19 Margaret L. King, *Women of the Renaissance* (Chicago and London: The University Press, 1991), pp. 99–100.
20 For reasons of space I have not included the short summaries of each chapter which are given in most German editions. These are not Caritas's words and thus nothing that she included in the *Journal* has been sacrificed.

simply left the order. Nürnburg as a "free," imperial city enjoyed the advantage of owing allegiance solely to the Emperor. When the city became Lutheran, however, it was forced to walk a precarious and religious tightrope since the Emperor had not accepted Lutheranism and the city did not want to lose the privileges it had enjoyed, many of which allowed the city to grow into a great center of commerce.

The *Journal* documents the period from the spring of 1524 until December of 1528. The last entry is dated 4 December 1528. The cloister had always held a special position in the city, since it was only open to Nürnberg women, and many daughters from the foremost families of the city served in the order. The City Council planned to replace the Franciscans who had been the preachers and confessors to St. Clare's with different preachers who were proponents of the "new doctrine" of Lutheranism. What was probably imagined as a rather simple matter of persuading the nuns to accept the new scheme turned out to be more complicated and problematical than anticipated. Caritas Pirckheimer proved to be a thorn in the side of the City Council. She did not yield to the pressure that was exerted on the convent and showed remarkable courage and determination in defending her sisters' rights to continue to practice their faith as they felt they were entitled to, having made oaths to God alone and not to men. This was a position of independence that was, after all, not so very far removed from some of the fundamental tenets of the new Protestant faith, although it was often clothed in theological language which served to obfuscate the issues rather than highlight their similarities.

The efforts of Kaspar Nützel, the superintendent of St. Clare's who was also a respected member of the City Council and served as its liaison to the convent, to persuade Caritas and her sisters to voluntarily accept the City Council's plans, proved unsuccessful. The 111 sermons from preachers such as Osiander proved fruitless. What we might even call an early attempt at "brain-washing" failed completely. The sisters were not used to such long-winded, dogmatic sermons (some of which lasted for hours) and only sat through them because they were forced to. Neither Caritas nor the other nuns granted their "undivided attention" to them. Indeed, among the "captive audience" they became the object of humor rather than serious discussion, since the sisters could hardly wait for them to be over. Caritas adamantly insisted on choosing their own confessors, instead of those proposed by the City Council, but was unsuccessful in persuading the City Council.

On Good Friday 1525, priests were forbidden to say mass at the convent, and on the Eve of Ascension Day the City Council's order that the new rule be accepted went into effect. The cloister was not closed, however, but no novices could be accepted, so that the convent would eventually "die out." This is what happened. The most important events described in the *Journal* include the forced removal of three nuns against their will (Chapters 33–34), where the sense of impending doom, possible mob violence and the destruction of the cloister itself make for high drama; Melanchthon's visit (Chapters 46–50) at the end of November 1525, which proved to have a surprisingly positive influence when he recommended to the City Council that they allow the convent to continue to exist; the visitation of the cloister by city councilors in November 1527; Anna Schwarz's decision to leave of her own accord; and the final chapters, which describe the efforts of the cloister to deal with the problem of taxes. It is worth noting that Caritas's last words towards the council were an appeal for God's mercy towards the council and for God's Grace towards her cloister, a sign that her faith remained strong even to the end.

The *Journal* begins in 1524, with a pessimism stemming from a time of great turmoil and prophecies of doom. The Peasants' War had brought about considerable acts of violence, torture, execution and death, and the citizens of Nürnberg had every right to fear that the city might not escape unscathed. With the acceptance of Lutheranism by the City Council in 1524, the fears expressed in the early pages of the *Journal* were largely justified. This dark undercurrent serves to warn of the imminent end of a once glorious and proud era, and this pervades the entire document. Caritas recognized the significance and importance of these years and had these memoirs recorded for posterity. Many of the chapters duplicate letters which can be found elsewhere in her works. The *Journal* thus represents her attempt to offer a history of the period when she defended the cloister in the face of a major attempt to close it and force the members to renounce their vows and accept the doctrine of Lutheranism. This was something which neither she nor her fellow-sisters (with but one exception, Anna Schwarz) agreed to do. It will be shown in the interpretive essay to what extent the relationship between Caritas and Kaspar Nützel grew to reflect a surprising degree of tolerance, respect, and love, despite the growing impatience of the City Council in its efforts to bring a conclusion to what must have seemed a long, dragged-on process. Caritas's occasional displays of humor serve as a welcome contrast to the sometimes dogmatic efforts (as in the case of Wenzel Linck) to use complex theological arguments to wear down her perseverance.

A note about the original manuscripts

There are four manuscripts of the work in the Staatsarchiv Nürnberg: Codices A, B C and D. Codex D is the oldest and Codices B and C are based upon it. Codex A is a pure copy of D. Codex B and Codex C are by different hands. Codex C was probably copied by P. Christianus Koppius, who was the father-confessor of the Bamberg cloister ca. 1628. It contains a list of abbesses of the Nürnberg cloister and their dates of service. Four different hands have been identified. Unfortunately they are also designated A, B, C and D, which tends to obfuscate matters a bit. A fifth hand, E, might be that of Caritas herself, since it appears in marginal notes, corrections and additions.[21] After the Nürnberg cloister had "died out" the manuscript was taken to the cloister of St. Clare in Bamberg. Eventually Codices A–D were returned to Nürnberg and kept in the Staatsarchiv, where they remain today.

---

[21] An excellent discussion of the manuscripts and the different hands can be found in Frumentius Renner, ed., *Die Denkwürdigkeiten der Äbtissin Caritas Pirckheimer* (St. Ottilien: EOS Verlag, 1982), pp. 164–170.

A Journal of the Reformation Years 1524–1528

Caritas Pirckheimer

Chapter 1

What follows are descriptions of some of the things that happened to our cloister here at Saint Clare's in Nürnberg in those dangerous, rebellious times, along with some letters written at the same time.[1]

We all know that for a very long time it has been prophesied that in the year of our Lord 1524 a great deluge[2] is to occur by which everything on earth will be twisted and changed. And, although this has generally been understood as a flood, experience has taught us that the stars did not indicate water as much as misery, fear and distress, and later, bloodshed. In the year noted above it happened that many things were changed by the new teachings of the Lutherans and much dissension befell the Christian faith. The ceremonies of the Church have been done away with in many instances and the clerical class has been almost completely destroyed in many areas. At that time Christian freedom was being preached as well as the idea that the laws of the Church and even the oaths of religious orders were invalid and no one was obligated to keep them.

And so it happened that many nuns and monks made use of such freedom and ran away from their cloisters and threw off their robes and habits; some married and did whatever they wanted. From this we suffered much distress and affliction. During the day many of the powerful as well as simple people came to their relatives who resided in our cloister. They preached to them and spoke of the new teachings and argued incessantly that the cloistered were damned and subject to temp-

---

[1]   This introductory note occurs on the first page of manuscript D only. The collection was obviously compiled shortly after the dates given.

[2]   The same fear is expressed by Felizitas Grundherr, a nun at St. Clare's, in a letter to her father written in July 1524. See Josef Pfanner, ed., *Caritas Pirckheimer Quellensammlung*, Vol. 3. *Briefe 1498–1530* (Landshut: Solanus Druck, 1966), pp. 249–250.

tations and that it was not possible for them to attain salvation there. We were all damned.[3] Therefore, some wanted to remove their children, sisters and aunts from the cloister by force and with many threats and also with many promises half of which, without doubt, they could hardly keep.

This fighting and quarreling lasted a long time, often with great anger and foul language. Since, however, by God's grace no sister could be persuaded, the Franciscan friars were then blamed and everyone claimed that since they had instructed us it would, therefore, be impossible to convert us to the new teaching as long as we had them as preachers and confessors.

When we learned that the honorable City Council had decided to force us to stop using the Franciscans, I reported this to the convent and sought the sisters' advice. Then they considered what would happen if the cloister were cut off from the usual service of these monks and placed under the control of the wild priests and renegade monks. Not one sister wanted to be subject to the latter. They all agreed to the plan that we should not wait until the fathers were removed from us by force, because then it would not be easy to have them return, even if we complained a great deal. Instead we should submit an appeal and make it abundantly clear to the City Council what burden and injury would result from such a change in the hope that such potential harm to us would touch their hearts.

And so I followed their advice and composed the petition which follows. I read it aloud to the convent. All the sisters, with no exceptions, agreed with it. At the same time they advised me in addition to the petition itself to write to the superintendent[4] and to Hieronymus Ebner[5]

---

3   This could also mean "crazy" in the sense of "taking leave of one's senses" which is the more modern sense of the German idiom, but in the highly charged rhetoric employed in the Reformation period "damned" seems more accurate.
4   The superintendent (*Pfleger*) Kaspar Nützel was appointed by the City Council and served as the intermediary between the City Council and the convent. It was he who brought the petitions to the City Council and who relayed the decisions of the council to the convent. In many respects the journal reflects the dialogue between Caritas Pirckheimer and Kaspar Nützel.
5   Ebner (1477–1533) was a prominent member of the City Council, a patron of the arts, a friend of Albrecht Dürer and, more important, a member of the Sodalitas Staupitziana, a local group of men who were enthusiastic supporters of the teachings of Johann Staupitz, Luther's mentor in Wittenberg and vicar general of the Augustinian order. The group first met in 1516. In 1517 Wenzel Linck was sent by Staupitz to become leader of the Augustinian church in Nürnberg and meet with this group.

as well as to Martin Geuder[6] so that the petition might be all the more successful.

Chapter 2

I wrote this letter to the superintendent Kaspar Nützel.

Prudent, wise, kind, dear gentleman, faithful father and superintendent[7]
    I am sorry that you are ill. May Almighty God in His benevolent Will bring healing soon. I believe I have felt the time of your illness for almost as long as you yourself have, for I need your advice and help more than ever in a matter which without doubt has not escaped your honor. They want to deprive us of the services which the Franciscan fathers have faithfully performed for almost 250 years. I have brought this issue before my convent, your kind-hearted children, and listened to their opinions, desires and advice, as is my custom. I have found them to be of one mind to such an extent that I firmly believe if your honor had been present, you would have been moved, even if you had had a heart of stone. Without exception they earnestly desire that your honor oppose such a change in view of the extensive and serious damage which would result if this matter were not considered now rather than later. It would be better to speak about this rather than write about it.
    However, since your illness precludes our speaking about this matter in person, we have all decided that we would enter an appeal to the honorable City Council so that our conscientious, dear gentlemen may yet learn a little of our affairs. We assume, of course, that the matter was undertaken for our benefit and not for our detriment. If the gentlemen hear the opposite side, that such action would be unbearable for us for many reasons, then we have the most faithful hope they will let love prevail which does for everyone what he wants to happen and spares him from what he wants to be spared from. I am sending the same petition to your honor to peruse, for I do not want to act behind your back. I humbly beg for advice about to whom I should send it so that it will be read tomorrow and not merely placed with other letters and not read. This is a far more serious matter for us than many believe.
    In 45 years I have never seen the convent more troubled than in this

---

6   Caritas's brother-in-law.
7   Many of the salutations in these letters seem somewhat formal as well as formulaic. It is fascinating to note how they change through the course of the journal as the relationship of the abbess and the superintendent matures.

matter. I know that your honor, although without our deserving it, has such a faithful, paternal heart for us, your poor children. If you fully recognized our plight in this matter, for honest reasons you would do a hundred times more than just helping and advising. In temporal matters your honor has done many good things for us for which we can never thank you enough. But in these spiritual matters which concern the Eternal your faithful help and advice is ever more important.

Therefore, I beseech your honor humbly as if I lay at your feet, that you would protect your and my dear children from such a change. For if they should suffer harm in matters which concern the salvation of the soul, that would be worth my life to me. I have faith in your caring wisdom and know you will act, for the children belong to both of us. May God help us that we may deliver them to Christ the true Shepherd who has offered his soul for his lambs. I commend your honor and your family to His Grace eternally.

Chapter 3

I wrote this letter to Hieronymus Ebner.

The blessings of Jesus who was crucified for our salvation!
Prudent, wise, kind, dear gentleman.

Your prudent honor knows about the plan of my lords[8] concerning removing the Franciscan friars from our cloister that is to me and the entire convent without exception an enormous concern in regard to temporal and spiritual matters. Therefore my dear sisters have recommended that I send an appeal to the honorable City Council in which we present our grievance. For we do not doubt that this was planned for our benefit, not for our detriment. At the same time we maintain the great hope that if your honor and the other elders favorable to us knew the basis of our real concern and the lack of truth concerning it, you would in no way compel us by force in this matter, but would instead deliver us.

Therefore I, along with the entire convent, appeal to your prudent honor as our special patron, lord and father and beg for God's sake that you graciously accept the appeal mentioned and that you would be a faithful servant, supporter and protector of the poor cloister that was founded by your pious forbears for the glory of God. Do not destroy the good order which the pious, dedicated old gentleman Friedrich Ebner

8   The City Council.

began. After he had become a Franciscan, he was the confessor of the cloister and then our superintendent from 1295. For the entire period since then the Franciscans have served our cloister in spiritual matters. This has kept us in good order, in peace and in unity without discord, bitterness, scandal or evil. They have grown accustomed to us and we to them. If in these dangerous times which people are experiencing now we had different priests there would be innumerable troubles which would be unbearable for all of us.

Therefore I again beg your prudent honor as humbly as if I lay at your feet to kindly help us so that change is not made in these matters which concern our soul for which Christ died. For I know that your prudent honor loves God. If you had as much experience in the affairs of the cloister as I have had for 45 years, you would disapprove of this plan rather than approve it and not allow it in any way, so that you would also not be responsible for the subsequent evil which come from it. In this matter act as a faithful father and founder to whom our cloister is faithfully devoted. Help protect my dear lambs from the wolves that could divide or harm the vineyard of Christ. It would be worth my life if the pious children who serve God with such good will and joy, and whom I have now instructed in the love of Christ for 21 years, were led away from it against their will and brought to frivolity. I do not need to write much about that to your caring honor. I hope the Holy Spirit will make His will be known to you. Follow this and none other.

Your dear little Katharine who has written this with complete devotion earnestly seeks such things. She sends her greetings to your prudent honor as well as to her dear mother.

I beg your honor to help arrange things so that this petition is read before the honorable City Council tomorrow and that everything possible is done in this matter. May Almighty God be with you!

Chapter 4

This letter I wrote to my brother-in-law Martin Geuder.

Considerate, wise, dear sir and loving brother-in-law.

Since I have always heard many good things about your honor, I come to you now in an important matter as to my especially faithful lord and father from whom I hope to find help and advice. I come to you with a troubled heart. Men and women have often told me how the gentlemen of the honorable City Council are ardently pressing to separate us from the order of the Franciscans and supply us with lay priests.

It would surprise me a great deal if that were so since in truth no one can provide real evidence that during the 250 years our cloister has been ruled by these fathers in spiritual matters by God's grace any disgrace, trouble or scandal has come to us because of them. They have kept us honorable, peaceful and in good order without any discord or any disputes and also without any noticeable temporal burdens. In honor and faith we have given no money or anything else to their convent nor to our superiors nor to the two fathers who perform divine office for us, except in the case of the two fathers to whom we have given food and drink and clothing. You can honestly and truly believe me as one who has experienced this for 45 years and knows more about it than those who say many things about us and the poor fathers out of envy and malice. The Franciscans can well do without us, but we cannot do without them. You can imagine what excitement and gossip would arise among the simple people of the city if the priests were taken from us now as if we had engaged in disgraceful acts and vice.

Moreover it would be most troubling for my cloister and me if we were given lay priests. The way things are going with them now it would be better and more useful to us if you sent an executioner into our cloister who would cut off all our heads rather than sending us fat, drunken, immoral priests. One does not compel a messenger or a beggar to confess to whomever his master wants. We would be poorer than poor if we confessed to those who do not believe in confession themselves, or if we received the Blessed Sacrament from those who abuse it so disgustingly that it is upsetting to even hear about it, or if we were obedient to those who are obedient to neither the Pope, the bishop, the Emperor nor the entire Holy Christian Church. If they were to do away with the beautiful divine service and change it according to their ideas, I would rather be dead than alive.

I beg you not to be moved by what is now being said untruthfully, that the clear, bright word of God is concealed from us, for by the grace of God that is not true. We have the Old and New Testament here within these walls just as you do outside these walls. We read it day and night in the choir, at table, in Latin and in German, in common and each on her own as she will. Therefore, by God's grace we have no lack of the Holy Gospel and of St. Paul's writings. I consider it more important, however, to follow it and live it and achieve it with works than to give lip service to it and perform no good works. But when they say it has never been interpreted and preached to us except by means of mere human chattering, then I answer that we want to abide by the text of the Holy Gospel and neither death nor life shall keep us from it. If we are to accept interpretations, then I will more certainly believe the interpretations of the dear, holy doctrine which are approved by the Holy Christian Church than interpretations of some alien mind which has been rejected and scorned and are preached by those who are, after all, merely human beings. Their evangelical fruit differs so much from the fruits and virtues of the dear saints whom they reject. And so, according to the council of the Gospel, we shall shun such people for our Savior taught us to know them by their fruits which in this case produce vain, sinful freedom and carnality. We will in no way mingle with them, for we can assume that our cloistered abbey would soon become an open house where everyone comes and goes, as he likes. Since according to this false freedom everyone can do what he likes, we will not allow ourselves to be forced into it.

We certainly would not want to be burdensome or annoying, but if there is a complaint about our conduct, then show us the abuse and we will be glad to correct it. For we confess that we are frail human beings who do not always do the right thing. We do not rely on our works at all as has been claimed. At the same time, however, we do not want to be a burden to anyone, but also want the same treatment for ourselves so that no one shows violence or injustice towards us, nor force that would endanger our salvation, our reputation and our honor, all of which constitute the basis of our cloister in spiritual and temporal matters.

I shall be full of good cheer and trust in the integrity of your honor and the other respected gentlemen of the honorable City Council and that you, say what they will, will not dare to do something which lies beyond your jurisdiction. For you are not our pastors. I fervently hope that you will not send wolves among my dear lambs who have willingly obeyed me in the love of Christ for 21 years. It would be too bad if so many pious, peaceful, orderly children were ruined so shamefully. That would be worth my life. I fully realize the fear such a group of people creates. Whoever wants to feed the wolves with money will have to be silent about the spiritual damage he brings about. Therefore I beg your honor as my special lord and father as humbly as if I lay across your feet to protect my dear children from such wolves and also to speak to the good gentlemen of the City Council and your friends and tell them of our troubles in spiritual and temporal matters. Do not be put off by those who advise against this, for they know as little about occupying my cloister with people and running it as I do about their houses. Believe me as one who has done this for a long time. If it were true that we had difficulties or great burdens in temporal and spiritual things from our priests, I would certainly report it to you because I trust your prudent honor as my father to whom I look for protection and kind assistance in this matter. I also request a nice, short written answer, which I shall await. May God's Grace be with you and your family. Your honor's troubled daughter the abbess of St. Clare's.

Chapter 5

This is the appeal that we sent to the honorable City Council during Advent in year of Our Lord 1524.

Prudent, wise, kind, dear gentlemen.

From our fathers the Franciscans we have been informed that your honors have instructed them to refrain from attending our cloister. It is unnecessary to go into detail because this is still fresh in your memory. Although we do not doubt that this was done by your honors with no other intention than your considering it good and useful, someone who has not listened to us cannot fully understand what this means to us, nor what difficulties it may cause us both physically and spiritually. Therefore, we poor, miserable children beg your honors for God's sake to consider our letter without prejudice and to take it to heart graciously. Please include us faithfully and paternally in your deliberations as those who have, after God, no one but your honors to appeal to.

Honorable, wise gentlemen, we hope your honors have not forgotten how we and our predecessors have always behaved towards you in the past and up to the present time, and have always done everything that was asked of us. We followed and obeyed, regardless of whether it sometimes proved rather difficult for us. Thus we have simply agreed to make an account to your honors of all our income and expenses, even writing down accounts, although this was not the custom previously. We did this so that your honors might know what our accounts look like and how we manage our holdings, obligations and household accounts. In particular we wanted to refute the charge that we made significant gifts to our fathers the Franciscans.

Moreover, in accordance with your honors' request we have arranged to have our interest deposited in this city as you desired and all our holdings reported to your honors and the city. Other orders have refused and not agreed to do this at all.[9]

We mention this only because we hope that we have never acted in any way that would displease your honors or cause you problems. We

---

[9] Caritas is trying to show that the abbey of St. Clare's in Nürnberg is far more accommodating to the City Council's wishes than the other religious orders in the city.

are also completely willing to obey your honors in all things that we consider appropriate and possible. We have the greatest confidence that we will continue to merit and enjoy this relationship. Moreover, we hope that in our everyday actions as well we have behaved toward the common man in such a way that (without boasting) no one can truly accuse us of being unreasonable or dishonest. We do not doubt that such could not be said of your honors either. If our fathers who have served our forbears for two and a half centuries in spiritual matters should be recalled from us and taken away from us in these troubled and stormy times, the common man who is inclined to think the worst would, without doubt, interpret this action unfavorably. He would believe that your honors had been forced to such action by particular behavior by the fathers or by us. That would bring discredit to our reputation and, indeed, not just ours but also yours, as well as that of our fathers, our relatives and those who support us.

Since all suspicion should be avoided wherever it is possible, it behooves your honors not just for the sake of those who are in cloisters but also for your sake to deliberate wisely because our disgrace can only mean dishonor for you too. We are also aware that many people suspect us of making many gifts to the fathers mentioned above. Our misery and poverty prove this charge to be groundless. How could we give away so much, when we ourselves have barely enough to live on and from the past wars and misfortunes, as your honors well know, we are so impoverished that we must suffer privation daily, so that it would be more necessary for us to take than to give away? Your honors know and understand this yourselves from our annual accounts.

It is also true that the two fathers who preach and hear confessions for us and provide us with other spiritual things receive no more than food and clothing from us. The "worldly" priests would not serve us and be satisfied with that in return. If we were to give them more and for that reason suffer even more want, that would be, in our opinion, not only difficult, but also unreasonable. In regard to our finances we hope that your honors will not place any further burdens on us, nor force us to do something that is absolutely impossible for us, not only because of our beliefs, but also in view of our few worldly possessions.

We are also of the opinion that in the event that your honors keep the same plan and want to proceed with it – something we do not hope for – it would encounter many difficulties on account of a lack of suitable persons and that you would find it impossible to carry out. Because competent leaders schooled in the teachings of St. Paul are unfortunately rare, are we to be burdened with incompetent priests or those whom we would really not want, but are forced to have? Do you honors realize what fruits and what benefit would result when the spirit wants to be and must be free and unfettered? No one in the world is forced to serve a master he does not like.[10] No less is a master forced to accept servants which are not compliant. How much more is it fitting in spiritual matters to leave things free and unconstrained if they are to function well and properly. The suspicion is deeply rooted in some people that our fathers forbid us to read the Holy Gospel and other books. In this instance they are unjustly accused. Even if they were to forbid us to do that, we would not follow them at all. We would much rather appeal to your Honors for help than to suffer that the word of God and other useful books be forbidden.

We can say to your honors in truth that we read and use the Old and New Testament in German and in Latin daily, and that as far as possible we attempt to understand it correctly. We read not only the Bible, but also what is necessary and suitable for us every day, except for the theological discourses that trouble our consciences and, in our opinion, do not always illustrate Christian simplicity. We hope, of course, that God will not hold back His True Holy Spirit at our heartfelt requests, so that we may hear the Word of God correctly and in its true meaning, not just literally, but also spiritually. Although some people have claimed that we rely on our own works and hope to be saved by them alone, by the Grace of God we fully realize – whatever people may say – that no man, as St. Paul says, can be justified by works alone, but by faith in our Lord Jesus Christ. The Lord Jesus Christ himself teaches that even if we have all performed good works, we should consider ourselves useless servants. Yet we also know that good, true faith cannot exist without good works, as little as a good tree without good fruit, and that God will reward everyone according to his merits, and that when we appear before Christ's judgment each person will be received according to his works, be they good or evil. Therefore, St. James also says that faith without works is dead and anyone who does not prove his faith through works is like a person, who looks at himself in a mirror, goes away and does not know what he looked like. Therefore, faith does not exist in merely speaking, but we are saved if we believe correctly and act well.

We also know that we should not attribute our own good works to ourselves, but if something good happens through us, it is not our work, but God's. Hence we are unjustly accused of boasting of our good

---

[10] Here Caritas is speaking within the context of "serving," i.e., using, a father confessor in whom one has confidence. Certainly the Peasants' War showed many instances where peasants were "unhappy" with their masters.

works. Our boast is solely in the spurned and crucified Christ who tells us to take up His cross and follow Him. Therefore, we confess our guilt, that we are also commanded to suppress the old Adam and subject the body to the spirit by penance, although we have more reason to hope within the cloister than without. We also have no hope of salvation outside of the cloister, but wish to remain in the calling to which God has ordered us. Truly we are not in the cloister because of a good life, not do we receive our reward here. God and the world know that we are poor, miserable people. Our hope extends beyond these walls because we know that we have no permanent residence here.

We are also not unaware that salvation cannot be found in eating and drinking, or in fine dining, or in food and drink or abundance. We must, nevertheless, pray, be watchful, suffer hunger and thirst, if the mortal body is to be suppressed and the enlivening spirit is to win the upper hand. But whoever thinks that the kingdom of heaven can be obtained in this life through sensuality is deceiving himself and not obeying the Holy Scriptures. For Christian freedom exists not in the flesh, but in the spirit.

We also do not despise marriage. For we know that whoever marries does the right thing. But according to the teachings of St. Paul we also know that whoever does not marry does even better. In the event that we decide to serve God as virgins, truly no intelligent person can hold that against us. If, however, someone is not so inclined or does not want to join us, we have nothing against that. We, therefore, do not plan to hold back any sister by force or to keep her from her parents. We also do not want to condemn anyone, but let every man judge himself; everyone will be judged when we all come before God's judgment. But just as we do not want to force anyone, we also do not want to be forced, but instead we want to be free in spirit, not body. But that may not be possible if we are burdened with different preachers. This would really lead to the destruction of our community. For even if we are provided with God's Word and the sacraments, if the Franciscans are to be taken from us and the bishop is not to have jurisdiction over us, then the visitation of clergy would cease upon which not the least part of cloistered life is based, not to mention the events which occur daily in the cloisters.

Why would your honors do this to yourselves and allow the poor little garden that has existed so long to be destroyed? Why should you trouble consciences with such acts and place a burden on us which would be no less terrible and gruesome than temporal or physical death? God knows we would be more willing to suffer death than endure this heavy burden, not because we would have to do without the monks, but because we foresee the danger to the salvation of our souls and the dissolution of our community. In these dangerous times it is really unnecessary to give more cause for anger and improper action, since, as your honors know, this already happens in excess every day. If your honors consider this carefully we are truly more justified within the cloister than without because we freely desire to be there without being forced. I pray God that your honors consider this reasonably beforehand and not experience it in fact. Of course we know also that if your honors considered our worth as we do you would not only have pity on us, but also, even if you had hearts of stone, have mercy because this concerns not only temporal matters, but, as mentioned above, the salvation of our soul and our eternal life. If we have behaved improperly or done something wrong, we will gladly improve if it is made know to us, and even suffer punishment. If, however, we have not done anything for which this heavy burden has been placed upon us – we pray to Almighty God that this has not happened – ,what then do your honors want to charge us with? We are and profess before God to be poor, miserable sinners, because before His eyes not even a new born child can be pure. But before the world and your honors we know that we are free and innocent of all blame.

In view of all these things we beg your honors for our sake and that of Almighty God and of Our Lord Jesus Christ who became man, and His Holy Passion, and His Precious Blood which He shed for our salvation, for the sake of Christian Love and Hope which all men have for the life to come, be gracious and give up your plan. Allow us poor, miserable children and simple women to continue forever in our former, innocent, long-accustomed manner and to serve the Lord God. Be gracious and remove this heavy burden so that God might be gracious and merciful to you on His great day and do to you what you have done to others. If, however, it should not please your honors to cancel your plan right now, we earnestly beg you again for God's sake to postpone this action and to let it rest and have a longer time to study it in these dangerous and wretched times. Perhaps, in the meantime, God, as we hope, will be gracious and peace and order will return. In case the world is not to be punished for its sins or the Day of the Lord should approach, we and the Christians of other faiths must wait and place our hope solely in the Grace and Mercy of God. May it grant your honors the proper, true spirit to act in the best way for the salvation of your souls and that of us poor, wretched, troubled children. Since we have placed our hope and faith in you after God, we await a gracious reply.

We received no answer to this appeal, except that the honorable City Council desired to let the matter rest for the time being until further notice.

Chapter 6

What happened to Sister Tetzel.

In 1525 on the day after the feast of the purification, the wife of Friedrich Tetzel[11] called on me and with many serious words demanded that I allow her to enter the cloister because she needed to speak with her daughter Margaret alone on a matter affecting the salvation of her soul. I refused and told her that she knew that up until now it had not been the custom to allow anyone to enter the cloister who was not needed. She then used many threats, saying that this procedure must be changed. In addition she demanded that the door be opened and her daughter be brought to her alone so that no one could overhear them. I refused this too and said that I would not begin such a practice just for her. Other people would want the same arrangement. Even her daughter implored me fervently not to open the door. She was afraid that her mother would want to drag her out of the convent by force and that she would not be able to defend herself when the door was opened.

After much discussion we agreed that I would leave her daughter alone in the chapel and open the window through which we receive the Blessed Sacrament. For more than an hour she spoke alone with her daughter. No other sister was present or listening in.[12] After her mother had left, the dear child sister Margaret Tetzel ran to me and the other sisters with much sobbing and bitter tears. With heartfelt tears she related how her mother had cruelly tormented her in every way. With love and anger, threats and promises her mother had wanted to take her home by force, but she had defended herself with all her strength and had said finally that no one should take her from the cloister. With God's help she would keep the vows she had made to God. Her mother then ran away from the child full of anger and finally saying Margaret

---

11 In this chapter, as in the later chapters dealing with attempts to remove relatives from the cloister, Caritas follows the custom of the times so that the wives' and mothers' names are based on their husbands' names. Thus Mrs. Friedrich Tetzel appears here as "die Friedrich Tetzlin."

12 This arrangement was an extremely "liberal" departure from the normal procedure in which the sister was not alone and was separated from the visitor by a grate and effectively could not see the person she was talking with.

should prepare herself because she would not leave her in such a depraved situation. The child was in such a pitiful state that all the sisters and I felt sorry for her. She pleaded with us most earnestly not to let her be torn away from us or else she would demand her soul from us on Judgment Day. She desired me to seek advice from the superintendent. I wrote him the following letter:

Chapter 7

Prudent, wise, kind dear superintendent and loyal father.

I thank your honor for all the effort that you expend on our behalf every day. May God Almighty reward you in eternity! Once again I seek your faithful council in a matter which I have never encountered before. Therefore I do not know what to do about it without your advice. Last Friday the wife of Fritz Tetzel visited me, demanded to enter our cloister and to speak privately with her daughter. I told her I would not grant admittance to her or anyone else without just cause. But I did not refuse to let her speak with her daughter just this once. At the same time I would also be willing to allow her to see the child if she did not believe she could find salvation here or did not want to remain in the cloister.

Nevertheless I also demanded that she use no force with her daughter to get her to change her mind. It seemed to me that the responses I received were not very "evangelistic."[13] When I noticed that she was very upset, I said that in place of her late father I wanted to have Sigmund Fürer present who would probably act in a reasonably way. But she showed neither reason nor patience and wanted to speak with her child privately. I answered I would allow her to go to the window in our chapel where we receive the Holy Sacrament. If the child wanted to leave, then I would open the door and the gate. She then spoke with her child for more than an hour, but was unable to persuade her to want to leave the cloister. In addition she said she wanted to come back again and deal with her daughter further. Every day the child runs up to me and begs me not to force her to leave.

Your honor knows we take in no one without the permission of the City Council. I also deem it reasonable that we do not release anyone against her will or let her be removed without the advice and consent of the City Council. She indicated to her daughter that she intended to take

---

[13] Usually this term means "Lutheran" but here it could be interpreted as "Christian" in an ironic sense due to the rather rude behavior of Frau Tetzel.

her home for a short time and then afterwards bring her back, something which neither I nor the convent approve of.

In this matter I beg for your faithful advice as to whether I should send a petition to the honorable City Council or what else I should do in this matter which is almost too burdensome for me. In my opinion such people should leave us in peace. We do not want to become a nuisance or live in conflict with the Holy Gospel and proper virtue. But from such people whose children we educate in sisterly love so faithfully and with considerable difficulty we do not, in my opinion, deserve this at all. Yet we commend this to Eternal God. May He find the best outcome for this and other matters and support your honor forever. Amen.

I received no answer to this letter.

Chapter 8

After a few days Frau Tetzel returned with her brothers Sigmund and Christoph Fürer. With harsh words the latter demanded that their sister's daughter be returned to her. From the clear Gospel[14] and the preachers she had learned so much that she could not in good conscience leave her daughter here. At the same time they condemned the religious life and reviled all our actions and customs.

I replied I had already told Frau Tetzel that I would not keep her daughter if she herself did not want to stay. I was prepared to make the same offer today. To drive her away from us against her will did not seem appropriate, for that would not be in accordance with the Gospel and also against the principle of our sisterly love. Then the Fürer brothers said I should let the daughter stay with her mother for only four weeks so that she could be instructed in the true faith and hear the Gospel as it was being preached in the city. Then I said she had recently spoken with her daughter alone for more than an hour and explained her opinion to her sufficiently and had not needed to worry that anyone else was listening in. I would also be willing to let all three of them go to the window. If they could persuade her to go with them then I would open the door and the gate. But if the child did not agree to leave, I demanded that no force be used. I was not able, however, to bring it about that either the mother or her two brothers would listen to a single word from

---

[14] Such expressions were frequently used by the Lutherans, whose preachers stressed that they were making the Gospel clear. Similarly many, including Frau Tetzel, felt that they had "seen the light" from such teachings.

the child either at the window in the chapel or at the regular conversation window. They said they knew in advance that she would not want to leave of her own free will, but they did not want to leave her here. After much quarreling I declared that we had taken in the child with the advice and consent of the City Council and we do not want to let her be taken away from us without its advice and consent. We would sent a petition to the City Council and let it decide what is just and reasonable. They said that was fine with them. They wanted to file a petition also. And so they left for the time being.

The dear pious child Margaret Tetzel was greatly troubled that her relatives would not listen to her because she loved them very much. She believed that by speaking with her relatives she could persuade them to force her mother to give up her unreasonable plan.

After several days our superintendent Kaspar Nützel came. I explained to him at length the events described above. He believed I should not be so deeply troubled about it, for even more would happen. They[15] were being informed by their learned councilors that cloistered life was meaningless and would not last much longer because it had no basis in the Gospel and many other words of a similar nature.

Sister Margaret explained to him her troubling situation with many fervent tears and pleaded and begged him most sincerely to speak with her relatives so that they would listen to her for God's sake before they used force on her. But the superintendent's heart was not touched. He only made light of it. He finally said she should write to Sigmund Fürer himself, which she did. She wrote him most humbly and begged him fervently to visit her with his brother. He sent her the following answer:

A letter from Sigmund Fürer to his niece in the cloister.
My dear little niece.

I have read your letter and your request and shown it to my brother. Since we have a fair understanding of your thoughts and know the desire of your mother, we do not consider it necessary to visit you now. We commend all actions and plans to God alone. He will arrange all of this as it pleases Him, not man. So be happy and trust in God alone.

Sigmund Fürer

---

15 The members of the City Council.

Chapter 9

I sent this little letter to our superintendent and included in it the following opinion:

Prudent, wise, kind, dear superintendent.

Sigmund Fürer sent this letter to his niece and she is deeply shocked about it. She said, God have mercy! Even a thief is heard before he is hanged. What have I done that in a matter that means so very much to me they will not listen to me. Nothing good can come of this. We must console the poor child.

Once again I desire your honest advice and appeal to you as a father to whom God has committed the care and administration of our cloister in these times. I beg you, for the love of God, let me know whether I should direct my petition to the honorable City Council and let my lords there be informed about whether it is reasonable and just that a sister in such a case is forced to leave against her will without even being heard or if your honor yourself will speak before the City Council for all of us as your children. Your honor can well realize that we are seeking no temporal advantage in this matter, but only the honor of God, sisterly love, loyalty and friendliness in which we have raised this child for almost ten years. We are truly sorry about her problems. We would not want to drive this one away, nor anyone who desired to remain with us, just as we would not desire to keep anyone here by force against her will.

I believe we do not deserve the arrogance of the people at all, for it is neither Christian nor evangelical, nor fraternal to repay good with evil. From now on we will, in full confidence, commend this affair to your honor as our faithful father and lover of justice since we do not want to be a burden to anyone and do wrong. Your honor along with the honorable City Council, our kind, dear lords and uncles[16] will once again protect us from violence and unbearable burdens. Finally, my sisters and I have come to the conclusion that if it must be that we release this child against her will, then we do not want this important act, the likes of which has never occurred in the previous 300 years of our cloister, to be carried out secretly in some remote corner, but openly in the presence of your honor and the other gentlemen. We implore them humbly and

---

16 Perhaps more in the general sense of "relatives" since some members of the City Council had daughters or nieces in the convent. Kaspar Nützel's daughter was a member of the convent too.

ardently as our protectors and defenders and loyal lords and gentlemen to all enter our cloister personally, observe this act and hear our side so that they can bear witness to the truth of the matter. In this way much of the gossip, unrest and untruth, as is the case now, will be avoided on both sides. We want to act as properly as other people and therefore we do not want to flee from the light.[17] We humbly request an answer today if it is possible so that I can prepare myself for tomorrow accordingly. I would be grateful if you saw fit to have this letter read to the old gentlemen by tomorrow.

Chapter 10

In answer to this letter the superintendent sent me the following letter:

Grace and peace from God the Father through His Son our Redeemer. Honored abbess and mother.

On Friday I left you. Yesterday, as promised, I spoke with Sigmund Fürer and explained the desire of Sister Tetzel to speak with her uncles herself. He answered that his sister, Frau Tetzel, had asked him and his brother about the removal and had indicated at the same time that she had decided not to agree to her daughter's plan. She knew she was not only justified in her appeal, but also within a short time no one would consider it odd. They then told her not to proceed against their wishes, but to write to their niece.

I should like to note, in addition, that she is willing to achieve her wish through a petition to the honorable City Council. This is how things stand now, and I know how my colleagues are accustomed to act. In an action they do not answer the parties without hearing them. They have certainly also considered this will not be the only appeal. Others could be made in the same way toward your cloister. My advice would be to wait until she enters her appeal. When I hear of it, I will say you told me about this matter and of Fürer's plan because it is important that the appeal be sent to you. Then you can honorably and irrefutably make a response as seems necessary because you will be able to act in good council. That will serve you better than an oral presentation. I do not doubt at all that both parties believe they are acting in a Christian manner, and, therefore, I earnestly implore God to make His will known

---

[17] Here Caritas is perhaps using "light" in an ambiguous sense to mean not only the truth in general, but also in a religious sense, as it was often employed by the Lutheran reformers.

in this matter. Therefore I will not have your letter read to the elders of the council because you might want to consider other necessary steps after the petition is received. The Lord be with you!

I also believe that the parents will not act behind the backs of the City Council in this matter.

Kaspar Nützel, the elder.

After this Frau Fritz Tetzel presented her complaint and petition to the City Council. The superintendent enclosed it with his letter.

Peace and salvation in Jesus Christ our savior!
Dear Abbess.

Enclosed is the petition which Frau Tetzel sent to the honorable City Council. I reported that you had spoken to me in person and by letter concerning this matter and had objected to the request and, in view of the present state of affairs, had not expected it. Be that as it may, I was charged by you to see that it be sent to you. Then you would not hold back your response to it and your concern from the City Council. That was considered reasonable, and it was sent to me so that I could turn it over to you. The City Council will await your reply and then announce their decision. In accordance with my last letter and the order given to me, I did not want to keep this from you. I stand ready to assist you.

Kaspar Nützel, the elder.

Chapter 11

This is the appeal of Ursula Tetzel.

Prudent, wise, kind, dear City Councilors.

With your assistance my dear departed husband and I helped out dear daughter enter the cloister of St. Clare years ago, since we knew nothing else to do but to give God a living sacrifice and thus achieve the washing away of her sins and the advancement of her salvation within the cloister. Now, however, I have learned so much from listening and reading that I believe that the cloistered life is unknown to God and is nothing but a human invention, a heretical deviation. Therefore my conscience has forced me along with my two brothers to demand that the honorable abbess give my daughter back to us. She responded that after she had taken in my daughter with your advice and consent it would not be proper to let her go without your honors' approval. There-fore she wanted to report the matter to your honors by a petition. Since this is not forthcoming, the salvation of me and my daughter forces me to approach your honors in God's name and request that you earnestly consider that my daughter came into this prison in her innocent years, without knowing the difference between good and evil – that is when she was 14 years old. Your honors might also consider that in the Last Judgment Christ will not be concerned with prayer, fasting, silence, clothes, eggs or meat, but faith alone and the love of one's neighbor. I would that you could help me and arrange for my daughter to be transferred to my home for a while.

I promise your honors and, if necessary, I will take an oath with my brothers, that she will be instructed in the Word of God which she cannot receive from monks since she suffers a hunger of the soul because of them, that she shall then be completely free and not under any pressure. She can choose to remain outside the cloister with me, the poor widow, and her siblings, or return to the cloister where perhaps she will have a better and more abundant life, so that my troubled conscience may find peace. If this plan is rejected by the worthy abbess of my daughter, then I will hope your honors as our higher authority will know how to make a favorable decision concerning the disobedience of my child toward me, toward the position of her mother and of both our souls in this matter. I therefore request that we both be commended to your honors.

> Your prudent honors' obedient widow,
> Ursula Friedrich Tetzel.

Chapter 12

This answer and petition which was voted on by the convent as a whole we sent to the honorable City Council.

Prudent, wise, kind, dear gentlemen.

We have humbly read the petition filed by the honorable Frau Ursula Tetzel and sent to us. Let us say first that it is true that because many requests by Friedrich Tetzel and the plaintiff we did, with the permission of your honors, accept the daughter mentioned and she is not without skills. Recently Frau Tetzel visited us alone and later with her brothers and demanded her daughter be removed from our cloister. We have educated her for nine years with great diligence and shared our poverty with her in sisterly love. The action of her mother is very difficult for us, for we do not believe we deserve it.

That we neglected to appeal to your honors with a petition stems from the fact that the woman named came to us and wanted to break into out cloister by force. After much negotiation we asked her if she would be satisfied if we sent her daughter to her alone and let her see her and, if necessary, speak with her. This actually happened and she spoke with her daughter alone for about an hour at the small window through which we receive the Blessed Sacrament. But after this conversation her daughter came back with much crying and complaining and begged and implored us most earnestly not to desert her, but to keep her with us. She does this every day. Although the woman has come to us again with her brothers, they did not want to deal with her daughter at all, which really hurt her. Therefore her daughter wrote to her uncles and asked them to visit her and listen to her. This was rejected with the observation that her mother had told them she would not give up her plan either. She made a great protest at the same time, in view of the fact that a criminal is heard before he is condemned to death. This and nothing else at all is the reason for our delay. We refer to our superintendent in this matter.

We have already informed your honors that we would not want to force those who do not want to stay with us to remain. However, that we should drive someone away by force against her will weighs heavily on our conscience, just as the mother is troubled that she should leave her daughter with us in the cloistered state which is unknown to God, as she maintains. That disturbs us in no small way, since God is, after all, the Eternal Wisdom, without whose will no leaf falls from a tree or a hair from our head, and to whom the depths of all hearts are known and before whose countenance no creature is invisible, and before whose countenance no one can hide. He shall not know us, his poor little creatures, where we are called through His Grace to Christian faith in which we alone hope for His Grace and place our hope in the bitter sorrows of Christ. We desire to love Him from our hearts according to His commandment. This love compels us to perform works in the cloister which the Lord Jesus and St. Paul teach us and who order us to be watchful, to fast, to pray and to praise God with Psalms and spiritual songs. We should not rely on such works, but instead, if we had everything consider ourselves useless servants. God has indeed given us a reasonable soul that we also wish to offer for salvation. How much more we would prefer it if it were possible to reach heaven the sweet way rather than the bitter way. But because Christ teaches us that we should take up our cross and follow Him, we nevertheless desire to remain in the state[18] for which we have been called according to the teachings of St. Paul. It is not true, as we have already explained, that we rely on this

18 Cloistered.

alone. We know, of course, that a true Christian's life is bound neither to time, place, food, clothes and the like, but instead it is free not in a physical, but spiritual sense of freedom with which Christ redeems us. For this our plan and our opinion neither our conscience, nor the Holy Scriptures trouble us. Whether men punish us is not important to us. God will judge. Before him all will appear and it is his judgment we must await, not that of men. Every action rises and falls before the Lord. Christ says, judge not, that you be not judged. It does not matter if we suffer humiliation, disgrace and evil talk, for Christ our Savior has suffered more for us, the Innocent for us guilty men, the Just for us unjust men. Praise and honor be to him for what he sends to us, for the unpleasant as well as the pleasant, for it is He alone whose Grace and Mercy are without end.

Would that God grant that the plan of this woman come from a good conscience and not from some other source, for although it is true that her daughter entered when she was young, she has now reached the years of knowledge and reason so that she can distinguish between what is good and what is evil. Although they should be reasonably honored by their children, mothers do not have power over their children as the fathers do, not even over those who are not under the control of mothers or fathers as the laws dictate. Thus the plaintiff does not have the power to take her daughter from the cloister against her will. Her daughter is not obligated to follow her either against her conscience. Therefore, the woman cannot say her conscience is troubled because she has done her part and expressed her opinion to her daughter, but the latter will not give in. The daughter must bear the responsibility and not her mother who is excused. The woman might well maintain a clear conscience if she took her child from the cloister against her will. We will let God decide that. We, on the other hand, are obligated to clear our conscience and do our part. What we cannot do, we must leave undone.

In order that your honors may get to the real basis of the matter, we ask you in all humility to choose someone to represent you not for our sake alone, but for the daughter's sake. Then we will let her appear alone and publicly so that she may be interrogated as much as necessary. If it turns out that she desired to leave the cloister, we will certainly not prevent her from doing so. But if she desires to stay with us, then we hope your honors will not allow force to be used, but will graciously protect her from such things. After all, the poor child should be listened to and her opinion heard. May your honors achieve what her relatives refused her, because no one should be condemned or incriminated without being heard.

If this is not the verdict of your honors, but instead the daughter must leave, something that we do not expect, however, then we can and will do nothing to oppose it. We offer instead to open our gates and set the daughter free. Whether you will sanction this with violence against her will or according to the will of another, we will commend to God. That we should drive her away from us against her will is very distasteful to us as your honors as highly intelligent men can well imagine.

If, however, the woman finally agrees that it should be her daughter's choice after she has been instructed by her mother to return to the cloister or remain without, we say we cannot teach the daughter so many good things that we cannot offer her even more later. We also hope it will be proved that we have also taught her nothing evil. But to take the daughter back into the cloister after she has left is not possible. We also hope your honors will not force us to do something like that in order to preclude different and greater disorder. For you know well from experience what kind of disorder can result if a disturbed or falsely instructed person enters a convent. We would much prefer that Frau Tetzel agreed with her brothers so that if she removes her daughter, she will then leave us alone. It would be very difficult for us to be confronted with such things all the time. Other people would act the same way and there would be no end to the running in and out.

If, however, the woman indicates a better and more fulfilling life for her daughter exists in our cloister than in her house, then we must commend that to God. We do not want to respond to harsh words with harshness because that is against God and the love of one's fellow man. Your honors know enough of our income and expenses and costs and we are content with that. We thank God that we have it and at the same time we hope that it is a work of charity if we are more sparing in food and disdain benefices.[19] Thus the holy alms that we enjoy are immediately distributed as much for those who bring nothing in as to those who bring in something. We want to follow the example of the first Christians of whom it is written in the Acts of the Apostles that they were all together and shared everything in common, both possessions and money. They sold there possessions and distributed to everybody what they needed. They went to the temple daily and praised God. This was a true cloistered life too.[20]

Thus, in all humility, we want to submit this matter to your honors as our kind, dear lords and faithful fathers in the hope Almighty God will arrange all things to His Praise. We ask Him to grant us patience in all

19 Benefices were a major source of friction for the reformers.
20 Here Caritas is presenting a Biblical defense of the cloistered life.

our troubles and make His yoke sweet so that we may bear His Cross
with joy. Amen.

> Your honors' humble children,
> The abbess and convent of St. Clare.

We received no answer to this appeal. Everyone remained silent. Later
on Thursday after Ash Wednesday, it was St. Kunigunde's day, they
began the discussion at the city hall. It went against the Franciscans for
the most part. They attempted to find a reason why they would be justified in taking them from us.

Chapter 13

Anno Domini 1525, on Oculi Sunday during Lent,[21] it was the 19th day
of March, Christoph and Bernhard Baumgartner came in the afternoon
saying that they had been sent by the honorable City Council and had
been ordered to bring a message to the entire convent. Therefore I was to
admit them into the cloister. I said I would call the convent to the
speaking window where they could deliver their message. They said no.
They had been ordered to present their message to the convent in such a
way that all the sisters could see and hear them. And so, with great
apprehension, I let them in and called the convent into the winter refectory.

The two men began a long speech on how they had been sent by the
honorable City Council with the best of intentions so that they might
offer us their paternal goodwill and concern that they had for us as their
children and relatives. Therefore they did not want to deprive us of the
grace which God the Lord had shown in having brought to light the clear
word of God and the bright Gospel and they could now recognize how
pompously they had been preached to previously. This had been shown
in the Christian disputation which had been held for several days at the
city hall and in which their preachers and highly learned men had
brought to light the truth of the clear Word of God so brilliantly that the
members of the religious orders present had to admit to themselves that
they had been mistaken in many things.[22] Up to now the Gospel had lain
under the pew and had been very much obscured by those who were

---

[21] The third Sunday of Lent.
[22] This is stretching the "truth" a bit here, since the Catholic representatives realized they had no chance of prevailing and left before the discussion was over,
thereby admitting defeat, but not necessarily guilt.

supposed to have preached it. Since now the city had been greatly illuminated by the preaching of the Gospel with the clear Word of God, the honorable City Council wanted to share this grace with us too. In doing so they would spare no expense. Therefore they had assigned to us a highly educated, excellent preacher by the name of Poliander from Würzburg. Therefore on Monday tomorrow he would begin to preach the bright Gospel. And from now on, on every preaching day he would preach until the honorable City Council appointed someone else. It was the earnest desire of the City Council that we should listen diligently to this enlightened man and that I should see to it that the sisters listened diligently to his sermons.

Next the honorable City Council wanted to supply us with much better confessors than we had had before, with highly educated, courageous, intelligent, experienced men. They suggested several we could choose from. They suggested two Augustinians, one of whose name was Karl, the other Dorfer, and the third was a secular priest from St. Sebald. From these three we were to choose one whom we wanted.[23] They praised them all so much and gave them so many titles that it seemed they were as holy as John the Baptist.[24]

On the third issue they said it was the City Council's honest opinion that we should separate ourselves completely from the Franciscans who had served us up to now and that we should have nothing more to do with them. That was the final word from the City Council. They would also inform the guardians of the Franciscans and the others. This was done with much appropriate deliberation as well as paternal love by the City Council which valued our cloister above all others. We were being cared for in this as we had been in other matters for as long as anyone can remember.

To this I replied on behalf of the convent roughly as follows: We are grateful to the honorable City Council for all the good will which they showed is. We would recognize that up to now they had shown us paternal loyalty. But the sudden dismissal of the Franciscans disturbs us in no small way, especially the separation from the order from which, by God's Grace, we had been provided Christian preachers and who also preached the Gospel clearly. In regard to the confessors, with our whole hearts we especially desire that the honorable City Council not take our

23 It is worth pointing out that the City Council did allow the convent a degree of "democracy" here, but since none of the candidates was a Franciscan, none were acceptable.

24 Caritas's sense of humor shows she was not swept up with the same enthusiasm as her guests.

pastors from us since our cloister has been well served by them for 250 years. The Franciscans who have heard our confessions until now have conducted themselves courageously, honorably and peacefully so that there has been a gentle peace among us and never disgrace or scandal toward the outside world. We do not want to accept any of those who were proposed to us. We hope and trust the honorable City Council will not apply pressure in matters which concern our conscience where no authority forces a servant against his will to confess to the one the authority wants.[25]

In regard to the third point, that they want to release us from the jurisdiction of the Franciscans, I answered that both orders[26] were so closely bound together from their founding and linked to one another by popes and emperors in their privileges and bulls that in no way do we have the power to release ourselves from our agreement with them. In addition, we have neither the means nor the right, for up until now we have received only good things from the order of the Franciscans. If we are to be subject to force in this matter, then we must leave it to God before whom we protest that we are compelled against our will and that in all points presented to us we expressed no agreement or approval. This was the general content of my response. Then the entire convent stood up and indicated to me that they concurred with what I had said.

Then the gentlemen became angry. They said in regard to the first point concerning the preachers, there would be no change for the learned Herr Poliander had already been hired and it had all been arranged that he was to begin on Monday tomorrow. We should also not take the second point with the confessors so hard. They were, after all, pious, well-educated, experienced men. If we were afraid of the lay priests, then we could choose one of the two Augustinians who were members of an order and monks too. Then I said if you want to give us monks, then leave us the monks whom we know and of whom we know what courage and good morals they have. We also are familiar with the monks you mentioned. We are well aware of what a loose life their order now leads. They said we should not take offense. They would not remain monks, but would cast off their cowls and assume another status. I said, surely nothing will come of it. If we were to accept as pastors apostates who have perjured themselves before God, what good should we expect of them? They would teach us nothing but what they do them-

---

[25] Here Caritas may be a bit idealistic and naive at the same time. She is trying to defend the right of individuals to choose a confessor to their liking at a time when the City Council is effectively removing that right.

[26] The Franciscans and the order of St. Clare.

selves. Since they take wives, do they think perhaps, we should also take husbands? God protect us from that! You really must not think that we would enter into such an arrangement.

Thus we argued for a long time about the confessors. They stuck to their opinion just as we did to ours. As far as the third point on releasing us from the order of the Franciscans was concerned, I desired that they give us the reason we deserved that. Had we done something bad or angered anyone? If we were informed of any such act, we would like to improve and stop the improper action. They answered that the honorable City Council knows of no abuse or problem ever caused by us or the Franciscans either. They know of nothing but complete discipline, honor and a good reputation. I said they should be reasonable and let things stay as they are. They answered that in other orders, however, things went differently, that is such things did occur and for that reason it was reasonable to take the Franciscans away from the female cloisters. If this were done in one location and not in another, nothing but discontent and discord would result.

After much talking back and forth, when they saw that the convent was earnestly troubled and the sisters were weeping so bitterly, they said they noticed that we were ungrateful toward the honorable City Council and did not accept their good, paternal opinion. For our sake they did not wish to report this to the honorable City Council. We should think about another answer. We, however, gave them none. And so they left us with neither side having an advantage.

When they left our cloister they went immediately to the confession house and sent away our pious old confessor Erhart Horolt and the preacher Nikolaus Liechtenstern. They told them it was the decision of the honorable City Council that henceforth they should neither preach nor hear confessions or have anything to do with us. The dear fathers obeyed and left immediately on the same night for their cloister.

After this the men went to the guardian of the Franciscans, at that time father Michael Fryeß. They told him also what they had done at our convent and by authority of the City Council they ordered that him and all his brothers to cease serving us and to have nothing to do with us from then on. The City Council would now provide for us themselves.

On the same day the men also went to St. Katharine's and did exactly the same thing to the monks and nuns there as they had to us.

Chapter 14

On the next Tuesday our confessor and preacher returned and fetched their belongings and what they still had in the confession house. They held mass in the chapel with a sermon and renewed the Blessed Sacrament so that it might remain all that much longer. Afterwards they returned home before mealtime. Since that time they did not return for a single day, nor has the father guardian, nor our superior, nor any other Franciscan come. Yet many lies have been told about us, how they come to us secretly, hear our confessions and administer the Holy Sacrament. This and other gossip we must leave to God. Since then we have been deprived of confession, the Blessed Sacrament and all sacraments, not without our consciences being rather troubled, especially in the time of a death, when our dear late fellow-sister Karla Löffelholz desired the Sacrament from the depths of her heart. She did not want to put soul in danger despite the heresy that many now exhibit in regard to the Blessed Sacrament. May this spiritual want be lamented to God in heaven. May He have mercy on us and send us a good solution through His boundless Mercy.

On the same Tuesday afternoon after Christoph Koler and Bernhart Paumgartner came back and once again wanted to enter the cloister. I asked them whether it was about the matter which they had recently discussed since I wanted to give them more information. They said no, they had had something else to present. Therefore I had to let them enter the convent again. Then they started with many serious and harsh words. They had been with us last Sunday and had observed and seen and heard things about which they were understandably upset. For from our contrary answers and the great weeping they had noticed that we desired to be disobedient and obstinate toward the honorable City Council. We wanted to despise the paternal favor which they showed toward out cloister particularly and not accept the good things they were doing for us. That would rebound to our great disadvantage. For that reason they had refrained up to now from informing the City Council about such things, for they hoped we would have considered a better answer in the meantime. They also did not want to keep from us that they had been to St. Katharine's. There they found a different, humble obedience toward the City Council than with us. They had, of course, given in without objection from the beginning. What the City Council decided for them they would accept and whomever they were given they would accept graciously. They saw no weeping about the monks being taking away from them, but instead they were happy. We should follow their example and that of others, for in time we would be grateful to God and the authorities that they had delivered us from the monks. Tomorrow they must deliver their report to the City Council. Therefore we should give them a different answer from what we gave them the last time.

Then I answered first and admitted my guilt for the entire convent and myself and asked them to forgive us if we had at first behaved inappropriately and not as they would have liked. They should not be angry with us because the sisters wept so much, for that was due to the unreasonableness of women[27] and shock, since at this time we had not expected such a sudden change at all. Perhaps the sisters at St. Katharine's had a different reason than we did, for our fathers have behaved with us in such a way that we couldn't be happy if they are taken away from us.

On the second item I said we would give them no different answer than what we had given before. Yet we begged them when they made their report to defend us before the City Council and not look upon our refusal as obstinacy and disobedience, but instead to consider our great distress at the same time. They knew very well that we had always obeyed them before in all temporal things. For what concerned our soul, however, we could follow nothing else but our own conscience.

They would not be satisfied with this, however. With many threats they continued to press hard and firmly for a different answer. Since we could not get rid of them, I said we wanted to answer the City Council through our superintendent, for we thought we could be more successful in making our superintendent yield than these young me, although unfortunately, that did not happen either. When they heard that we wanted to deal with the superintendent they let up a little. They said if we would promise them that we would give an oral answer through our superintendent and if this would happen soon, they would report the best about us to the City Council. They believed, however, we would submit a petition. In addition, they wanted to tell us that it would not be of any use. They would not accept a petition, for the entire City Council had decided that it had to be this way and no other way. With that they left us.

On the next Wednesday I held a chapter meeting. I asked the sisters for advice on how we should proceed. Previously we had intended to

---

27 Here Caritas is appealing to the vanity of the men and attempting to use a "feminine weakness" to her advantage. This is but one example of her debating technique.

enter a petition, but since the two men had rejected that, we did not know what else to do. Nevertheless, the convent voted to write a petition and present our grievances fully in it and request that the superintendent visit us. We were to read this appeal to him and listen to his advice about whether he should submit it to the City Council or make an oral presentation of our opinion. They were very hopeful that they could bring him over to our side. And so I wrote to him and asked him to come.

He wrote me this answer

Honored lady and mother.

I am with you more than you can all imagine. I wanted to be with all of you within the cloister, although you know that I would never seek to go inside out of mere curiosity. However, since you requested I come and, although I may prove to be more flexible than I believe I am and seem to be in this matter, without considering my own affairs, and in God's name and in true brotherly love and God willing, I intend to come to you tomorrow afternoon at three and accept your report and make my own report as much as God's Grace allows me. I write in haste and do not want to delay. I ask God to grant to you His Grace which I desire also and nothing else. May His Grace be with us all!

Chapter 15

In accordance with this letter he came on Thursday evening. Contrary to our custom we let him into the cloister along with only our accompaniment since there was no one among our lay staff we could trust. And so he entered the convent with great joy and was full of jubilation that we had requested his advice. He said that when he had told the entire City Council about his upcoming visit, everyone was happy about it. Of course, they sincerely hoped that the Holy Spirit had come to us and that we had made the right decision. For that reason he wanted to assist and advise us and be kind and good to us.

He began a long sermon in which he praised the preachers most highly and told us how splendidly they had fared in the disputation at the city hall and how they had made clear the bright Word of God to the members of the clerical orders although previously it had been very confusing in some places. They decided that by virtue of Christian freedom no one was obligated to obey rules pertaining to the time of day, food or other statutes devised by man.[28] They considered the

---

[28] All of these were, of course, essential elements of cloistered life.

accursed ceremonies and teachings of the clerics to be meaningless. The preachers of the parishes had forced these and other items onto us in such a way that no one could respect the clerics any longer. Everything must be changed and brought into a unified order. Therefore we needed only to volunteer to agree and we would stand in great favor with the City Council and the whole community. After all, the entire city had accepted the new doctrines except for us. We would not be able to maintain our order and the old ways. If we desired to retain our old beliefs, we would cause great bloodshed and such a disturbance that the whole city could be destroyed by it. He knew, of course, that there was a great gathering of peasants. Every day more were coming who wanted to defend God's Word and the Holy Gospel and destroy all the cloisters by means of the sword. Therefore we should consider very carefully that with our particular life style we do not give cause for great bloodshed which might result. He told one story after another, sometimes with threats and at other times with promises.

When he had finished his speech he wanted to leave and hoped that we would be receptive to his paternal warning and that the brilliant Word of God would move us to follow obediently what the honorable City Council planned for us. Then I spoke. "Dear, wise gentlemen. We have heard your speech and hope it came from a loyal heart. Yet nothing was mentioned concerning the matter for which we asked you to visit us. It is this.

"Last Sunday Christoph Koler and Bernhard Paumgartner were with us, and on behalf of the City Council they dismissed the Franciscans from us for confessions, preaching and everything else. They named some persons who are to serve us. We protested against this as a matter that would serve to destroy our cloister and all spiritual life. They came back last Thursday and wanted the final answer we had decided on. I told them I wanted to give your honor the answer. And so we sent for your honor in order to ask you as our loyal superintendent, who has always done many good things for us, for your advice as to how we should act in this matter so that we could answer to God for it. It is extremely burdensome for us that they want to remove us from the administration of the pious fathers by force. For over 250 years, as you yourself well know, they have served our cloister courageously and honorably so that neither disgrace nor scandal has ever occurred to us on account of them. In addition, they want to saddle us with persons we do not desire and who, as you yourself know, lead a life that we will in no way accept, above all because we realize that all this has been specifically set up in order to force us to accept the new faith. In no way will we accept it until it is accepted by the one, holy, Christian Church. We have, you see, decided together that with the help of the Living God neither in life nor in death will we be separated from the mother of holy Christianity[29] and from the things which we promised God. What I am speaking here I speak at the command of the entire convent."

Then all the sisters stood up and acknowledged me. After that I spoke further. "So that I am not accused of forcing my sisters to do and say what I want, I will leave. Then ask all the sisters in common or some alone what they think and hear what each one's will is in this matter." But he did not want to let me leave, saying it was not necessary to interrogate the sisters either. Then for the third time I asked him to interrogate the sisters alone. I would trust him in this matter so that the blame would be mine alone. Then he spoke. He knew well what they will answer and could see from their gestures that no one would follow him.

After this he began a long speech again about how sorry he was that we found it so difficult to accept the paternal good intentions of the honorable City Council. In these matters he was not seeking his own benefit, but solely the salvation of our soul. The new preachers had been proposed with great diligence as a comfortable means by which our cloister could remain intact. We must know after all that some people had demanded their children back, only because we had not been enlightened in the Holy Gospel. Even more people would do this who had children with us. Up to now they had been restrained by being assured that we intended to provide learned persons who would enlighten us. With this reassurance they had been calmed down and restrained so that up to now they had kept still. If that were not so, then some sisters would have long since left the cloister. Therefore, we should accept such a splendid scheme with gratitude or else we would be responsible for great bloodshed and unrest. Within a short time we would see what would happen. We were always pressing him for different advice and a better way, he said. He could not give us any other advice except that we should generously agree to this, for it would be impossible to change the decision that had been courageously deliberated and had been signed. Among other things he said everything is possible for God, but it is not possible through human persuasion that you will ever again in all eternity come under the jurisdiction of the Franciscans before my lords leave any stone unturned. Then I asked what the Franciscans had done. He answered that the fact of the matter was that the members of the City Council did not want to tolerate them any longer at all.

[29] The church of Rome, the "Holy Mother Church."

After that I told him we had composed a petition to the honorable City Council in which we presented our grievances. We hope when they heard it they would not use force in this matter. I asked him to read it aloud and to advise us what we should add or remove. But he did not want to read it. Then I ordered the prioress to read it aloud before the superintendent and the entire convent word for word as follows:

Chapter 26

Prudent, wise, kind, dear gentlemen.

After the decision of your honors was presented to us in recent days by Christoph Koler and Bernhart Paumgartner, to wit that you are removing from our cloister the Franciscans along with their sermons and hearing confessions, we have requested at the same time to declare to your honors our grievances about it in the certain hope that you might listen with paternal kindness to your poor, humble children, not as disobedient children, but as those who have been oppressed. We know very well that your honors have planned this for our well being and not our oppression.

First, we are not troubled so much because of the preachers, that the Holy Gospel was not preached to us with Christian understanding, without combining it with the human element so that it would be heard as the word of eternal life by one who seeks it openly, earnestly and with a thirsty heart, although, by the Grace of God, we have not lacked that up to now. But last Monday your honors appointed another preacher and we listened to him, although it has been said unjustly of us, that we despised hearing this sermon and our superiors forced us to listen, locked the choir and took away the keys. That does not conform to the truth in the best of faith, for no sister was forced or forbidden to do such things. Our choir cannot be locked this way. Accordingly, may your honors not look upon us as despisers of God's Word, for by God's Grace we are Christians who desire to hear and believe in the Holy Gospel with all our hearts. May God help us to also live according to it as we, according to the teachings of St. James, should not just hear, but achieve the Word.

Yet the removal of the confessor is very difficult for us for the reasonable grounds which we mentioned in our first petition. This concerns, of course, not only temporal things, but also our conscience, which cannot be shared with anyone, especially in these dangerous times when one must protect oneself from the people, as the Holy Gospel says. Indeed, one sees and experiences openly what fruit results from some spiritual

and worldly priests at women's cloisters. For that reason our fear of such
priests is justified. Not that we were so devoted to the Franciscans,
except that up to now we have experienced nothing from them but
courage, discipline and piety. Nevertheless, as we have been truly
informed, our honor and our good reputation is being destroyed so
terribly as if we had engaged in dishonorable things and scandal and had
secret passages in the confession house to our cloister plus many other
disgraceful things.[30] These charges are contrary to all fraternal love and
the Holy Gospel when one Christian slanders the other without valid
reason. With St. Paul we do not care the least that we are condemned by
a human court. We do not condemn ourselves in this matter at all, for we
know we are innocent of such acts. For this we take God as our witness.
Our reputation is proof of our conscience, that we want to avoid hard-
ship by being guilty. For this reason and so that the truth might come to
light, we desire that you have our confession house inspected inside and
out to see if a single footprint of an intruder can be found. If you find the
truth at this place, then do not continue making such wild accusations in
other matters so that you accuse us or the fathers out of envy. We are
favorably inclined to you for no other reason than your piety and sincere
courage and would very much like to remain in such a relationship with
you even longer. In our opinion we have neither the means nor the right
– it is also not within our power – to separate ourselves from this order.
Our rule, which we do not want to deny, states that we are to receive the
Sacrament of Penance and other Christian sacraments from those who
receive their power from the Cardinal to whom this order is entrusted.

If one does not allow peasants and other people to place themselves
under a different power than what is proper, then, in our opinion, it is
also not appropriate in spiritual matters. Your honors know well that in
temporal matters we have always been subordinate and willingly
obedient. But if the spirit and conscience are to be free, we beg your
honors as humbly as if we lay at your feet for the sake of the Love of
Jesus, who cleansed our conscience from dead works with His precious
blood, do not force us in matters concerning our conscience. It would be
a terrible, pitiful affair if we, in addition, to the physical enclosure to
which we have willingly submitted, would also be imprisoned in our
conscience at a time in which the freedom of the Gospel is being
preached. It has not been customary to compel and force someone to

[30] Obviously whatever "abuses" had been discovered in other cloisters were
considered possible at St. Clare's too. The reformers in Nürnberg as well as elsewhere often tended to paint their pictures of abuse with a broad brush which was
applied generally, not specifically.

confess to someone who does not suit him or to believe what someone else wanted. Your honors would not deny us the general Christian freedom either, although some may say what the preachers correct, the confessors destroy. This has never happened to us up to now. For in respect to faith, our own confessor never got involved in public matters or caused trouble because of it, but instead he kept us in peace. Therefore we implore your honors as much as we can, to leave him with us longer for God's sake. If that does not suit you and you do not want any more Franciscans with us – which we do not expect – then we ask most fervently not to burden us with any other ones. Since it is now believed that spoken confession is no longer necessary, we will, if it cannot be otherwise, do without it and will confess our manifold sins with heartfelt sorrow to Him, to Whom all abysses of the heart are known. We will trust completely in His infinite Mercy, that He will forgive us graciously through the bitter suffering of His only begotten son. And thus, if we do not want to confess, we will not need any confessor. We hope the honorable City Council as understanding men will not be upset that we poor, simple women, who have no great understanding and cannot debate and who could easily be misled in these times of dissension and discord in which many changes and innovations are being undertaken and then done away with and altered, desire to remain in the faith of the Holy Christian Church and with its good, praiseworthy customs. With God's help they can be kept until the changes are also accepted and evaluated by the holy, general, single Christian Church. Let us also, if you will, remain in the same faith with the help of the Living God until the end, since we have made the same declaration in the sacrament of Holy Baptism. And so, according to the promise of our Redeemer, we hope to attain salvation not by our own justification, but through His endless Mercy.

We ask humbly that you grant our request graciously and console our troubled conscience. God knows we do not like to act against your honors, nor would we be a hindrance to your order, if it did not concern our conscience and the souls which Christ has purchased with His precious blood. For that reason they should not be minimized, nor endangered after God, our Lord, considered them so precious. When we weigh the pros and cons, we are perhaps speaking with St. Susanna: From all sides we are full of fear, yet it is better to fall into the anger of men, than into the hands of the Living God.

Chapter 17

When this petition had been read and the entire convent affirmed that this was everyone's opinion, this did not please the superintendent at all. He became almost angry. He said he was not of this opinion at all and that we should earnestly reconsider it and let ourselves be better informed.

We said that we would not decide differently, but would stay with what the petition contained. Therefore we desired humbly that he deliver this petition to the City Council himself or that he present it orally, something which I consider most suitable for him. He said it was not possible to enter it in written form, for he did not believe that was mandatory. The honorable City Council had, of course, acted deliberately in these matters. Now they had their other activities also and all kinds of innovations and changes and ceremonies which they conducted, all of which had been written about to his imperial majesty by a special messenger. They had no doubt that his imperial majesty would be graciously pleased.[31] Many cities were also following their example. Hence it seemed neither good nor necessary that this petition be entered in writing, for we could not achieve anything with it after all. If we did not want to give up the idea, he would present it orally in good faith. He believed that the long letter contained only two points. The first, that we desired that the old confessor be returned. Then everyone said, O yes, very much so. Then for a while he seemed to act as if he really wanted to help us and return the confessors. After some time, however, he said it was impossible for all eternity.

The second point was that we desired that our fathers not be removed and that the City council would not burden us with any others. To that all answered, yes, that would be our final decision, that we would accept no confessor but one who suited us. Then I said, among other things, grant us the freedom that you have outside. If you think nothing of confession and never want to confess, then we inside these walls do not want to confess either except to the highest priest. If we never want to confess, then we need no confessor. Then he asked why we did not want

---

[31] Here we see an example of the special relationship of the free, imperial city of Nürnberg to the Emperor. The city enjoyed "free, imperial" status and was therefore responsible only to the Emperor, not to any other authorities. The Emperor Charles V remained Catholic while Nürnberg became Lutheran, a fact which put considerable strain on the city's imperial politics.

to be Lutheran in anything except in this one point, that we never wanted to confess.[32]

Many other words were spoken which would not have been recorded if he had not employed his greatest diligence and had not wanted to convert us. He was very sad that none of his efforts had been successful.

When he stood up and was about to leave the refectory, the sisters ran up to him, something that was not customary, kneeled before him and fell at his feet begging him with all humility most earnestly to help us and be our protector and patron. They did not want to let him leave the refectory. He told then that they could not force us to comply in spiritual matters. Then he took great offense, became angry and vehement and tore himself loose from the sisters by force.

As he was leaving the refectory, he said he desired to speak with me alone. He led me into the choir and spoke to me for more than an hour employing many pleasant words, but also threatening ones. He sought to influence me in every way. He asked me most fervently to convert to the proper path. I would then do him and the entire City Council the greatest of favors, for they liked me very much and were well inclined toward me. If they only had me on their side, then they would have the entire community. After all the prelates in the men's cloisters had shown good will. They all wanted to conform. Only I was headstrong and made the convent disobedient towards the City Councilors. If I agreed and urged the convent to do so, he had no doubt that the sisters would all follow. There was a rumor about me, that I was advising not only my convent to oppose the City Council, also all the nuns' cloisters in the area. They all sought advice from me and said they would behave as I did. If I converted, the whole area would convert. If, however, I continued in this error, I would do great harm to my soul and be the cause of much bloodshed and unrest. Thus he spoke with many long, forceful statements by which he showed from what sense of great love he was doing all this and also from what sense of duty after he had been our superintendent.[33]

When he was through speaking I took courage and told him how I

---

32 It almost appears that Nützel was thinking out loud here. He may even have been making an attempt at humor, although this seems out of character for him, even allowing for the fact that he was probably rather tired.

33 This is not the only time Caritas reveals a keen sense of appreciation for the difficult role which the superintendent had to play as a sensitive father figure and as an obedient representative of the City Council. It is obvious that she feels sorry for Nützel, whose failure to win her over has all but broken him.

felt. Among other things I said, my dear wise man, I am overwhelmed at how ardently you are concerned with the salvation of our souls, since by virtue of your office the care of our souls is not your responsibility. You are only the guardian of our temporal goods. Thus you have assumed a power which you do not have and are removing from us our regular pastors which popes, kings and emperors have appointed. For this you have no power or right. Therefore I cannot change my will either a lot or a little, for I see and know that this change will serve to ruin our cloister and all ecclesiastic order. You desire of me that I should direct the sisters to do things that are against my conscience. That I will not do out of fear or favor of anyone. I know my convent is very devout and honest. If I were not here by no means would they enter into something that is against their consciences. In these times there is so much division and error that no one really knows what to believe. For this reason we have all decided to remain in the old faith and in the clerical state and do not want to accept anything which has not been accepted by the Christian Church. My sisters have also specifically forbidden me to consent to anything at all. If I should, however, they would not agree and would never obey me. You have undertaken the order regarding the priests. You should have asked us beforehand whether it would be possible for us to carry it out. You have taken our pious confessors from us without just cause and you want to burden further with wild rabble.[34]

Then he spoke. Dear mother, if you do not like those who have been recommended, then just name a different one now. If he does not reside in the city but many miles away, then we will see if we can bring him here and will pay any expense so that you are taken care of. But I want to tell you, they will not give you one from the old sect.[35]

Then I spoke. Then we really do not want anyone from the new sect. If, however, you force one upon us, then be aware that we will neither trust him, nor confess to him, nor receive any sacraments from him, nor attend any mass he celebrates. Therefore I will not name one for you to bring here either, for I know that you will not give us one for our consolation. I am very familiar with the fellows being brought here. May God protect my dear little children and lambs whom I have raised in the love of Christ for 21 years now against these wolves. We are not used to the adventures these fellows engage in. I have known the Franciscans for longer than 45 years, but I have never heard an irreverent word from

---

[34] By this she means the Lutheran preachers, many of whom were former priests.
[35] The Franciscans.

them. We need them not just for hearing our confession, but also for visitation and all that goes with it.

He spoke. Don't you think that the convent would give in to my lords on visitation? Then I spoke. Absolutely not. Do you really think that we would give up the abbey's freedom of election? According to our rule we have the freedom to choose whomever we want as abbess. No one has the right to interfere. Similarly, no one has the power to give us one against our will. Under that method it could happen that you might give us an abbess you like. We have no desire for that. We know as little about who is acceptable in your council as you can know who is acceptable in our cloister. Up to now our fathers have not forced us to do anything. They have merely accepted the votes from the sisters and then confirmed the election.

In this way we argued with each other for a long time. He believed we should trust the City Council in everything. I felt no. For if they were our good friends right now, who knows, what might happen later?

Next he got to the preachers. He could not praise his Osiander and Poliander and others enough. How inspired they were and how they expounded a great deal concerning the new faith and how reasonable it was to do away with the accursed ceremonies. Among other things, however, he said he had to tell the truth. He had never really liked the German mass, but our preachers claim it is the correct apostolic mass. In addition he spoke of many errors and praised the preachers most highly.

Then I spoke. My wise friend. I like you and wish you well. I pity you from the depths of my heart because you have been led astray and blinded so terribly. In the times of Arius and other heretics things proceeded the same way when people were misled with sweet-sounding words. Truly now you too are agreeing to lead the people astray to such things that you will regret in your heart and will cause you fear and distress.

Then he answered. No. There is a thaw and more grace is raining down than in a hundred years.

In this way we argued with each other for a long time. Each believed the other was blind and mistaken.

When we both stood up, his daughter Clara appeared and, along with the other sisters whose fathers served in the City Council, fell at his feet. They implored him most earnestly to ask their fathers to allow them to remain in the cloister. But he turned away from them coldly and left the cloister very troubled and serious. Then he spoke. I entered the cloister with great joy in hopes that I could bring good news to my lords in the honorable City Council. But this grace has not been granted to me. I do not know what answer I should give, for I do not yet feel the Holy Spirit.

The next day his wife[36] came to us in great anger and gave us a stern lecture about how we had treated her husband. He had not slept the entire night. There was no place for such behavior. We really should not be so obstinate. We should follow the people or else we would encounter misfortune.

We still hoped that the superintendent would come over to our side. Then, on the next Saturday, it was the Saturday before Laetare and the Ascension Day of Mary, he wrote us this angry letter from which we could see how things stood with us.

Chapter 18

Grace and peace from God our Father and His only begotten Son Jesus Christ, our Savior and our only Interceder!

Honorable lady and beloved sister in Christ.

Last Wednesday I appeared before your assembled convent and, as usual, on the Thursday after that, I reported to the honorable City Council, our gracious lords. In proper fashion I reported my impressions. On the first item, the City Council was pleased to note that you, worthy mother, would allow me to interrogate the sisters together as a group and individually.

On the second item, I reported that you had composed a petition whose purpose, as I perceived it, was not to appear defiant, but, if it pleased the City Council, to proclaim God's Word to you through an appointed preacher. But in regard to the confessor, you have made things extremely difficult by including many supporting arguments. You requested that they reappoint the same one, or, if they did not wish to do that(which you do not hope for), then not to burden you with a different confessor. All of you intended to confess to God until the situation improved.

My lords were troubled as well. They feel that you did not understand their plan, which they have designed, sincerely for your sake with Christian charity. They say that they know well that you will agree to do whatever the Franciscans request. Now, for good, logical reasons the Franciscans are not considered appropriate for such things any more, some of which I reported to you orally. They believe, therefore, if you do not like the people appointed by them for this purpose or for other

---

[36] In Chapters 33–34 she and two other mothers attempt to remove their daughters from the convent.

purposes for which the Franciscans served, then they will not force you. You should seek others and not just the one whom my Lords cannot tolerate who is deemed inappropriate.

When I told them that you wanted to consider the matter, listen to God's Word with diligence and let it take effect, my lords were content, since they do not want to rush you. Finally, I reported that you announced that you want nothing more than to know what pleases God and what He wants. Then, without recourse to other principles, you will follow His highest pleasure uniformly. But it is very difficult for you to act without the Will of God and against your own consciences in matters concerning salvation. In addition, you beg them not to be angry and not consider it disobedience or stubbornness. Such a report pleased the City Council very much, since it never wanted anything else either, nor ever will. If both parties in this matter call upon God the Almighty, you can be confident that His Grace will be granted also. Through it we attain true wisdom. May God, the Father, the Son and the Holy Spirit help us! Amen.

My faithful advice would be that you, worthy mother, not avoid speaking, as you do so well, to the preacher, for you will find complete modesty in him. I believe that if you do not speak with him, that would not be interpreted in your favor by the City Council and the community, since he is very well respected.

I met him only yesterday and requested that he visit you and your sisters. In a very honorable and Christian manner he stated that he would learn from you at the same time. I beg you, do not make this difficult. If you want me present, then I will be there too.

Verily, verily I say to you – not I, but the Lord – you are blind and up to now have been led by the blind. Do not trust yourself or your leaders so much. For I have seen such things at your convent that I am sorry to say that you were led astray by men who were very much mistaken. You consider it appropriate to fall down in humility. That belongs in your heart and not in external gestures, before God and no one else. It is difficult for me to have to observe that your salvation is based on the Franciscans alone. To them alone you want to confess. Salvation does not lie there. In your opinion no one else is worthy enough to serve you. You alone are the ones who possess the correct Christian view, and nobody else. God help us! The man with the greatest power in our empire has long said this of himself. Every day more people are finding the new path and become aware of their errors. At the same time much Christian blood is being spilled. If you do not change, then you will also be responsible for it, although I trust God, that He will not let that happen. I must confess that on the whole with you and your group your error lies in the reason and wisdom that you ascribe to yourself. If that were not so, then you would change and then show that you recognize and obey your subservient obedience to God and willingly accept the authority and its report and have no doubt at all that your salvation does not lie with the Franciscans alone. According to God's Will I must speak more forcefully and clearer. You want to be those who cause the spilling of blood, murder and all manner of misfortune such as is happening now in the Swabian League. Certainly the violent ones believe nothing else, but that they must hold fast to that long impressed error by which, according to their reasoning, they can accomplish something good. God's Will demands action, and in the end, even despite their artificial and false ceremonies, they will be successful. Years ago it would have been strange to hear what is happening now, that is that we are informed about two to three day's ride from here, a group without a leader and of about 50,000 men strong has gathered. Every day even more people, even Imperial cities and Federal cities have joined in four days, having left their land in order to wipe out the sects by whom the Gospel is falsely interpreted and to reestablish Christianity. They are willing to take on anything that could be done against them. I cannot help thinking that in this way God looks down upon us graciously every day and lets His Grace and Peace rain down on us. I will die for this faith. Once again I beg you earnestly to accept the advice of understanding people, as you have always done up to now. Perhaps from this you will attain further understanding, which you really need. You also have the choice of whom I should send to you for a friendly conversation, one or several of the eight preachers who have now appeared here by the Grace of God. Among them there is one father from the Carthusians, a very devout Christian, old and experienced man. It would be no trouble for me if you wanted to have me present for one or several of them.

I do not desire of God to live any longer than when His Will is done for you and grants you the reputation of willingly accepting guidance. Through your enthusiastic works you may have occasion to believe that it will happen with a superintendent who comes after me that you speak truly and from your heart and say, why yes, we did not want to follow Kaspar Nützel, our superintendent, despite his faithful advice. We wish we had, but perhaps that was not yet the time for it. Now we want to follow and accept advice. I only worry that we have waited too long, that the bishop who is now in power will not always be there and there will be great sorrow. May God protect you and give you Grace! I commend this matter to God, the Almighty, and all of you and me to His boundless Mercy.

Kaspar Nützel

I read this letter before the convent. Then the sisters were deeply touched. I heard some especially, but all agreed that they did not want to accept the new faith under any circumstances. They wanted to leave neither the Christian Church, nor their cloistered life, nor be subject to renegade priests, even if they should have to be without confession and the Blessed Sacrament for a long time. They suggested that this should be written down very clearly for the superintendent, so that he might know how we felt. He should also let the elders read it so that they would finally know how we felt about them. And so I composed the following petition which I read aloud to the entire convent again. All the sisters agreed and requested to sign it. They wanted to faithfully share any burden that might come of it.

Chapter 19

Prudent, wise, kind, dear superintendent.

Your letter has been read aloud to us in the convent. We note from it that your honor has presented our case to the honorable City Council in the best manner and we are grateful to you for that. At the same time we noted with special concern that you were very upset at our actions and particularly at our falling down on our knees, which (in your opinion) was done out of hypocritical humility, something we are not accustomed to doing otherwise.

However, we considered that this matter concerned more than mere temporal affairs and we kneeled in order to show your honor that we were appealing to you for God's sake as children before their faithful father, of whom we expect only goodness. We might not have done this otherwise. But, be that as it may, for God's sake, please pardon our behavior and do not get upset, for with God's help it will never happen again. Help us to ask God, our Lord, who sees all the hidden motives of the heart, for the grace of true, honest humility and for the illumination of our darkness.

We confess that we are surrounded by darkness and that is only as it should be. If we should think that we belonged to a group of visionaries, then, according to Christ's teachings, we would retain our sins. If we confess our sins, we hope for forgiveness and for illumination from our blindness. We seek this most earnestly, since in our judgment we do not rely on our own understanding and our own knowledge, which is folly before God, nor on the blind leaders as they are called.

Instead we desire to be ruled by the true Shepherd and Bishop of our souls who lives now and will never die. He himself is the way, the truth and the life. We beg him with our hearts not to let us be led into temptation. Upon him alone and on no living person in this world we place our hope, refuge and salvation, and not on the Franciscans as we have been accused of doing, for we know well that a person is cursed who puts his trust in any man.

Believe us indeed, if they wanted to give us Franciscans who are like those who have been suggested to us, then truly, as we recently said to your honor, we would oppose them just as much. As we said previously, we are not attached so much to confession as to other things because, of course, both our orders were deeply linked to each other. Later we received privileges from emperors, kings and popes. Because of this and other things, we do not have the power to separate ourselves from them of our own volition. If we have to suffer force and pressure then we will have to commend that to God the Almighty. May He protect us through His Grace from bloodshed and other evil. We do not want a bread knife, let alone a sword to be raised on behalf of the fathers who have provided for us in spiritual matters. It is also well known that the peasants claim that they belong to no one and want to use Christian freedom in order to be subservient to no one according to the bright, clear Gospel. Therefore, we hope that we are no cause for such revolt, for we have no supporters among these people. For God's sake do not hold it against us then that we do not give up His Freedom in the cloister. We have no power to do so, for we did not build it. It is also not fitting, therefore, to surrender it, or let ourselves be released from our vows which we made to God by some human being, as reasonable as this is made to appear, as if our vows were not binding and were impossible to keep too. In this way it would be impossible to keep what we promised God in the sacrament of Holy Baptism. Although we know that we can do nothing without the Help and Grace of God, we speak with St. Paul, "I can do everything in that which strengthens me."[37] With this power we hope to accomplish what we promised to God. For that reason we are not terribly afraid of all those who would give us reasons to leave the faith, just as we also protect ourselves from all those who are recommended and given to us, who are, for the most part, renegade monks and priests. What would they teach us but what they themselves do? With God's Help neither the sword nor death will bring us to perjure ourselves before God, out Lord.

Our God, to whom we have committed ourselves, is a jealous God. Thus in good conscience we cannot approve any of those who have

---

[37] Phil. 4:13.

perjured themselves against God and their bishop to whom they have sworn to maintain celibacy. And so they take wives, engage in other evil activity, abandon the priesthood, leave their order and relinquish their cloisters which, after all, are not their property. It is said that the priest assigned to us has a wife also. Today, after he criticized the clerical estate several times, he finally said that no one should give credence to the idea that many pious, holy people were in the orders – something that is probably true. But it is also certain, he continued, that no pious or holy person has remained there. God has helped him to leave before they are eliminated. With these words we believe many pious, holy, old fathers are trod upon too much. These statements are dangerous for us too. We can well assume from this what the end of this game will be, that they, of course, want to drive us out of the cloister. Unfortunately, this has happened to many a poor soul who was led astray by such stuff. Afterwards they became the laughing stock of the people and now their conscience suffers. May God protect us from that! Why should we have anything to do with them? Should we trust in them and expect good things of them when they have acted so badly and not done for God the Lord what they swore to Him? Therefore, it would be in no way fitting for us to grant the eight preachers a friendly conversation, for we hear that not much good resulted from the friendly conversation which was held at the city hall and which was also announced as "friendly."[38] At the same time, it was said the orders could do what they wanted, but in the end, what had already been decided for them would happen.

We know well that among these preachers are some who do not act in a Christian manner, but under the mantle of the holy, clear Gospel they attack us from the open chancel in an non-collegial way. Some have even said they would not rest until, by means of their sermons, they drove out the nuns and monks from the city and a bowling alley is made out of our cloister, something which has been proposed to us often. If such were decided for us too, then it would be better to drive us out beforehand, before we were compelled and forced to do so by means of disputations and the like. Although the aim of such things is our death,[39] we do notice, however, that all activity is directed towards our joining the new sect voluntarily. No sister can in good conscience be respon-

---

38 This is the first time Caritas makes direct reference to the "religious dialogue" at the city hall that sealed the fate of the cloisters in Nürnberg when the new Lutheran faith was accepted.

39 Ultimately the City Council did allow the cloister to remain in operation, due in no small part to Caritas's perseverance, but it could not accept new members, so that, in effect, it received a death sentence.

sible to God for that. With God's help we want to remain in the faith of the Holy Christian Church and neither death nor life can separate us from it until this division is brought into unity by the Holy Christian Church, but not before, for, after invoking God in heartfelt prayer, we cannot find in our conscience that we should believe and hold fast to what everyone wants us to, that we should reject the long, good tradition of Christianity as everyone is doing today according to his own vision, even though he is only a human being, and abandon the faith and order of the Holy Church which has been ruled by the Holy Ghost until now according to the promises of Christ. From this we will not allow ourselves to be separated and will suffer what God gives us to suffer. For it is always better to suffer all evil than to give in to it. Of course for what we suffer we do not need to account to God. But to agree to something and give a reason for our fall, for that we must pay a high price before the stern Judge, for we cannot be responsible for this for the whole world.

Therefore, for the love of our Creator, Redeemer and Savior, we beg you honor to have patience with us poor creatures. Do not force us into a faith we do not believe in. Even the Turks allow everyone to remain in his own faith and do not coerce anyone.[40] Every day we will pray earnestly to God that he might increase His proper, true, Christian faith in us. If He makes us of another mind, we will not keep that from you. No one's faith and conscience should be subject to coercion since God, our Lord, wants consciences to be free and not forced. Therefore, it is not appropriate for anyone to bind them or imprison them. We earnestly and humbly desire that your honor accept our petition. It comes from the depths of our being and is without any temporal or spiritual advice and with no pretense, as we will indicate, but from our own consciences and our troubled hearts.

It is especially burdensome for us that this is a matter in which we simply cannot follow your honor and the honorable City Council as we have done up to now in temporal things. We consider your honor to be a man of such great wisdom that you know full well that we must obey God alone as judge of our consciences more than men. Even St. Paul teaches us that each person should keep his own counsel, for everyone will have to bear his own burden. No one goes to heaven or hell for someone else.

---

[40] Caritas's idealistic attempt to champion religious tolerance was, for the most part, unsuccessful. Using the Turks as an example may have been historically accurate, but was not something which would make the City Council change its mind.

We have no doubt that if your honor, along with our older, kind, dear lords to whom we ask you to read this letter also, could look into our hearts and consciences, you would be content and commend this matter to God, our Lord, alone without any human involvement, haste or force. He would conduct this matter better than all of us. To His Grace we commend your honor forever.

Your honor's poor children, the abbess and the
entire convent of St. Clare, some sisters individually.

Chapter 20

The superintendent wrote this answer to our petition:

Jesus. Worthy mother and sister!

From the letter you sent to me I can note that I am experiencing what others do who take on too much. For even though I wrote with love, as I proclaimed a long time ago, God does know my heart after all.[41] I beg Him to be gracious in the future.

I have done what you desired. I have had your letter read before the older gentlemen. Neither they nor the whole City Council considered themselves so wise in these matters that they wanted to give an opinion about what you mention in your letter concerning what goes on with the preachers of Christian life and Christian teachings whom you never knew before. They want to consider the matter, however, not by themselves, but in the entire City Council and where ever else they consider it will be necessary. Then they want to proceed graciously and trust in God alone.

Please let me know (so that I do not neglect this matter) whether you want to let the City Council to know more or less or whether you desire that this letter which is addressed to me and was read before the elders should remain with the City Council so that they may have it read aloud there. You will soon find out whether you were correctly informed by those who pointed out that the attack of the peasants and the cause for it are based solely on serfdom and their not wanting to pay any taxes.

It is certainly true that you poor people are not the cause of that. However, I will not enter into whether the sect leaders from Rome and their supporters should apologize for these and even greater evils. I will

---

41 Nützel is attempting to say that he is disappointed, if not frustrated, because his labor of love was so negatively received by the convent. It is apparent that his heavy workload has taken its toll on him.

show discouragement to no one but myself in trying to straighten things out for you.

Today my lords sent their excellent messengers to two cities near here, Rothenburg ob der Tauber and Windsheim, because the citizens of both places have made prisoners of the City Council and the mayor because their evangelical[42] preachers were taken from them and replaced with charlatans. Likewise Salzburg has taken the concubines from the spiritual and temporal leaders and requested they marry them, something the godless ones would not promise to do. They want to conduct themselves completely according to the local order, as truly as God lives. If the Grace of God had not removed the false preachers then we would have had to share something that some weak-kneed pastors were not up to. I do not doubt that you would be more inclined to believe me if you could see better. I hope that with God's help only a small number of these disobedient ones come here, or at least, as I hope, commit no evil acts as a few or even some are inclined to do.

Thus I commend us all to God.

Kaspar Nützel

Chapter 21

I gave the following answer to his letter:

Prudent, wise, kind, dear superintendent!

I have read your letter and with a troubled heart. I understand your honor's uneasiness on account of the last letter. We did not write it against you or want to treat you with contempt, but instead from our loyal hearts and without flowery words we indicated to you what our fears and our grievances are in this matter. I read what was in your letter to me and the convent before the entire convent and asked each one individually, both young and old, what she wanted to answer according to her own will. Thus each told me what she thought as the letter states. Then, with my own hand, I wrote these opinions on the slate and gave them to the scribe to be copied. I report this so that you do not have to accuse any other people. Then, when the letter was about to be sealed, I had it read before the convent again. All the sisters again forbade me to present a position they were opposed to. If I did so without their knowl-

---

[42] Lutheran.

Journal of the Reformation Years 1524–1528   59

edge, I was told, they would not stand for it and would no longer obey me.[43]

If, as ordered by my sisters, I have written something awkward and unreasonable in which we attacked some person too much, then, for the love of God, please ascribe this more to our feminine irrationality and our limited intelligence than to our scandalous judgment or haughty attitude. Of course God, our Lord, knows the depths of our heart, and that in these matters we are only afraid of people who could be the source of apostasy. Your honor should not hold that against us, since, according to the Holy Gospel, it is necessary to be on guard against people. It is true that we demanded to have the elders read the letter as our kind benefactors and faithful fathers. If they become acquainted with our situation, which stems from our love and fear of God, they will take that to heart and appreciate it in the best light.

I charge the same gentlemen and most importantly you most of all as our loyal superintendent and provider to decide whether it is possible for this letter to be read before the entire City Council or not. For the Honor of God and of the Holy Gospel we desire that in this matter you act as someone who would want the same thing to happen to him. We also ask humbly that you have patience with us poor souls until God lets His benevolent Will act within us. Nevertheless, according to the request of the honorable City Council we listen to the Word of the Holy Gospel and have released the Franciscans. Please do not burden us any more in the future.

With God's Help we will maintain our faith and tend to our affairs and not interfere or hurt anyone. Also, since I was judged to be biased, I promise to permit the convent to be interrogated. I will also leave the room so that every one can freely express what she feels, whether in my favor or not. I can and will not force my convent to do anything else. It is also inappropriate for me to do something without its knowledge. I hope the Holy Ghost will not hold back His Divine Will from you and from them, since we are, after all, gathered in His Name.

Thus I commend your honor to God's Grace, that he always grant us the ability to act correctly.

---

43 This is an important point for Caritas to emphasize. The notion that Caritas was "forcing" her sisters into a position which they did not share was one which reappears in the negotiations between the convent and the City Council. This was the reason why attempts were made to interview the sisters individually so that they might feel free to voice their opposition to Caritas's positions.

Chapter 22

After our fathers were taken from us as ordered on the Monday after Oculi, a Lutheran preacher began to preach to us. His name was Poliander. He also had a wife and had been canon in Würzburg. Because of his Lutheran teachings he and the prior of the Carthusians were driven out from the city. They were not permitted to be there any more.

From the Monday after Oculi to the Tuesday after Judica[44] this same Poliander held eight sermons. He enjoyed great popularity. The people liked to hear him so much that the superintendent told me if they could only keep him they would give him 600 gulden[45] a year to convert us. But neither I nor any sister spoke a single word with him. For this reason I made many enemies among the people because of this Poliander. The superintendent wrote me the following letter:

Chapter 23

The Mercy of God, the Father and the Grace gained from His Son be with you all. Honored, dear mother and dearly beloved sister with whom I wish to deal no differently than I would wish to be dealt with even in the case of the highest truth which is God Himself.

Your last letter that you sent to me I read aloud (before the City Council). Although, due to the absence of some of the elders, I neither could nor wanted to do anything before we could all meet together, something that did not happen until today. I was ordered to tell you that after diligent negotiations with the Count of Mansfeld he will allow Poliander, the preacher assigned to you now, to stay here a while. There are indications of much good work resulting from this as the City Councilors had hoped. The City Council has spared no expense so that he is provided for. The count, of course, has this consolation, that through his God-inspired teachings he has brought all his estates and people and even some of his brothers, cousins and friends to a Christian life and to unity. Moreover, he has been urgently pressed by those of both high and low estate to preach the Gospel in the land of Prussia, so that perhaps he

---

[44] Passion Sunday.
[45] For a brief discussion of money in Nürnberg see Gerald Strauss, *Nürnberg*, pp. 92ff.

will not be able to stay with the count very long, something that probably does not shock you at all.

May God grant that you carry out this arrangement better than Poliander believes you will and may He grant you the consolation that you will be far better served with the father from the Carthusians than with him. In this matter it has been arranged for the Carthusian mentioned above to begin preaching to you on next Thursday morning at the usual time.

Perhaps God will be gracious so that you will find him pleasant. I pray for God's help constantly. If he is enlightened by Him then this will be fruitful, since some divine effect stays with a true believer. The reasons and requests mentioned in your letter have all been postponed for now until they can be weighed at a suitable time by the entire City Council.

In some outlying cities there is much unrest, all truly by those who cling to the Roman Church. At Windsheim they detained the ambassadors of the council and after eight days while the city was closed off they finally negotiated. But first of all they had to reinstate two preachers which the City Council had looked upon unfavorably and had sent away. I am concerned that they are not yet indoctrinated firmly enough, as is the case with many whom we have. I still hope that you yourself will confess that just because of your own willfulness and the stubbornness of those who assist you there could be all sorts of trouble. If, however, you and your sisters want to be taught the Holy Scriptures from the correct foundation and at least believe that you could have been mistaken, then I will not at all be concerned about you and all of us who would have to await the misfortune which could threaten us, if you did not.

For God's sake it is my great request that you understand that all this comes from a truly fraternal and caring heart. All the members of orders have yielded to our request in part, except for you and the Franciscans. I have the very modest hope that you will come to the vineyard late. You will not miss all the reward. May the Lord of the vineyard grant you what He desires. I ask this of Him from my heart more than for myself. Amen.

Your willing and devoted servant, whether you want him or not.

Kaspar Nützel

I gave no answer to this letter. Then things changed, however, and he wrote me this letter.

Honored woman.

Although I wrote you yesterday that the honorable City Council arranged that the father from the Carthusians would preach to you, he gave many reasons why only Thursday and Tuesday have been left open to him to preach to you. On Sunday the preacher from St. Sebaldus is to preach to you in the afternoon until the City Council considers this matter further. I did not want to keep that from you on orders from the council. Our Lord God does make strange rods to punish us with because otherwise we would not want to stop our idolatry. I commend you and me along with those who are entrusted to us to the Grace and Protection of the Almighty. Amen.

Kaspar Nützel

Chapter 24

And so on the Thursday after Judica, the Carthusian was to preach for the first time. Then he became ill. On Palm Sunday the preacher from St. Sebaldus, Dominicus, preached, on Monday the preacher from St. Giles, on Tuesday and Wednesday the preacher from St. Lawrence, Osiander, on Maundy Thursday the one from St. Giles again, on Good Friday and Easter Sunday Dominicus, and on the second and third Easter days Osiander, on Saturday the Carthusian for the first time, and on Quasimodo Sunday[46] Dominicus for the last time.

Thus for the whole passion week we had to hear all the preachers so that we might be converted by force since there was no escape. Truly we had a difficult passion week, with a great deal of commotion, shouting and unrest in the chapel.

The entire convent was compelled to hear the sermon and no sister could miss it. Whenever we wanted to say anything, they did not believe that we were all present. They threatened us that if they learned we had not listened to the sermon they would let people enter who would sit with us during the sermon and keep watch to see if we were all there, how we behaved and whether or not we stuffed wool in our ears. Some people even boldly suggested that the door to the chapel be broken down and a grill installed in its place so that we would then have to sit publicly before everyone during the sermon.

And so on the Monday after Quasimodo that Carthusian began and gave two sermons every week, on Monday and Saturday. Osiander, the preacher from St. Lawrence preached every Sunday and holiday until the Feast of St. Michael. But not everything can and may be recorded: in

---

[46] The first Sunday after Easter.

what an unchristian manner they forced a strange meaning onto the Holy Scriptures; how violently they overturned the laws of the Church; how shamefully they cast aside the Holy Mass and all ceremonies; how disgracefully they criticized and reviled all religious orders and the clergy. They spared neither pope nor emperor and openly called them tyrants, devils and antichrists. I will not relate the coarse and unchristian manner contrary to all brotherly love in which they attacked us and the greatest conceivable sins they preached to us about in order to stir up the people against us. In good faith they exhorted them to wipe out our godless community entirely, tear down the cloisters and drag us out of them by force. We were, you see, in a state of damnation, heretics, idolaters, blasphemers and would belong to the devil forever.

All that cannot and may not be written down, but we can be grateful to Almighty God, always and everywhere, who has protected us so mercifully that despite these wicked sermons, they could discover no arrogance in us. During many sermons, however, we were in such fear and anguish that we expected our cloister would be attacked any minute. We should also thank Almighty God who has protected us so paternally that no sister has been poisoned by these harmful, heretical sermons, although we had to suffer much disgrace and insult. The preachers have also spared no effort to poison us. Yet the more they preached, the more we noticed what trickery and falseness and errors they employed. May God continue to protect us through His Mercy!

Meanwhile, some good friends advised us to choose a pious, honorable priest to whom we could then confess when necessary so that we would not be judged as being contemptuous of the Holy Sacrament. For there was very much talk about us, that we would rather die than confess to anyone but the Franciscans. I shared this opinion with the convent since it would mean nothing else but that we could not confess to any father (Pater).

Then the sisters decided that we should choose Conrad Schrötter who was a pious, courageous priest about 65 years old. We did this with the advice and consent of our worthy father guardian, at that time Michel Fryeß. He agreed and gave the man we had chosen the power to serve us for a while. He assured us that in this way we had not broken with the order of our worthy fathers as some sisters feared. This priest was, of course, also a member of our order, for he observed the third rule of St. Francis. Therefore our father guardian advised us to ask the City Council to grant us this priest, although he was very worried that the City Council would not give in any way. For what they wanted to avoid from the Franciscans, they would find in this priest.

The sisters commissioned me to send for the superintendent and to present to him immediately the gist of the opinion that was later written down. The superintendent came on that very Friday evening. I told him the following: After the City Council had robbed us of our dear fathers and councilors we had, we would end up with no councilor and, yet, after all, we were all mortal, and did not want to have to die like cattle without confession and the Holy Sacraments. Not long again, when he was talking to me in the choir, he asked us to choose someone as confessor. We were to choose whomever we liked, as long as he was not a Franciscan. Even if he were not from the city they would bring him here and spare no expense. This I reported to my convent. They commanded me to act and even the council sisters who were present considered it so that he and the honorable City Council might see that we did not want to proceed arbitrarily in these matters and had not set our hearts on the Franciscans alone. And so we wanted to choose a devote, old, honorable, courageous priest whom we had known for years and who always had a good reputation, had led a priestly life and whom we could trust and relate to. But we did not want to name him at this time, until the honorable City Council had assured us that it wanted to give us this one and not one we did not want. We desired this only on the condition that if, at some time sooner or later in the future, these dangerous times should improve, we did not want to give up anything by this action regarding our worthy fathers. We would also reserve the right to have the power to choose another priest if the priest we wanted should leave. We did not want anyone to take this freedom away from us. We wanted to confess to the person who was right for us and to no one else.

At that time there was a lot of other discussion concerning the confessor, so that we presented our superintendent a clear picture of our grievances and also told him how much it meant to us. We admonished him most fervently and begged him as out loyal master and superintendent to take this matter to heart and thus present our final decision to the honorable City Council.

He was very receptive to this speech, but, at the same time, he noted that he was worried if we chose such a simple, inexperienced and uneducated confessor, the City Councilors might not like it. We should choose one who had a reputation. Then I spoke. The one we want to name is experienced enough, for he has heard confessions for many years. We do not need any highly educated person, for in the confessional there is not need for a great deal of discussion. We also need no confessor who has a great reputation, for the less we have to do with him in the confessional the better. Instead we need a loyal, discreet father, who listens to our sins patiently and absolves us, rather than one who talks a lot.

He responded well to all of this and said again how he wanted to present the matter before the honorable City Council. We were therefore of the opinion, more or less, that to please the honorable City Council we would name a lay priest we liked to whom we were prepared to confess so that they could see that we did not insist on the Franciscans alone. We wanted to insist, however, that as far as our (Franciscan) fathers were concerned, we did not want to give up anything. If things should improve again and also if the priest should leave, we wanted to choose another one and retain the freedom to choose. Yet at the end he added that we would also tolerate the sermon.

Then I spoke. Yes, we have to suffer even that, for we cannot defend ourselves against force. But first we did not agree to that at all. When they mentioned that to us the first time, we answered that we certainly wanted to hear the clear, pure, Holy Gospel from anyone, but without giving up our freedom. At this time, however, we cannot, unfortunately, defend ourselves from force. As often as I spoke, at least three times, he listened quietly, when I said that unfortunately we had to endure this pressure. And so he departed from us in friendly terms, so that we even thought we had been successful. But on the next Saturday, the Saturday before Palm Sunday, he wrote me this letter.

Chapter 25

Grace and peace in God the Father! He has granted it so mildly in His Son Jesus Christ, especially in recent times, when we really might have deserved to have strayed until the end of the world. We can never do enough for Him except for the works that He has assigned us. Through Him alone and not through our efforts they are completed in us.

Honored woman and mother. I have carried out the order given to me by you and your advisers as diligently as I could and brought it before the honorable City Council and also explained that you, along with the whole convent, are willing to listen to the preachers whom the honorable City Council will choose for you. In so doing you have reserved the right, in case one or several of them should say something unchristian, to report this to the council in the firm hopes that they would look into it.

In the matter of the second item. The Franciscans and your order have been linked since time immemorial, so that it was, therefore, not in your power to finally break these ties. Because you now have to do without them upon the solemn request of the City Councilors, and do not want to be thought of as having given up all other confessors as the resentful rumor has it, in order to squelch that rumor you now make the humble request not to be forced to accept a confessor contrary to the will of the sisters. You believe that no one outside the cloister would put up with that either. Therefore, you request that the choice of naming a confessor be left to you. You and your convent decided to name a priest who does not yet know your perspective, but you hope will be someone who up to now has not joined one side or the other, but has behaved well and in a priestly manner.

You also do not need to argue and fight in the confessional, but instead desire to continue to simply confess in the fashion you did previously and accept absolution and leave it at that. If the Word of God, which, as you promised above, you still want to hear, should have a further effect, you desire, as always, to remain faithful subjects of the City Council with simple words, respectful requests and humble trust.

Then the City Council again decided to provide you with sermons from one or several persons. It was agreed that they would not permit anyone to preach in a manner unchristian, non-collegial or unfriendly. You have good reason to believe this because many in the City Council have daughters and relatives in your convent, and believe they are obligated to aid their salvation. Truly, if they noticed that they were being deceived, they would probably cease supporting them and working on their behalf. This work and support is being carried out conscientiously.

As far as the second point regarding confessors is concerned, the City Council considers it a difficult issue. First, you have taken it upon yourselves to admit and agree to a worldly priest and to choose and name one you consider appropriate. Your naming of a confessor should be preceded by the City Council's permission. The council interprets this to mean that you join the City Council with its permission, but you are free to choose and name him.

On the second point, you want to obligate a confessor to only listen to you, but forbid him to speak to you about the imperfections of your consciences, to reveal to you the consolation and light that God causes to shine and to liberate you from false ideas. I will let you judge how the Council views that.

After all, what kind of confession and admission would that be for a sinner who would not allow her confessor to point out the imperfections of her conscience and her faith? The councilors worry more than you give them credit for. So that you will understand their paternal, Christian attitude better and understand that they have the same concern for you as they do for themselves, they propose that if you name a priest for them now who seems suitable and acceptable to you, they will inquire about his understanding of what is Christian and unchristian, his life and his personality with as much diligence as if they were entrusting him with their own souls. If they find him to be appropriate and suitable as a Christian confessor, they will accept and approve him as your choice and suggestion much more readily than if they had assigned him to you themselves. But the City Council will not hold back if one of them behaves improperly or offensively toward you instead of behaving properly, as he should.

Yesterday the councilors sent off to the Bishop of Bamberg a reply that took up ten sheets of paper. That is an answer to a letter sent by his grace a few days ago. If I were not worried that I would burden you and perhaps anger you even more in this matter, I could not help but send them to you and let you read them, for in them you would find not only what has already happened, but what else they consider their duty to do.

In the conclusion it is very humbly stated, that if he or any of his staff in present or future questions can prove from the text of the Holy Scriptures that it deserves to be changed, lengthened or shortened, he should proceed in a Christian manner and in such a way the City Council's just, brotherly and very moderate attitude would be noticed. If he wants that then there is no hesitancy on the part of the councilors to be instructed in a Christian manner. Nevertheless they will not be satisfied with untruths.

It is getting late for me. I record this of myself honestly.[47] I ask God to grant me the Grace not to give advice or write or say anything against His Will, but instead His Will alone.

Your devoted superintendent,
Kaspar Nützel the elder.

Chapter 26

On Monday of Holy Week I sent the superintendent the following answer to his previous letter:

Hail to Jesus Christ the Crucified!
Prudent, wise, kind, dear superintendent,

From your last letter we have gathered that your honor faithfully presented our concern to the honorable City Council. May God the Lord reward you for such action and good works. At the same time, however, we notice also, that they did not accept our suggestion about the

---

47 Nützel is obviously both physically and emotionally tired. Once again he is showing doubt as to whether he is up to the challenge and demands of his office.

confessor. We sought him as a reasonable means to remove the burden from our sisters and also the gossip from people hostile to us and in order that the City Council might see that we do not persist in our stubborn opinion in all matters. It is true that we wish to retain the selection as we recently told your honor when last we spoke and that we do not want to give up anything as far as spiritual matters are concerned. We know well that in temporal matters we should yield and obey the honorable Council for the sake of peace and good relations. But in the affairs that deal with conscience, such as confession and other things, no one can show us from the Holy Gospel that anyone is to be coerced or put under pressure. We truly believe that the honorable Council is doing such things for specific reasons, as your honor mentions.

Therefore we bear no mistrust toward our kind lords and fathers. We truly believe they want to do the best for us, but they cannot, after all, see into people's hearts. One looks at a person from the outside and does not know what is inside. After long acquaintance and a good life a judgment can be made, but more in one respect than in the other. As true as it may be, that we wanted to ask the City Council to give us a confessor according to our taste, it is also true that if we give in on this issue and let ourselves be forced to confess to those we do not trust and in whom we cannot confide, our consciences, which God wants to be free, would be very troubled. A person who is physically sick is not helped by the advice of a doctor in whom he has neither faith nor trust. What would happen then to someone with a troubled conscience?

Since our proposal is not going to be carried out, we think it would be better if we do not name the one we have in mind. If we should propose someone whom other people do not like, we would perhaps not only achieve nothing, but also cause trouble for him, if he did not want to believe and follow what suited other people. Although we have truly not spoken with him yet, we consider him to be such a man who will not do anything from either fear or favor against his conscience, but only what is right.

For although one should give in in many things, to burden one's conscience by believing what goes against one's conscience in order to please others goes against God and oneself. No one bears his burden alone. No one will have to account for others, but everyone will bear his own burden before the eyes of God. As we have already said, the new teachings are, in many respects, too ambiguous when compared with the old Christian faith and yet both sides have the Holy Scriptures before them which each uses for his own cause. Therefore, for us poor simple folk, the most practical thing is for us to retain our faith in the Holy Gospel until this matter is cleared up through God's Grace.

With God's Help we will hold fast and give no one cause to get upset. For what business is it of the people outside who we confess to, since we attend the sermons in public as you have ordered. We are, moreover, condemned as despisers of the Holy Sacraments, but we desire them from the depths of our hearts as we bear witness with God and His holy angels. This holy time has been taken from us against our will and we must commend to God that we are looked upon as godless heretics, blasphemers of God and the like. Christ our Redeemer had to suffer vicious abuse from men himself. As minor limbs of the body we do not want to consider ourselves better than the Head itself.

Let us speak with St. Paul's words. It does not matter the least to me that I am condemned by you or a court of men. It is God who will judge me. He looks at the heart. Before His eyes we are neither better not worse, say what one will. To Him we will confess our sins in the bitter contriteness of our heart and trust in Him alone. Perhaps He will send some blessed means by which the honorable City Council will find peace for our sake and we will find it in our conscience, since we desire to act according to the Council's benevolent will if our conscience permits it.

For God's sake have patience with us poor souls and read this letter in the best light. It comes from the depths of our conscience. May your time be blessed!

> Your caring honor's humble daughter, the abbess and
> All the advisory sisters of St. Clare's.

Chapter 27

On Monday, it was the Holy Evening before Maundy Thursday, the abbot of St. Giles came. He reported that our cloister had been reformed. The abbot of St. Giles had been installed as executor and from now on all abbots of his cloister were our conservators. For that reason he wanted to introduce himself as our pastor. He was surprised we had not sent for him a long time ago since there was so much going on. He really did want to help and advise us. He admonished us most strongly, that we should always follow the honorable City Council as our superior authority ordained by God. He spoke with many condescending statements.

I answered the first point curtly. We would recognize Christ as our true Shepherd who risked his soul for his lambs. Otherwise in these troubled times we would, unfortunately, be furnished with such pastors whom we would fear as much as wolves. As far as his other pastors were concerned, it would be no wonder if the wolves had not long since torn the lambs to pieces. On the second point, we were not willing, however, to follow those people in matters which ran against our conscience and our oaths. We had decided amongst ourselves that we would let no one drive us away from the unity of the Christian Church and our order.

Then he wanted to argue for a considerable time that we should receive the Holy Sacrament in both kinds in addition to other ideas. But I would not accede to him. I said we were simple, uneducated women and would leave such things to the learned men and until there was unity in the Church we preferred to stay with the old faith and not be driven off by anyone. Then he wanted to know how I liked his preacher from St. Giles. He could get no other answer from me but that I liked one as much as the other.[48] We really wanted to hear and believe the text of the Holy Scriptures. The explication which each of them came up with we could not fathom.

After the sermon on Holy Good Friday the superintendent came once again. Then I took the council sisters along with me. On this same holy day he kept us until our small meal. He told us again what transpired in the City Council when he presented our opinion about the confessor. The honorable Council was not at all content that we did not want to take to heart their paternal loyalty. Whenever they wanted to do their best for us we would not trust them, but retain the selection of confessors for ourselves. That would not turn out well for us. He was utterly ashamed that he alone among all the cloister superintendents had such trouble with us. All the other cloisters had told their superintendents that they would do what the councilors wanted. We alone were so stubborn and so very clever that we would follow nothing but our own notions. Truly we would lead ourselves astray this way and other similar statements like that.

He also said that although we had not named the priest to whom we would want to confess, he and the honorable City Council could imagine that it was no one other than Conrad Schrötter. Among all the councilors he had not noted one who liked this preacher. No one would vote for him either.

Then I spoke. It is really not necessary that we confess to the one the council likes. If they will not let us have those we like, then we do not want those they like. Then he spoke. Everything will change with those greedy servants of the mass. We should disabuse ourselves of the idea that they would not give us anyone who was not on the Lutheran side. I spoke then. If they do not believe in confession, then we will do without them too. You do not have to be in a hurry with the confessor, if you will not leave us our freedom.

He went back to speaking about the renegade Carthusian who had been driven away from Würzburg because of his Lutheran teachings and who had been engaged to preach to us. He could not praise him enough, that is how he had been a visitator and a prior of his order. We would be well served by him if we accepted him as our confessor and visitator.

I spoke again. We are Sisters of Saint Clare and not Carthusians. Therefore we want no Carthusian, for we would probably have to accept his order too. Then the superintendent spoke. He would guarantee that he would not remain a Carthusian or a monk and would not keep his habit. Then I answered him. Then let death confess to him! Are we to confess to a faithless apostate? If he does not keep faith with God, how is he to display faith to us? What else should he teach us but what he does himself? Then we would all have to become apostates! May the Living God protect us from that!

Enough of such talk. The more the superintendent praised this monk, the more I swore on behalf of myself and the whole convent that we truly did not want to ever confess to him. Nor did we want to have him as a visitator or as a superior.

Both this time and at other times this quarrelling about the monk lasted a long time. They wanted to force us to confess to him. I said more or less the following to him. Today or tomorrow this monk will take a wife too and then it would be a fine thing for us to have to take care of a pastor and his wife and their children. What could we respond to the charge that at night he would tell his wife what we had confessed during the day? Then the superintendent spoke. Yes, it would be a fine thing and he and the other councilors would also be in favor of not letting any confessor into the convent if he had a wife. We would not have to worry about him, if he had a wife.[49] Then I replied. You may think it is fine, but we do not and we truly will not be coerced into confessing to such people.

49 The text is a bit ambiguous. It could also be interpreted to mean that if the confessor had a wife, they (the sisters) would not have to worry about him, in the sense that they would not have to worry about possible sexual advances or the like, one of the "abuses" which the reformers were trying to put an end to. Since Nützel replies to Caritas's rhetorical "It would be a fine thing" with "Yes, it would be a fine thing," perhaps the interpretation just described is the correct one.

Since he could not win in this matter, he began once again and spoke of the gathering of the peasants who were now standing in the field with a large army with the intention of destroying all the cloisters and bringing down and driving away all those called clerics. He was of the opinion that they would be in Bamberg[50] on this coming Good Friday. He believed that on that day there would not be one sister left there in the cloister of St. Clare.[51] Therefore we should consider what we had in mind so that we would not be the cause of great bloodshed. And even if the peasants did not reach here, the common man would still be instructed by the clear Gospel and the clerical estate was nothing. Therefore we could not maintain our ways and should have the good sense to stop.

With these and many similar threats we spent Holy Good Friday and in like manner Easter Monday when the superintendent returned and once again used his greatest efforts to convert us. But with God's Grace it was of no avail. In truth we had a long, sad Lent full of fear and distress, horror and fear from within and without, with nothing of the Passion and other good things which belong to the holy season. We had to raise the holy cross ourselves and sing the Alleluja, since we could not have a priest.

Chapter 28

As we were coming out of Lent in misery and distress, things got much worse after Easter. On the Friday of Easter Week all the priests were summoned to the city hall and forbidden to celebrate the Latin mass. The council said they had learned from educated men that the mass was such an idolatrous, blasphemous thing that they could no longer permit it, especially because of the canon. All lay priests and the priests in the monasteries with the exception of those in the parishes were forbidden to hear confession and to dispense the sacraments.

Unfortunately, from that day on we have not had mass in our church, except on the day of our holy mother, St. Clare.[52] Then the Lutheran women along with the Lutheran pastors and the cantor from the

---

[50] Bamberg lies less than 60 km north of Nürnberg.

[51] In 1852 Josef Pfanner discovered Caritas's journal in the Bamberg Staatsarchiv and published it under the title of *Die Denkwürdigkeiten der Äbtissin Caritas Pirckheimer*.

[52] 12 August.

hospital[53] arranged to sing a German mass in our church. We all ran from the choir, however, and did not hear it.

On the same Friday they also forbade our worthy fathers the Franciscans to ring the bells any more, to celebrate divine services either by day or by night and also to pray in common. This order was given to no monastery but the poor Franciscans. The others were forbidden only the mass, but were allowed to celebrate the divine office as they wanted. But soon, unfortunately, they fell away from the faith themselves. Without being forced, they began to sing the German mass and to perform different ceremonies in the parishes.

At first (the end of 1524) in Nürnberg the Augustinians defected; in May 1525 the Carmelites followed them and in July the Benedictines, and in November the Carthusians. At that time the Franciscans and the Poor Clares remained faithful to the old Church. They also dispensed the sacrament to the people in both kinds, with the exception of the Franciscans.

Also the lay priests had to become citizens and swore to pay the tax on wine and beer and the income tax[54] and in all things to behave like the other laity. At the request of the City Council in all the men's monasteries an inventory was made of all articles for church use, chalices and other jeweled items plus decorations, vestments worn during mass and altar cloths. This was all written down, even for the Franciscans.[55]

Soon afterwards the abbot of St. Giles relinquished his cloister with all that belonged on it, both movable and immovable possessions, and even all documents and treasures. All this the City Council took possession of.

The monks took oaths as citizens and for each an estimate was made as to what he was to receive annually, approximately 25 gulden for each one. But if anyone wanted to give up the monastic life entirely and marry, he would be given 50 or 100, or in some cases 200 gulden depending on what he had brought into the cloister.

After that they put off the habit of their order, put on worldly clothes, some a little costly, and stopped saying Matins or anything else that belongs to the divine service except what they wanted. The Augustinians who were the source of all this misfortune – Luther had been an Augustinian monk – did the same thing too as did the Carmelites and the Carthusians as well. In all the cloisters a wild life ensued. No order

---

53 The Heilig-Geist-Spital.
54 See Strauss, pp. 90–91.
55 Since the Franciscans had taken a vow of poverty, the reformers hoped to find "evidence" that this vow had not been upheld.

was observed any more, with each person doing whatever he wanted to. In these cloisters they ate meat even during Lent and on other forbidden days. Many monks ran away from the cloisters and took wives. The preaching monks would have been happy to turn over their monastery to the councilors and petitioned for it themselves. It was not accepted, however, for they were too poor, having not as much annual income as the other monasteries. Then all but nine of the monks left. The latter sold what valuables they could find and lived off that as long as they could.

Then all income in every church, all offerings, all anniversary donations, all alms, all endowments were taken away from the churches and placed in the general fund.

Oh, we were in great fear and distress night and day! They threatened that we would have to do that too. Then we agreed among ourselves that in no way would we give up the cloister. We had not made it. It did not belong to us. We had not built it. Every day they threatened to drive us off or plunder or burn the cloister. Sometimes rather angry, audacious fellows surrounded the cloister and threatened our servants that they were about to attack the cloister on that very night so that we were very afraid and worried and could hardly sleep from fear. In addition there was also considerable unrest in the city, so that every day there was fear of an attack.

In this way the community would go after the priests and monasteries first. We were hated and looked upon unfavorably. The upper as well as the lower circles were hostile towards us to such an extent that our servants could hardly let themselves be seen when they bought our necessities. They considered us more disgraceful than the poor women behind the wall,[56] for it was preached publicly that we worse than they were.

Only with great anxiety and secretly could our good friends visit us. The others who came to us tormented us to the marrow of our bones. For in all the pulpits the preachers were demanding again and again that no convent and no habit should be tolerated any more. Moreover, people did not want the convents to be called cloisters anymore, but hospices. The sisters also should no longer be called sisters, but pensioners, and not abbess or prioress, but manageress. There should be no difference between secular and religious persons, but all should be alike. Every day we were threatened again. Because of this we got so discouraged that we feared every night would be our last in the cloister. Every day we heard

---

[56] Prostitutes.

many awful, terrible things about how the peasants destroyed so many cloisters and drove away the poor inhabitants so dreadfully.

We had so much Easter joy[57] between Easter and Pentecost that it would not have been anything unusual if the marrow had dried in our bones. When the peasants got so close to the city, the sisters from Pillenreuth and Engelthal were brought into the city in great despair. They also had to turn over their property and land to the City Council. The plan was not to let them return to their cloister any more. The Swabian league came to their assistance, however, and arranged with the councilors that a few weeks after the peasants had run off, they were allowed to go home and their cloister and their holdings were returned. In the houses where they found shelter they suffered a great deal. Those from Pillenreuth left behind two professed sisters and two novices who belonged to their order, but those from Engelthal at least five.

And so we were in great fear and distress and every day we expected even more misfortune. We crouched down and bent down so much that we could hardly hold divine services or ring the bells in the choir. Whenever they heard anything from us, cursing, shouting and abuse would start up in the church. They threw stones into our choir[58] and smashed the windows in the church and sang slanderous songs in the churchyard. They frequently threatened that if we rang for Matins one more night they would do something terrible to us.

But we risked it, trusting in the Grace of God, and not for one night did we stop ringing the bells or holding Matins. Otherwise all Matins would have been done away with. The sisters at St. Katharine's have not rung for Matins for about half a year.

On the eve of Ascension Day the councilors sent their wine and beer inspector who was to check all we had to drink from our wine and beer cellar. On the Friday after that I sent a messenger on an errand to our superintendent. Then the superintendent's wife had me informed that she wanted to come next Monday and fetch her daughter. The councilors would come to us on the following Sunday and negotiate with us for so long that we would probably have to give her daughter back to her. Next Sunday the council would send a message to us and give us a different rule which we would have to follow from then on. Even Sigmund Fürer had been there[59] and with all his might had demanded

---

57 Even in the midst of such turmoil, Caritas did not lose her sense of humor, or, perhaps more accurately, her sense of irony.

58 Hence the crouching down to avoid being hit by stones and breaking glass.

59 Before the council.

the daughters of his two sisters, Frau Ebner and Frau Tetzel. When I learned of this I wrote the superintendent this little note:

Chapter 29

The Grace of God our Father, through our Lord Jesus Christ, in the unity of the Holy Ghost, be to your honor!

Worthy, kind, dear superintendent and faithful father,

It has been reported through our servant Wilhelm that recently Sigmund Fürer earnestly requested of your honor that I should send home the daughters of his two sisters, Frau Tetzel and Frau Ebner. Your honorable wife requested the same thing. Since then she has notified us that she will come on Monday next and wants to negotiate the matter seriously.

As I mentioned to you recently, I would very much like it if your honor were there personally, for if the father wants it so, then the mother has more control over the children. Accordingly it is my wish that this be put off until you are healthy again. May God grant that soon! But if you cannot or do not want to wait any longer, the I desire for your honor to let me know in writing what your will and opinion are.

I have raised these two and other children in all friendship and motherly loyalty. I still want to act as a friend and not send them home so that it cannot be said that they behaved in such a way that we drove them out. If, however, the father and mother want to fetch their children and not allow them to stay with us any longer, then I will not hold them back for an instant. We would keep one against her will as little as we would drive one away from us by force.

I would like to have your answer in this matter and your loyal advice as our loyal superintendent as to whether I should also convey this opinion to Herr Ebner and Frau Tetzel or whether I should wait until they come themselves.

Up until now your honor has always advised and acted in the best way. With the entire convent I desire nothing more than that God's benevolent Will be done in all things. I commend you to the Eternal Grace of God.

Chapter 30[60]

I received no answer to this letter. We had a very troubled church conse-cration, for every hour during the week we expected the gentlemen would arrive and undertake something strange.

Then early on Wednesday during Pentecost week at prime Sigmund Fürer, Sebald Pfinzing and Andreas Imhof appeared and demanded entry into the cloister. They had a message to deliver from the Council. They were in such a hurry that they were reluctant to wait until prime was over. And so I let them into the summer refectory and called the convent together.

Fürer began to speak. By means of the clear, bright evangelical Word of God it had now come to light that the special sects, that is the clerical, isolated cloistered estate, were immoral, mistaken, sinful and cursed estates in which people lived contrary to the commandments of God and the Holy Gospel. This and many other things had become abso-lutely clear to the common man. For this reason the community was so enraged about the clergy that they simply did not want to tolerate a cloister or the clerical estate any more and not only here, but also in all lands far and wide. That was also the reason for the great bloodshed caused by the peasants who had joined together in order to destroy and uproot the clerical class everywhere. Therefore, the honorable City Council as our faithful father is very worried about us as well as about themselves. With our nun's habits and our peculiarities we might give the community cause to attack us and this might spread out beyond us; or in some other way they might attempt to prove us guilty of haughti-ness. That would make them very sorry. Therefore out of its paternal concern for our well-being the honorable City Council had considered the issue and ordered them to present us five articles. If we accepted them and carried them out, they could protect and guard us from the community that much better. However, if we did not accept them, some-

---

60 The five point program of the City Council (Chapters 30–32):
    1. The abbess is to release the sisters from their oaths.
    2. Every sister shall be free to leave the cloister or, respectively, her parents have the right to take her from the cloister. The City Council will provide for her support.
    3. The sisters shall wear worldly clothing.
    4. A clear window shall be installed so that during visits relatives can see the sisters and also whether they are alone during the conversation.
    5. The sisters shall undertake an inventory of all their possessions.
    All of this shall be done within four weeks.

thing they certainly could not imagine, then they could not support us or the cloister any longer.

The first thing the honorable Council wanted from me as the leader of the convent was that I should release all the sisters from the vows they had taken so that they could make use of Christian freedom and would no longer be obligated or forced to do something. Instead whatever they did was to be of their own free will so that they could cease and desist whenever they wanted.

The second thing was that I should not keep any sister within the convent against her will. I should also not keep parents from their children whom they did not want to stay here, even if that were not the desire of the children. It was, of course, contrary to God's commandment, for children were obligated to obey their parents. Nevertheless, the Council was to be informed beforehand if anyone wanted to leave or if the parents wanted to take one out by force. The Council wanted to return to each person whatever property of the cloister she had brought in. Even to those who had not brought in anything they wanted to grant an appropriate pension if they left. To those who wanted to marry and take a husband they wanted to grant an honorable pension too. All of this was to be done according to the holdings of the cloister but ensuring that the old ones who remained within would also be supported and not become completely impoverished.

The third thing, according to the final decision of the Council and the community, was that we put aside our nun's habits and dress like other people. There was to be no difference between worldly and clerical persons and therefore no difference in their clothes. After all, the kingdom of heaven is not made up of clothes.

The fourth thing, as finally decided by the honorable Council, was that our 'speaking windows'[61] should be not just speaking windows, but also transparent windows. They were to be constructed with a grill in such a way that friends who wished to speak with a sister could see that she was the right one and that she was alone and had no one with her. If someone wanted to speak with a sister alone, that should be allowed. The other sister who listened in should be sent away so that the sister could speak freely about what was on her mind. This is the way the Council wanted it.

---

[61] The "grille" which allowed people to converse, but not see one another. The reformers wanted to be able to speak privately with the nuns without a third party listening in. The sisters of the cloister, however, preferred the old system which allowed another sister to hear the conversation and, should it be necessary, serve as a "witness" to what really transpired, lest the reformers make false claims.

The fifth thing was that after the honorable Council had undertaken an inventory in all the cloisters in the city and had had everything described, we should make one ourselves and turn it over to the Council. We should indicate all our income, all interest, pensions and monies, all land (where it was located and what income it brought in), all treasures and whatever each sister had brought in. The honorable Council wanted all these things done this way. They would give us four weeks. These points and many others had been decided upon not just for our cloister, but also for the sisters at St. Katharine's and for those in Pillenreuth and at Engelthal who were still there at that time.[62]

Chapter 31

When they had finished speaking, I responded to the first article concerning vows. The whole convent present here knows very well that no sister made a vow to me or to any living person except to God Almighty. Therefore, it is not fitting for me, a mere human being and useless creature, to dissolve in any way what was promised to God. I would not and could not get involved in any way, for that is not within my power. I have enough to bear from my own sins and would not burden myself with the sins of others.

The men made great sport of that. They said we would find in our own consciences and even in the Scriptures that oaths do not matter. They were not binding before God and had all been eliminated anyway. Nobody had the power to take an oath except at baptism. I was to just release the sisters from what they owed me. As far as God was concerned, it really did not matter.

In addition I said that I would gladly release them from whatever they owed me, for none of them had promised me anything, except if the convent wished to release me from my position, for I could not be in charge if they would not obey me. I had administered the convent with my dear children for 22 years now. Up to now they had always shown obedience willingly and humbly so that sisterly love, peace and unity could be maintained. I could never hope for that now. In the event they wanted to make the sisters oppose me, they themselves would have to decide what kind of governance they would have and what would come of it in time. There were also some children within whom their mothers while at the speaking window had forbidden to do anything I would

---

62 Some nuns had already left the latter two cloisters for safer quarters.

propose. The daughters would be obligated to obey them and not me and my prioress. This was unacceptable to me.

They said it was reasonable for them to follow me and obey me in household affairs. But the honorable City Council did not want me to force them to fast or pray and keep their vows, for all these things should be voluntary. The gentlemen did not want any sister to be obligated to keep any vows.

Concerning dress I said we knew very well that our habits did not assure us of salvation. We also knew, however, that in heaven there was no inappropriate attire such as coats of camel hair.[63] I also brought up the costs this would entail. It would not be possible to reclothe such a large convent. Up to now we had made our clothes and our coats ourselves. What should we do with the old clothes?

They said we should take apart our habits and have them dyed a different color. It would not matter if we spent 400 gulden on clothing this year. The cloister would die out anyway. There was no way they would allow us to continue to receive novices.

Therefore we were to spend lavishly on food, drink and clothes. Our possessions and money would be left when we had all died. Above all else they forbade us to let anyone wearing a habit go into the garden or anywhere else where she would be seen by the people from outside, for that would certainly cause a disturbance.

Among other things I said, "Dear sirs, you always maintain that because of our vows and our habits we might create a reason for an uprising. I am more afraid that your preachers, to whom we must listen, would cause an uprising, since they constantly scold and insult us from the pulpit and accuse us of such great sin and immorality that the people[64] later told us to our faces that if we did the things the preachers say then it would be a good idea to burn us all up in the convent. Some others say that the immorality we practice in the convent is now coming to light and that we are worse than those behind the city walls.[65] Therefore, we desire that you tell our lords if they want to prevent an uprising, they should advise their preachers not to preach in such an inappropriate manner. Many times we have sat through a sermon and we all trembled

---

[63] Perhaps the representatives of the City Council were wearing camel hair coats. If they were, Caritas again showed that she was not afraid to "speak her mind."

[64] These "Lutheran" preachers spoke in the convent's public church and as a result the public could hear the charges made against the nuns and, as is evident here, often reacted strongly to them.

[65] Prostitutes.

because we expected that the cloister would be stormed any minute. If that should happen, then the people might go even further."

Sigmund Fürer rebuked me on this point. He said that such things were not preached solely at our convent, but the Gospel's message concerning clerical dress was being made known throughout the entire world. I also had a great disagreement with him concerning the speaking window and speaking alone.[66] Among other things I said that I noted very well that they wanted to make this an open cloister. If they wanted to make a garden gate[67] out of this reformed cloister, they should have told me in advance. I would truly not want to remain in this cloister, for I do not believe that I could then find salvation for my soul here.

They said the idea was not to make it into an open cloister. For this reason the Council had suggested the grate as a means by which the cloister could continue to remain "closed." If we did not accept the grate and did not want to let the sisters talk alone with their parents, then we would have to allow the cloister to be entered. Many people were constantly coming to the Council with the request that they be allowed to go into the convent. In order to prevent this, we were to have three grates installed so that nobody would have to wait in line.

Thus we had a good discussion. Fürer shook the hands of some sisters and they left our convent on friendly terms. As I was about to let them out, I asked them when the four weeks would be over that they had given us to consider these issues and whether they wanted to come back for the answer themselves or whether I should send for them.[68]

They replied that in no way had they given us a month to deliberate since the matter did not need an answer. The lords wanted it done this way and that was it. The four weeks were given to us so that we could bring about the changes they had presented to us.

---

66 That is without another member of the convent being present.

67 The image she wishes to convey is that of an "open door" policy whereby "outsiders" could enter whenever they pleased. Such a change would, of course, destroy the whole principle of the "closed" convent with limited access from the outside.

68 Here Caritas appears very naïve in believing that the convent had a choice in these matters. Whatever sense of "give and take" may have existed in the past between the City Council and the convent (when the Council members were all believing Roman Catholics) had largely disappeared by this time. Although it could be said that the convent received "special treatment" this was mostly because Caritas refused to accept the changes mandated by the City Council as readily as the other convents in the city did.

Then I spoke. "How would it be possible to reclothe the large convent in one month?" He answered that I should first take 20 to be reclothed and after that more, until they had all been reclothed.

Chapter 32

As they were leaving the cloister, I called the sisters to a chapter meeting and listened to advice from all of them as to how we should proceed with these serious matters on which the very destruction of our cloister and all religious life depended. From each one separately I desired to know what I should expect, whether they wanted to accept the new rules which the lords had given them.

Without exception they all voted unanimously and each one separately that they would keep the rule which they had vowed to God and in no way obey the rule which the Council had given them. Humbly and willingly they stated that they did not want to be free.[69] They would gladly obey me and do whatever I wanted, if only I stayed with them and did not abandon them in their fear and distress. And so once again I promised to be loyal to them, to remain with them and to risk life and limb with them even unto death as long as they remained steadfast in the true Christian faith and religious life. If they wanted to become Lutheran, however, or be unfaithful to their bridegroom,[70] or make the convent open, then I would not stay with them a single day longer.

In this way we consoled one another in faith and with fervent tears and vowed once again to remain faithful to one another in sisterly love. As a whole convent we also declared before the living God that we would accept nothing willingly that was against God and our holy rule. If, however, we were compelled against our will, we wanted our Lord to see that we had to yield to a force we could not defend ourselves against. Once again we joined in the promise that even though we now had to accept something against our rule, we would not continue any longer than we had to. And, at the very hour that the whole situation got better, we would stop.[71]

Concerning the window grate which they did not want at all, the sisters voted that since it could not be avoided and in order to avoid

---

[69] That is leave the cloister as "free" citizens, no longer bound to the rule of the convent and therefore no longer nuns.

[70] Christ.

[71] Obviously they believed that these "reforms" would be short-lived and at some uncertain time in the future they would be able to return to the "old ways."

something worse, I was to have a single window grate installed and it was to be used according to our rule as much as possible. The rule did not completely prohibit seeing the speaker's face either. In the matter of speaking alone,[72] many sisters stated that they did not want it at all. They had nothing to say to their relatives that they would be afraid to say before a listener. It would be dangerous to speak with outsiders alone, because it might be said of us that we had stated something we had never said at all. As it was, our words and our works were already being distorted.

The issue of clothing proved very difficult. They wished to ask some good friends for advice about how we could defend ourselves against this and other changes. I did as they wished. I asked some who were knowledgeable in the subject and had our best interest at heart. They said it was unthinkable to oppose these people. We had to give in a little if we did not want the cloister to be completely destroyed. For these people[73] did everything with great force. They respected neither justice nor fairness. They feared neither Pope nor Emperor, not even God Himself except in their words.[74] Nothing else mattered to them except saying it must be this way. This way and no other. For they let themselves be heard saying they were stronger than even the Pope himself. Our advisers said it was true that the window grate had been proposed as a method of avoiding the entering of the cloister itself. A few weeks ago it had been decided in the City Council that anyone could visit his relatives in the women's cloisters as often as he desired. The sisters were also to visit their relatives[75] if they were ill. If the relatives should want to have a party, they could also invite a sister from the convent. The abbess was not to deny that right to anyone, but was to supply a companion for the invited nun who was to eat with her outside the cloister and accompany her back again. At St. Katherine's they had already instituted this procedure. It gave rise to a great deal of coming and going, early and late. Even the Lutheran preacher Thomas at the

---

[72] Without another sister present.

[73] The reformers.

[74] The reformers believed they were doing "God's work" as much as the loyal Catholics did. They could quote Scripture to defend their actions too.

[75] By doing this they would be breaking their vows. On the surface this seems like a "reasonable" reform. What could be more "cruel" than to not allow a person to visit her sick relative? In truth, however, there was more behind this one change than might appear at first glance. It could well become the "first step" toward making the cloister open. If this change was agreed to, other changes could well be expected which would contradict the rule of the cloister.

Hospice[76] had changed his robes along with other good fellows and come into the cloister and criticized the young sisters in an unspiritual manner and had spoken to some of them very boldly, saying that they should promise to marry him. When he had come out of the cloister later he said many nasty, untrue things about the nuns that they could never have even imagined.[77] Then the sisters complained to the City Council about him. Some gentlemen who were on our side, that is Martin Geuder,[78] Hieronymus Holzschuher,[79] and Jakob Muffel,[80] took this to heart. They faithfully proposed that the right to enter the women's cloisters be done away with. At the City Council they said, among other things, "Gentlemen, what are you letting yourselves be responsible for by bringing this great disgrace upon yourselves! Many of you have your own flesh and blood, your children and daughters, your aunts and other relatives in these cloisters. Is every young man to be allowed to go in and out of the cloisters? You can imagine yourselves what could result from that. It will not go on without sin and disgrace and trouble. There will be more open, bad houses[81] than cloisters." These same gentlemen had proposed the window grate, for they thought it would be less troublesome for us to accept it for a while than to endure free access to the cloister.

Therefore these good friends advised us to have a window grate installed according to the will of the lords, since it could be used with discipline and honor and with appropriate modesty. But with the issue of clothing we should take some time, for they hoped some assistance would be forthcoming in this matter. The women of Pillenreuth had vehemently opposed discarding the habits of their order. Their leader, Magdalena Kressin, had asked her brother Christoph Kressen, who at that time was a member of the Swabian League, to help her to continue to wear her habit. He told the councilors he had asked his sister if she was not satisfied with one habit since she wears three over one another.

---

[76] The Heilig Geist Spital by the river Pegnitz still stands today. It was literally "down the street" from St. Clare's.

[77] On the surface this episode has all the trappings of a drunken prank, but there is no evidence to support such a claim.

[78] A member of the City Council since 1483 and advancing ultimately to the rank of first treasurer, the highest office, Geuder was married to Juliana Pirckheimer and was therefore Caritas's brother-in-law.

[79] Dürer painted his friend Holzschuher's portrait in 1526. Both were members of the Sodalitas Staupitziana. The well-known portrait shows a "typical" Nürnberg patrician. Holzschuher had been a member of the City Council since 1499.

[80] Dürer painted Muffel's portrait in 1526.

[81] In other words, brothels.

He would see who wanted to defy her and to remove those from her.[82] Here they thought, if she could keep them on, we might also enjoy the privileges of our cloister if we all just maintained our position uniformly.

Later, on the Saturday before the Feast of the Holy Trinity, Hieronymus Ebner and our superintendent Kaspar Nützel demanded from us their daughters Katharina Ebner and Clara Nützel.[83] Although the honorable City Council had ordered us to change our habits, these two did not need to dress differently, for during the coming week they would be taken away and would then be clothed appropriately. Oh, what fear and distress and heartache began for the poor children! One cannot imagine what a wretched time they had from that hour on. Nevertheless, they still hoped they could save themselves.[84]

Chapter 33

The next Monday Hieronymus Ebner, Frau Kaspar Nützlin, Frau Friedrich Tetzl and Frau Sigmund Fürer[85] came riding up in a carriage and wanted to enter the convent by force. When I refused and would not allow it at all they said they had permission from their husbands and from the honorable City Council to be allowed to enter as often as they wanted or desired.

I said, I had heard something different from the honorable City Council. They told me they did not want an open cloister. The mothers said even if they did go in, that would not make it an open cloister. I said that if you enter, other people who have children within will want to

---

82 This sounds like an attempt at humor. His sister must have been a very strong-willed woman. Anyone who might attempt to cross her was probably not going to have an easy time of it. If someone were to attempt to remove her habit whether by decree or by physical action, he might expect considerable resistance.

83 Here begins one of the most fascinating parts of the journal. The superintendent of the cloister is seeking to remove his daughter from the cloister. Although the young woman does not want to leave, her parents remove her. Afterwards Kaspar Nützel continues to be the superintendent and therefore must continue to deal with Caritas Pirckheimer as she defends her cloister and her charges from the City Council's attempts to chip away at her power and at the whole concept of the cloistered life. How helpful it would be if we had Nützel's private journal of this period.

84 In the sense that they might not have to leave the cloister.

85 It should be noted that it is the mothers alone, not the fathers, who come to remove their daughters from the convent.

enter too and in this way the cloister will be opened. With the help of the living God, I will not permit that as long as I am in charge.

When they saw that I would never let them enter, they wanted to force me to let their children go out into the chapel so that they could speak freely with them of God's word and the salvation of their soul. I did not permit that either. I said I had taken in the children according to the will of the Council and I did not want to let them leave without its permission. They said they had enough power at their disposal. Even if we did not want to release them, we would have to. I was simply to tell them whether I would keep their children against the command of the Council. They would then bring force enough so that I would see they were serious.

I said the children wanted to see their fathers so that they could tell them their feelings beforehand.[86] Then the women got angry and said that the fathers had brought the children here and now they were angry about it. They also asked where the window grates were which the honorable Council had ordered us to install. They could see very well that we were obstinate in everything the Council had decided. I said that it had not been possible to have them installed in so short a period. We had four weeks and I would have one made. Frau Ebner said that she would have to have one for herself alone before she could instruct her daughter sufficiently in the Word of God.

After much quarreling I offered to let them speak with their daughters alone at the speaking window[87] or in the chapel at the little window where the Holy Sacrament is given to us, or wherever else they desired. They were not sure that someone would not be listening to them in the chapel. And so they were extremely angry. They would not let the children choose for themselves. With many threats they said they would go away this time and would bring back enough force so that I would have to give in.

On Tuesday they attacked me very forcefully before the entire City Council through Nikolaus Haller, their attorney. I was said to have dealt with them very rudely, haughtily and abusively. Contrary to the command of the honorable City Council I had kept their children from them by force and had not wanted to let them speak with their children for either a brief or a long period of time. I had ordered them to lie. This stems from their charging me with allowing other women into the

---

[86] It seems clear that the young women believed that their fathers would be more sympathetic than their mothers.

[87] Where it was not possible to see the person speaking or whether that person was alone.

cloister at other times and they named some who in fact had never set foot inside the cloister. They said they would produce witnesses who had seen with their own eyes that I had let this one and that one enter. Since I had been untruthful and denied this Frau Ebner said she knew very well she would have to lie to me. I had done it to her before even more. I said I had not told them to lie; that was absolutely not true. These and other things I said they had twisted around so much and had accused me of many other evil things.

On the same day after dinner they sent two City Councilors to me, Sebald Pfinzig and Andreas Imhof. They lectured me about how the women had accused me and how the City Council was very angry with me because I had ignored their command and, in an illegal manner, I had kept the children from their parents to whom they owed obedience according to the divine commandment. I was also obstinate in other matters the City Council had decided. The lords were upset and with good reason. Nothing good would come of this for me or the convent. Contrary to all law I had not wanted to allow the women to speak with their children. Therefore we would soon know the final decision of the Council and its orders in case the people did not want to leave their children with us any longer. If the mothers wanted to remove their children on the next day, I was to allow it and offer no resistance. The honorable City Council wanted this done and nothing else, regardless how the children themselves felt.

I told them things had not proceeded as the Council had been informed. I had told the women many times that they could speak with their children themselves at the conversation windows in the chapel. They had not wanted to do that. They only wanted to enter the cloister by force or the children were to go out into the church. It was certainly true that I was opposed to that coming in and going out, yet not out of malice, but in accordance with the City Council's command. Both gentlemen had of course been present when Sigmund Fürer on behalf of the Council had agreed that no open cloister would be established. If people wanted to go in and out, then the cloister would, of course, become open. Then there would be a great influx, for what was allowed for one others would want too. I hoped they would keep what the City Council had promised. I would rely on that and, with the help of the Living God, I would allow no open cloister as long as I lived.

Then I began to speak again and told them the truth concerning what had happened with the women. They were very surprised about it and said the City Council had been informed of many violent and obstinate acts plus other things and that my behavior had been examined very carefully. I should just think about these things and no longer hold back

the children from them with force when their mothers came to fetch
them. We would truly have no peace as long as they remained inside.
Perhaps things would get better later and we would be relieved a bit
from this daily influx and unrest.

I told them how the children had begged from the depths of their
hearts that their fathers be sent to them before their mothers came back
so that they could discuss important matters with them. They said that
would really not happen. When they came to the houses of their fathers
they would have enough time to speak with them.

Finally I asked them to report my answer to the honorable City
Council and to clear my name of this unreasonable accusation. They did
this in good faith. Then Nikolaus Haller was asked why he had
presented such material to the City Council. He said he had only
presented what the women had told him. He believed they spoke the
truth. In this way they were shown to be liars.

Chapter 34

On Wednesday, the eve of St. Vitus Day[88] which was also the eve of
Corpus Christi which most holy day was not celebrated nor was the
slightest reverence shown to the Holy Sacrament,[89] the wicked women[90]
sent word to me an hour before meal time that they would come before
dinner[91] and remove their children. They would bring along other
people too, so that I could see that they had enough force. I then sent a
message to the city hall and demanded that they send me two witnesses
who would be present during this activity. Since they wanted to bring
along other people, we should have some on our side also so that the
women would not make unreasonable accusations as they had done
before. The poor children, however, did not know yet when this would
take place. They had many plans and still maintained hope. Even if the
confrontation were to take place soon, they would still defend themselves. No one would use such force on them against their will. When I

---

[88] 14 June.

[89] Already some of the "reforms" of the City Council had been carried out,
including repression of the traditional celebration of these holidays.

[90] Here, as elsewhere, we are reminded that this is by no means an impartial report.
As far as Caritas was concerned, these mothers were evil. The situation suggests
the classic Old Testament scene of the two women claiming one baby as their
own. Unfortunately, there was no Solomon present to arbitrate this conflict.

[91] This would be the noon meal.

called the poor children, however, and told them their mothers would be taking them away within that very hour, all three fell to the floor, and screamed and cried a great deal and behaved so pitifully that God in heaven could have been moved. They would have liked to have fled and hidden themselves. I would not allow that, for we were worried that they would break in by force and search for them everywhere. Then the situation would get even worse. The entire convent wept and cried out also, for these were pious, intelligent children who had conducted themselves well among us and with their heart and soul did not want to leave us.

Sister Margaret Tetzel was 23 years old and had been in the holy order for nine years. Katharina Ebner and Clara Nützel had both entered the order on the same day. They had professed their vows on the same day too, 3 May, the Day of the Discovery of the Cross. It had been six years since they entered the convent. Katharina Ebner was 20 years old and Clara Nützel 19 when they were taken from the convent. With many tears we removed their veils and girdles and the white skirts and put shirts and worldly girdles and headwear on them. With some council sisters I led them to the chapel. There we waited for almost a whole hour until the fierce she-wolves came riding up in two coaches. In the meantime, word had spread to all the common people outside. They gathered in great numbers, like when a poor soul is being led to his execution. The whole street and the churchyard were so full that the women in their coaches could hardly drive into the courtyard. Then they were embarrassed that so many people were present. They would have preferred that we had let them enter by the back gate in the garden. Then they sent to me the two gentlemen, Sebald Pfinzing and Andreas Imhof, who had been appointed by the City Council as witnesses as I had requested. I did not want to use the back gate, for I did not want to be secretive in this matter. I told them if they were doing the right thing they would not need to be embarrassed. I did not want to release them from any place except where I had first received them. That was through the chapel door.

And so at 11 o'clock in the morning the ferocious wolves, both males and females, came to my precious lambs, entered the church, drove out all the people and locked the church door. Unfortunately I had to open the convent door in the chapel. They wanted me to go out into the church with the children. I did not want to do this.[92] Then they wanted

---

[92] The chapel was for the exclusive use of the cloistered nuns. When a divine service was being conducted in the church, the nuns remained in the chapel and received the sacrament through a special window between the church and chapel. They did not enter the church where the public might be present. Caritas was not

me to use force and order the children to go out into the church alone. I did not want to do this either and left it up to the children. None of them would cross the threshold in any way. The mothers then asked the men to finish things up, for the crowd was getting closer. They were afraid there would be a riot. I then spoke to the men and told them to go in and speak with the children so that they would cooperate. I could not and would not force them to do what was repugnant to them from the depths of their hearts. And so the two men went in. Then I spoke and said I would bring them my poor orphans as they had ordered me to do yesterday at the behest of the City Council and would commend them to the highest Shepherd who has redeemed them with His precious blood. With countless fervent tears we took our leave of one another. The children embraced me, wept loudly and begged that I not let them go. But unfortunately I could not help them. I withdrew with the other sisters and left the poor children alone in the chapel. I locked the door from the chapel to the churchyard so that nobody could enter the convent.

Then the angry women ran in, that is the ferocious she-wolf Frau Fritz Tetzel along with a daughter Frau Hieronymus Ebner, Frau Sigmund Fürer, Frau Kaspar Nützel, our superintendent's wife, along with her brother Linhart Held who was there in place of the superintendent, and also the young son of Sebald Pfinzing etc. Then the women used kind words and ordered the children to leave. If, however, they would not go willingly, they would be removed by force. Then the brave knights of Christ defended themselves by word and deed as much as they could with great weeping, screaming, pleading and begging, but there was less mercy there than in hell.

The mothers told their children they should obey them according to God's commandment. They wanted them to leave the convent. For they were there to redeem their souls from hell. Here their children were in the jaws of the devil and in good conscience they could no longer allow that. The children cried out that they did not want to leave the pious, holy convent. They were not in hell at all. If they were dragged out, however, they would plunge into the abyss of hell. On Judgment Day, before the stern judge, they would demand their souls from them.[93] Although they were their mothers, their daughters owed them no obedience in those matters that could damage their souls.

Katharina Ebner spoke to her mother. "You are the mother of my

about to make an exception to the rule in this instance. The cloister was to remain "closed."

[93] From their mothers who, by means of this act of forcing them to leave the convent, had taken their souls from them.

body, but not of my spirit, for you did not give me my soul. For that reason I owe you no obedience in matters which my soul opposes." Of this and other statements the mothers made much ridicule. They said they would bear responsibility for the matter before God and would assume all sins themselves. Held held out his open hand so that Clara Nützel could strike it. He wanted to take all the sins that she would commit in the world upon his soul and bear responsibility for them on Judgment Day.[94]

Every mother argued with her daughter. For a while they promised them a great deal and then for a while they threatened them a great deal. The children, however, continued to weep loudly. The arguing and shouting lasted a long time. Katharina Ebner spoke very courageously and constantly supported all her words with the Holy Scripture. She found errors in all their statements and told them how much their actions ran contrary to the Holy Gospel. Afterwards outside the men said they had never heard anything like that their whole lives. She had just spoken the whole hour without interruption. Not a word was wasted. Each word was so well chosen that it carried the weight of several words.

Since neither side would give way to the other – the children would not leave and likewise the people from outside would not listen to the charge that they had used force in attacking them – Held and even the women made threats. If they did not want to go with them now and thought that they would give up, they should understand that they would not leave them inside. In short, they would have to go and that was that. They would send people who would be strong enough. They would have to tie their hands and feet together and drag them out like dogs. But all that did not help. The children would not give in.

Then the two gentlemen sent for me again and complained that they were very afraid and did not know how they should carry out their task. No side would give in to the other. Katharina Ebner was especially defiant and violent. She had fought them to such an extent that they were all weary. If they had known in advance what kind of battle would ensue, they would not have accepted 30 gulden to come here. They hoped that with God's help no one would ever again subject them to such abuse for the rest of their lives. They said if they gave up now,[95]

---

94 How Held was "empowered" to assume the sins of someone else is not explained. Such an act certainly runs contrary to Luther's teachings. From a theological standpoint, Held is making his niece Clara Nützel a promise he cannot keep.

95 If they gave up their role as "witnesses" on behalf of the City Council, there would be no stopping the violence which would result.

truly a great misfortune would befall the convent and me. We would be attacked with force and then finally it would have to happen after all. I was to speak with the children and persuade them to leave. I protested against this very much. They requested me to release the children from their vows. Perhaps they were uncertain in regard to obedience and whether they would not be permitted to leave. Then I spoke. "You have heard me say earlier that I have no power to dissolve what is vowed to God." Then they requested that I should return to those in the chapel so that the women might see that I was present. The gentlemen would be my protectors so that the women would not show arrogance toward me. And so I went back into the chapel with some sisters. There stood my poor little orphans among the vicious wolves and defied them with all their strength. I greeted the mothers and told them I had brought their children here without force as the City Council had ordered. Now they could see clearly how much they wanted to leave. Then they demanded that I should release them from their vow of obedience. Among other things I said, "Dear children, you know I cannot release you from what you promised to God. I do not want to get involved in that, but instead I will commend it to Almighty God. He will dispose of it in His own time. But I will free you from what you have owed me up to now as much as I am supposed to and am able to just as I have done for you even today when I was alone with you." The worldly people were content with that and said I had done my part and they did not desire any more. What had been promised to God was no longer valid anyway. Vows had already been dissolved except those made at baptism.

The three children cried as one, "We do not want to be freed of them, but with His help we want to keep what we vowed to God. If our worthy mother were to set us free and the whole convent heard it, we would, nevertheless, not want to leave. For we owe obedience to nothing but the vows of our order." Margaret Tetzel cried out, "O dear mother, do not drive us away from you this way!" I said, "Dear Children, you see that unfortunately I cannot help you, for the forces here are too great. You would not like to see even more misfortune befall the convent. I hope we will not be separated for this reason, but will meet again and remain forever with our faithful Shepherd. I commend you to Him who has redeemed you with His Precious Blood."

Katharina Ebner said, "Here I stand[96] and will not yield. No one shall be able to force me out. If I am removed by force, however, it shall never be by my will in eternity. I will appeal to God in heaven and to all the

---

[96] Ironically here she uses Luther's famous words "Here I stand."

world on earth." When she was speaking Held took her under his arms and began to pull and drag her away. Then I ran away with the other sisters, for I could not watch this misery. Some sisters stopped at the chapel door. They heard the quarreling, shouting and dragging away amid the great screaming and weeping of the children. Four people grabbed each one with two pulling in front and two pushing from behind. And so the dear sisters Ebner and Teztel fell over each other at the threshold. Poor sister Teztel almost had her foot severed. The wicked women stood there and blessed their daughters as they came out in accordance to all their rituals.

Frau Ebner threatened her daughter that if she did not walk before her she would push her down the stairs to the pulpit. She threatened to throw her on the floor so hard that she would bounce. When they broke into the church amid much cursing and swearing, an incredible screaming, shouting and weeping began before they tore off the holy garments of our order and dressed them with worldly clothes. They did not take the habits along with them. All the sisters in the choir heard the screaming and fighting as did the people from the city who were standing in front of the church and had gathered in such numbers as if a poor soul were being led to his execution.

When they were about to place them into the coaches before the church there was great weeping. The poor children cried out loudly to the people and complained that they were suffering abuse and injustice and that they had been taken from the cloister by force. Clara Nützel called out loudly, "O beautiful Mother of God, you know this is not my will." As they rode away many hundreds of boys and other people ran after each coach. Our children screamed and wept loudly. Frau Ebner struck her little Katharina on the mouth so that it began to bleed. When each coach arrived at her father's house, each child began to scream and weep all over again so that the people had great pity for them. Even soldiers who had gone along said that if they had not been afraid of a riot and of the city police who were also present, they would have drawn their swords and helped the poor children. Dear Katharina got out in front of Ebner's door by the fruit market and put her hands over her head and, with many tears, complained to the people that against her will force and injustice had taken place. Almost all the women in the fruit market cried with her.

What happened afterwards to the poor children among the vicious wolves we cannot know. But we were told that by the fourth day afterwards Clara Nützel had still not eaten one bite in the world outside and that the others cried unceasingly. Before God and mankind I give my testimony that they were very diligent. They never spoke evil of the convent later, but when asked always spoke very highly of us and had a great longing and desire for their cloister. May God help us to be reunited with joy! We were separated from one another with great sorrow. Truly we had a sad Corpus Christi eve. The convent did not sit down to dinner until the afternoon.

Chapter 35

After this we made an inventory as the City Council had requested. Through God's grace, however, it has not been picked up yet. We ceased working on clothes also, cut up nothing and dyed nothing like the other cloisters.[97] Then the people seemed to have forgotten about it, so that we were not criticized because of our habits. Therefore up to now we have not needed to dress differently. May God protect us further!

Unfortunately we had to have the window grate made. We did not do that until the very last day when four weeks had passed. By the grace of God we had no such surfeit of worldly visitors as we had feared. Although some people did attempt both earnestly and often to instruct their siblings and relatives in the Lutheran doctrine and about leaving the cloister, by God's grace no one was persuaded. Also, the sisters did not want to speak with their relatives alone, for they were worried that their conversation would be twisted if nobody else were there listening in. The sisters also behaved towards their relatives in such a way that whoever was there once, did not come back again soon. Praise be to God!

Afterwards, on the eve of St. Laurence Day, the inspector came who had visited us before and told us three things from the City Council. First, we were not to lay in a supply of any more wine without a form from the tax collector. Second, we were to have our wine and beer supplies inspected before we laid in any more. Third, we were to lay in all the supplies that we had arranged for. Therefore, from that time on, whenever we bought wine, we had to send for a form from the inspector. We begged the superintendent and Sigmund Fürer that we be allowed to lay in the wine with our staff as before. We also requested that we be allowed to give the wine merchants their money so that we did not have

---

[97] In the Middle Ages Nürnberg was well known for its cloth, much of which was woven in the cloisters. Here, however, the nuns are obviously backsliding as far as making "new" clothes is concerned in hopes that the pressure from the City Council to abandon their order's traditional habit in favor of more "contemporary" dress will subside.

to admit them to the cloister. The City Council gave in on this point, but only if the money were deposited into the general till. Therefore for each barrel we had to pay the merchants one penny as their pay and let our staff lay it down.

Afterwards, on the Sunday after St. Laurence Day, Sigmund Fürer and Linhart Tucher visited us. They demanded to see me at the window grate and said that they had been sent to us by Hieronymus Ebner, Kaspar Nützel and Friedrich Tetzel[98] They were to inform us that after we had educated their daughters at our cloister for several years, it had no longer seemed a good idea to the parents to continue to leave their daughters with us. Yet they could not help but notice that we had educated them well and properly, had showed them love and faithfulness and had incurred expenses for them. They really wanted to compensate us for that. They did not want us to have kept them these many years without pay. I was to determine a sum, which they would be glad to take from their accounts as compensation for their room and board. I said it was not necessary. We had raised their children with all our sisterly love and dedication but had refrained from speaking of it, so that we could receive the young ones. Yet, be that as it may, I made no demands but one. If they returned what had been stolen from the church, their three children whom they had robbed us of by force and against the children's will, then I would consider the accounts settled. Then Fürer asked why we wanted to take them back. After all he had advised us previously not to take back anyone who had once left us. I replied, "We will do it nevertheless. Those who ran away from us by their own free will and did not believe they could find salvation with us we will never take back. But it is well known with what crying, weeping and moaning these three children were taken from us by force against their own will. Therefore we would be happy to take them back at whatever time they might come."

They said they had also heard what a great struggle was necessary before they had been taken away from us. They also wanted to tell the truth. They believed that if it were up to the children, all three would come back to us before nightfall. Nevertheless, they knew well that the children's parents would never allow that. Therefore I should come up with another suggestion.

I said that as long as I had held this office I had never demanded money for board or anything else. I did not want to start with them. If we

---

98 These were the fathers of the three young women whose forced removal from the cloister (by their mothers!) was depicted earlier in Chapter 34.

had been given something, we would have thanked God, and if we had not been given anything, we would not have been upset. For that reason I would stay with my previous answer. They also left it there. They said they would inform the parents of the children.

Since that time nobody has offered us anything, nor offered us a heller or a penny. Fürer, however, said he could see clearly that we had not obeyed him. We were still wearing our habits and had not dressed differently as he had ordered. I said, "Nobody is guilty but you. You told the sisters they did not have to obey me and that I was not to force them to do anything against their will. And so now they tell me they will not obey me in the matter of putting on different clothes. They want to retain their habits and will not be forced by anyone."[99] He said, that might well work as long as the city had calmed down a little concerning the convent. If, however, there were an uproar like that three months ago, then they would have to wear worldly clothes. It had to be this way and no other.

Chapter 36

On Friday after St. Barthomew's Day Niklas Groland and Linhart Tucher came and requested I come to the grate window. They said they had been sent by the honorable City Council to give me a letter. The preacher at St. Laurence, Osiander, had directed it to the mayor. I was to read it. After that they wanted to talk further. The letter went literally as follows:

Prudent, honorable, worthy, kind, dear mayor,

Some time ago the City Council commissioned me to preach at St. Clare's until another preacher is retained. I accepted this position willingly. Yet I have not undertaken any particular material to preach about, but let it remain according to the old papal order. I was worried when I began that another preacher would replace me before I had completed my plan. Since, however, that papal order does not indicate the subject matter that is most important for the virgins there to know, I ask you sincerely to inquire from the City Council if they want me to continue to preach such sermons. I will do what I am ordered with all diligence and humility. And I will take it upon myself to preach on a different subject. The papal subject can, of course, never be presented as fruitfully as

[99] Here Caritas shows her sharp wit and debating skill. By shifting the "blame" onto Fürer she makes him look ridiculous.

when one treats an entire evangelist or a whole epistle of Paul in order. At the same time I would like to ask in case I am to help out at St. Clare's even longer whether the honorable City Council would consider it possible for me to preach at St. Clare's on another day of the week than when I preach at St. Laurence's. If that seems suitable, I would be relieved of the burden of having to deliver two sermons on one day. If the honorable City Council does not approve of this, I am willing to follow its wishes as best I can since I consider it my duty, I beg most humbly that you act kindly in this question and grant my request.

Andreas Osiander
Preacher at St. Laurence

Chapter 37

When I had read the letter they said the honorable City Council had ordered them to arrange the following. After we had learned from the letter what bothered the preacher at St. Laurence, the honorable City Council would ask us which of the two preachers we liked better, Osiander or the Carthusian. We were to inform them whether we wanted one or none at all, what topic they should preach about and on what days. We were to indicate this to them. The honorable City Council was eager to know our opinion and to do the best thing in this matter.

I said the matter did not concern me alone, but my whole convent and I wanted to discuss this with them.

Then they said they would wait half an hour.

When they returned I gave them more or less the following answer, for we were well aware that it was only an experiment and a trap. "Dear gentlemen, after my lords in the honorable City Council during Lent took our fathers the Franciscan preachers and others from us, they assigned preachers at the same time according to their own taste. They had us informed that the clear, bright word of God, the Holy Gospel, was to be preached according to correct Christian understanding without human interpretation. We want to leave it this way. At the same time we have neither determined nor even chosen a person, a subject or even a day, but whatever pleases the honorable City Council and what-ever it decrees that we must also put up with as long as God so desires."

Groland said the gentlemen were so kindly disposed toward us that they really wanted to know what we would like best.

I said the answer that I gave was given to me by my sisters. I had nothing further to report.

They asked whether we would be satisfied with how the City Council arranged it.

I said that we would accept it.

Groland said, however, that it would be good if we were grateful to the Word of God and to those who preached it to us.

I said we would very much like to hear the Word of God, without omissions and human interpretation, but with brotherly[100] love so that it promotes peace within the community.

He said he was of the opinion that no preacher preached differently in the whole city. The opinion of his lords would not be different.

I spoke and said that I commend that to God and to every reasonable listener. I did not want to complain any more, for we were well aware that this all was a clever game where we were to be caught by our own words.

After this Osiander preached until the Sunday after Michaelmas[101] when, by the grace of God,[102] he preached his last sermon to us. He preached 34 sermons to us and always said very little of the Word of God, but instead scolded us most harshly and reviled us and employed all his energy to make everyone our enemy and to demand that we should be completely done away with. May God forgive him and let him repent here!

The Sunday after Michaelmas the Carthusian preached for the first time. He preached three sermons a week on Saturday, Sunday and Monday until the next *Quatemberrorate*.[103] Then he no longer preached on Mondays, stopping by his own choice. We did nothing to cause this. May God in His Grace help us so that he stops altogether, for he is probably worse than Osiander.

Chapter 38

A few days after Calixus Day the tax collector sent us a bill for over 17½ barrels of wine which we had laid in before St. Laurence Day. Not until St. Laurence Day itself had they informed us that we should not order

---

[100] The use of "brotherly" here is a clever "code word" by which Caritas is really referring to the Franciscan brothers who were no longer allowed to serve them as preachers or confessors. It appears that such subtle use of language was wasted on Groland.

[101] 29 September.

[102] Once again we note that Caritas was able to maintain a sense of humor in the midst of these very trying times.

[103] In Advent.

any more wine ourselves. Then I wrote the superintendent the letter given below.

May the Grace of God the Almighty dwell within your heart! I wish this as a friendly greeting to your Honor.

Prudent, wise, kind, dear Superintendent,

I must once again involve your honor in a matter in which I for the love of God, our Lord, ask your help and advice as our father and provider. This is the subject. Last Wednesday the tax collector sent me a bill for 17½ barrels and one cask of wine which we laid in before St. Laurence Day. On the eve of St. Laurence Day we were forbidden by the City Council to order any more wine without a form from the tax collector. Therefore we did not think we should have to pay taxes on what had been ordered before this time. We would also have imagined that the honorable City Council would see our poverty and lack of resources and not burden us further. It is well known, of course, that otherwise we are not able to get along without incurring debts, although we live in the most frugal way. The people from Erfurt have not yet paid us the Walburgis amount and the same is true of those from Eger and also Schweinfurt. If we are also to pay taxes then we will have to drink water or, if it agrees with us, beer. In truth that would not be difficult for me. But when I think of the dear old mothers, some of whom are 80, many 70 and even more 60, who have been used to drinking mostly wine, then it touches my heart that in their later years they are to be nourished in such a poor fashion that their life might well be shortened by such a change. I am moved even more whenever I hear of their patience and whenever they say they would prefer bread and water, if only they can all remain together. If God provides for them, it cannot be bad for them. They hope nothing but death will separate them from one another, but certainly not food and drink, as little as it may be. Human salvation is not found in food and drink which only serves to preserve the poor body and not the salvation of the soul.

Such tax money cannot mean much to the honorable City Council or the whole city, although it is very damaging to us. Thus your honor knows well in what manner we are free. I do not mean from the Pope, but from kings and emperors. Your honor brought about the confirmation of this right[104] which is linked to a fine at Worms yourself. Perhaps the honorable City Council knows nothing about this. If your honor can ask it to exempt us in view of this freedom and also our poverty and the impossibility of our paying the tax. If that cannot be, then it could

---

104 That they do not pay taxes.

demand a specific amount as tax so that our obedience can be recognized. May that occur harmlessly and without damaging the imperial freedom mentioned above. If, however, your honor believes we would not receive a positive response, then we will not send a petition, but commend the matter to God.

We also beg your honor to advise us which of our land holdings we should first take and sell so that we do not suffer too much loss and can pay the council too. If God has given us something then it belongs to Him and He can take it away from us. May His Holy Name be praised and blessed forever. At the same time we hope your honor will act loyally and paternally for us in this matter as you have always done in similar cases. May Eternal God reward you abundantly in this life and in eternity. I commend your honor to His Eternal Grace. Please give our friendly greetings to our pious little Clara[105] from all the sisters.

Chapter 39

The superintendent gave me the following answer to this letter:

Grace and peace from God, our Father, and the growth of the true Christian faith[106] to his praise and brotherly love I wish to you and me from His divine Grace!
Honorable woman and sister in Christ.

There are all sorts of things that kept me from writing you and visiting you. Most of all it happened because your faith and my faith do not want to become completely the same. Time is thawing here and grace rains down daily so abundantly from God, indeed stronger, more powerfully and in a more Christian manner than has happened in many hundreds of years. My heart fails me completely so that afterwards I am so desperate to save you from the strong, crude bonds with which you have been shackled up to now and also from your own presumptuousness, your own reason and that of those who remain within the same faith. Nevertheless they do that not without personal gain. You will not be instructed any more so that I do not know how my letters or my

---

[105] The superintendent's daughter Clara was one of the three nuns who had been removed from the convent.

[106] This somewhat formulaic greeting, which echoes that of St. Paul in his letters, takes on a somewhat ironic tone when one considers that what Nützel the superintendent and Caritas Pirckheimer consider "the true Christian faith" is no longer the same thing. Nützel refers to this problem in the second sentence of his letter.

actions are to bear fruit. I can only plead incessantly to God for you more than for my father, my mother or anybody else. I do not intend to stop, although, as I have noted above, there is little hope considering what I have heard. Unfortunately, with no restraint at all the sermon and whatever we are commanded to do by God's Word are called blasphemy.[107] The individual, cursed and made up things and the sermons by which they lead us astray in a disgraceful, evil and, may it be lamented to God, in part deliberate manner are considered to be praising God.[108] Unfortunately it is as clear as day that God is to be lamented and pitied very much.[109]

I cannot see it any other way except that the sisters have placed so much value on earthly nourishment and the previously noted innovations that they would rather that the other part[110] be destroyed as has also happened in previous years. But many who previously considered these things gifts of God have called their wealth the works of the devil for the sake of the Holy Word. Indeed, many of them in many lands have lost their life in a chivalrous and brave manner for this reason.

Thus I hear so much about Christian dying which some are reasonably looking forward to. On the other hand I have also learned that through the misdirection of clergy the people end up in such mortal danger or despair that they are to be pitied. May God grant that you and your supporters do not carry out your will, but God's Will which you have all declared like King Pharaoh. I declare to God that it would be my greatest joy to hear that.

Some time ago I sent a relative of mine to you as a messenger about the contract concerning the time and board of my daughter Clara. You did not want to make any report about that, however. Since, however, I admit that when I sent her to you, I sought nothing but the kingdom of heaven, that is benefit for her and not me, I do not want you to suffer because of this, although it was I, after all, who made a terrible mistake. Therefore, I want you to name a sum by which I will acknowledge my compensation to you. I know very well that you not only gained nothing from my daughter, but also acted and taught her in the best manner you knew. I am grateful to you for that and always will be. But I did not want her to serve in your cloister as has happened up to now and, of course,

---

107 The actions of the "reformers" are considered blasphemy by the faithful.
108 The "reformers" look upon the traditions of the Catholic Church not as praise of God, but as blasphemy.
109 Nützel seems to feel sorry for God because He has to endure so much blasphemy.
110 The spiritual world.

solely because of her faith. For I cannot believe that it found shelter here. I also hope that it will be imparted to her in a paternally loyal and pure manner. I can well imagine that you will perhaps be upset about this letter of mine and think that I probably would not have written it years ago, which is true. But you must believe in the name of the highest truth which is God Himself, that I am now no less faithful than at that time. Indeed, I believe with complete Christian and fraternal care, in case I should ever doubt you, He will not desert you in faith. He alone has the power to grant it.

You have recently indicated that a small cask of wine was presented to you by Jakob Muffel from his own vineyard and you asked if you should accept it. I informed you I would take responsibility for that. A few days later I reported it to the Council, as is my duty. For some reason or other, however, they would not excuse the tax on it and as I left they commanded me to inform you of that. You write now concerning the tax collector who sent you a bill on which 17½ barrels of wine was written. However, it was only afterwards, on the eve of St. Laurence Day, that the order of the City Council was shown to you. The sisters from St. Katherine's have also made a similar report and received the word that before the City Council sent a valid message, none of your wines were taxed, and since you claim poverty, then that is valid as I understand it in order to help you out of this predicament for a while until the tax collector is again informed.

As far as the final elimination of the tax is concerned, I have seen to my consolation that the tax affects not just you, but many others. I have thought a great deal and feel that under no circumstances should you give up any part of the convent's holdings. In no case should you do that, for if you thought as I do, then you would not worry about the decrease in members of the convent. I, of course, think that there will soon be few nuns, and not, as you believe, many nuns again. At least let it be until Herr Ebner and I come to check your accounts which we plan to do shortly.

I cannot advise you whether you should send a petition to the council and thus obtain your freedom from taxes, not that one from the Pope, but the imperial one which I obtained for you in part with a threat of punishment. I firmly believe that even those who wish for you and other similar ordered communities to remain in existence advise this too so that no harm comes to you and all other communities are treated as before. However, whoever does not believe that God wants to or will look over these things and finally grant you something good will not advise this. Therefore, show your good sense here too. This is what I advise as you wrote at the end of your letter. To sell property and other things will still not be necessary in my opinion. If you are satisfied with paying your interest which falls due on St.Martin's Day, then let me know. I will not let you down, for I really want to see your temporal holdings unharmed and improved. For that purpose I will help and advise you in the future. May God protect us all!

Kaspar Nützel, the Elder.

Chapter 40

I gave the following answer to his letter:

The Grace of God be with us all.

Prudent, wise, dear superintendent,

I received your honor's letter with thanks and was happy that you so humbly want to appeal to God on our behalf. If only God granted that everyone did that, then we would be able to bear much. For one Christian does not criticize another, nor does he condemn him, nor scorn him. Even less does he insult or trouble him, but out of Christian love he has sympathy for him and appeals to God for him, if someone does not treat him properly.

I am so very sad that your faith and ours cannot become the same, for we hope that as Christians we also desire salvation and in the matters that we understand would not be right, here let us practice moderation. We also do not want to trouble anyone, even less blaspheme against God. We call Him who knows all hearts as our witness that we would not want to do anything against the faith, against reason or against own conscience out of presumptuousness. If we did that we would bring judgment upon ourselves. It is also difficult for us to act or believe against our conscience. For, if we were to say that we believed something that we could really not believe at all, then we would only be deceiving ourselves. Faith is indeed a Grace from God. It cannot be forced either and therefore it cannot be poured into people by force or threats. If, however, a person pretends to believe only to please someone else and he really does not believe, then that is hypocrisy. Thus, God knows, we also seek no selfish benefit from our acts, and even less are we instructed by any other person. Nobody comes to us anymore who would like to speak with us about these things. If somebody would like to instruct us, then we have, thanks be to God, enough intelligence to know that we should not follow him, because we can also read the Holy Scriptures. Therefore, God willing, neither man nor angel nor even less earthly nourishment nor selfish benefit shall mislead us to not want to act and believe properly. For this is our faith. We have learned from the holy apostles to attribute justification to God alone and to the works and sufferings of Christ. He is our justification and certainly not our works, for we read and know well that no one is justified by works, but by faith alone. If we could find salvation by our works, then Christ would have died for us in vain. We also know, however, that man is justified by the Grace of God and not by good works. Then as a good tree he will bear good fruit. These are a sign of his correct and true faith. By their fruits, says Christ the Lord, you shall recognize them. But where the works of faith and above all brotherly love do not exist and are not revealed, there is no faith either, even if it were so great that it could move mountains. Therefore, because we know that we are all justified by faith, as St. Paul teaches us, we also know that we are at peace with God.

This is and should be our faith in which we live and will die, let them say what they will. We also want to ask God always, in case we lack faith, to take this lack from us through His great mercy. May he grant us His Grace that we might confirm our faith as a good tree also with works, because God will judge each person by his works. But as far as our works are concerned, or our habits or our living together, our being silent at certain times, eating this or that food and similar external things which are, of course, voluntary, for we regard them this way, we could stop them or not, but we do not rely on them. For we know well that we should not consider our works worth anything. If we have done them all we are no better or worse because of them. We do or we stop doing such external things. But where there are so many people together there must be order so that everything, as St. Paul says, proceeds correctly and orderly. May God grant us His Grace to do what is right and avoid what is wrong.[111]

Your honor, however, might excuse us for one thing that we cannot understand, that we should not keep what we have promised to God, although we have allowed anyone who cannot remain with us in good conscience to go wherever she wanted. But those who really want to stay and who, with God's Help, without which we can do nothing, hope to keep what they promised to God are taken away by force against their will. This I do not consider just. And so I can picture our sister Rechel

---

[111] Here Caritas shows her solid foundation in theology as well as her ability to defend her order against the many accusations of the reformers. The argument of faith versus good works was used by Luther and the reformers to criticize the cloistered life. Here Caritas cites St. Paul (just as Luther did) in defense of her position. She proves to be a far more effective apologist for her faith than Nützel.

before me who will soon be 50 years old and whom her brother and sister want to force out of the cloister against her will. What would happen if we all ran out of the cloister at the same time? Would we be better because of that or closer to God, if we just praised him with our mouth and our actions showed that they were contrary to our faith?

I can absolutely not believe that your honor values the life of some monks and nuns who have left their cloisters and behave like well-to-do daughters. They all say they have faith. Yet God in His time will let just judgment fall on them.

Therefore, wise, dear gentleman, I beg you for God's sake not to despair of us or to judge us with prejudice. God knows our hearts, of course, and that we have nothing to boast of except Jesus Christ crucified. Pray to him for us, and we will do the same.

In the matter of your honor's daughter, let's let it stay as I stated in my previous reply. We cannot name a sum to you, for we did not accept her because of money or property. If we could have done many good things for her, we would gladly have done so. What can we do for you, however, since your honor cannot believe that faith resides with us? May God's Mercy make up for what we lack. It is not necessary for your honor to excuse yourself on account of your letter, for I understand it very well. I hope your honor will understand my simple letter[112] in the best way, no differently than I intend and, as far as your honor is able, you will help, protect and guard us so that under the mantle of faith and brotherly love no unfaithful and unbrotherly things are forced upon us.

In regard to the tax I give your honor my greatest thanks for the position which you have taken. After reading your letter, however, I am still a bit uncertain. If your honor comes to us about the bill, I will be better able to inquire about it. If the final elimination to it is impossible, then let us hope the honorable City Council will be completely gracious to us in view of our poverty. We will maintain our position of freedom from the tax as your honor advised. We commend it to God whether there will be more or less sisters. Because we have shortages everywhere, we must consider how we are to limit ourselves. We pray to God that he will not abandon us. Nevertheless we must confront the matter ourselves. Excessive concern is forbidden, but justified concern is not. We would not like to come up short, but if there is something left over, then we will know where it should go. There are many poor people who will need this and that. But perhaps distress will teach us to hold back and to bear our losses.

---

[112] Here one could accuse Caritas of false modesty. Her letter is certainly not "simple."

At the present time they preach to us that we should leave and hire ourselves out to work. Good God! Many sisters are 70 years old and many more 60. How are they supposed to find employment and what work should they do, since they themselves are in need of good care? If I had not pitied them so much, I would have quickly sought employment, for, by the Grace of God, I do not need alms. But what is to become of these poor, wretched dears? If we borrow a great deal, we will have to pay it back in the end. I cannot imagine how this is to happen without selling our holdings or demolishing the convent. Nevertheless, we don't want to do anything without your honor's advice, but in the future we do want to discuss this and other matters with your honor and Hieronymus Ebner when you visit us about the bill. In the meantime we will commend ourselves to God and your honor. Thus I wish you many blessed times!

Chapter 41

Afterward, on St. Simon's and Judas' Day, the young Tetzel girl came to her sisters Ursula and Justina Trollinger and wanted to remove them by force. The pious children, however, defended themselves against her with force. They said they owed her no obedience, since they were only her stepsisters. She behaved so inappropriately that we told the superintendent about it in the following letter:

Prudent, wise, kind, dear sir,

I want to make your prudent honor aware that yesterday the young Tetzel girl visited her two stepsisters who live with us. She spoke with them alone at the window grate and urged them to leave. Among other things she said your honor had sent her and would give her further instructions if they do not give in to her demands. She did this all with so much impetuousness and angry threats and profanity that would even make people in a common tavern blush. I find it impossible to believe that such things really happened on your orders. The whole thing went on, you see, in such an uncharitable, unchristian and unevangelical manner that her two sisters were deeply troubled by it. They begged me in the most intense way to beg your honor on their behalf not to allow their stepsister to do anything like that again. If there is any doubt that they want to stay here then people should be appointed to hear them who will act with modesty and not with such impetuousness violence. They hope, of course, that their stepsister has no power over them since they have neither mother nor father any more. She gave them to understand that they had to leave if she wanted them to, even if it angered God. We do not give any credence to these words, for the honorable City Council promised us that such sisters could only be removed by their father and mother, but not by relatives or siblings. The children wanted to abide by that. They are fully aware that it is a question of the dowry which they brought with them and which we had not expected at all when they entered. She also said that she had heard from the council that if they leave within 14 days, they will have to be paid to the penny for what they brought in with them. If they stay longer, however, and what is planned happens to us, then she will let it be, even if moths crawl out of them.

In addition, there were other such words from which they could detect her sisterly attitude. She also threatened to inform your honor what answer she had been given. Although we do not believe all that of your honor as our loyal lord and father, the two troubled children beg you humbly and from the depths of their hearts to be on guard if she comes to your honor and wants to make a big fuss. They do not want to be forced by here to do anything. They did not like speaking alone with her because their words are immediately twisted and untruths are reported. Other sisters are also afraid of this too. We are afraid of saying something bad, even when we are speaking alone. If only they would stick to the truth! We were also informed that we were not to speak alone with anybody, only with our mother and father.

I did not want to keep this from you at the request of the two children named above. I must state, however, that I do not believe a word of what was said about your honor. It is, however, good for your honor to know how to deal with the people when they come to you and that you see to it that we are spared any further tempestuous entering of the convent. May that all be commended to God!

Chapter 42

The superintendent wrote the following reply to this letter:

May God grant us all His Grace in the true, proper faith which, I am certain, cannot exist without the love of one's neighbor.

Beloved woman and sister in Christ,

Recently I wrote to you from the goodness of my heart and as a brother in response to one of your letters. From the answer you sent me later I understand all to well that my spirit is too simple and weak to move you in any way toward something in which I could find consolation or joy. As I note my inexperience in the Holy Scriptures, my simplicity and inability to please God and every day find tremendous errors and godlessness so flagrantly among the richest, the well-to-do and the wisest people whose intellect far surpasses mine, so that even children could speak about it, all of this nevertheless causes me to write to you again out of Christian love and to ask God the Lord to make my effort fruitful.

I have also been prevented from writing to you because I was involved to some extent in the marriage of Andreas Osiander.[113] In a variety of ways and for very evil reasons the devil and his minions wanted to prevent it. Thanks be to God, the practices of these evil people referred to above became known and the wedding was held. It is not necessary to note at this point that it is without doubt a Christian act from which the kingdom of the Antichrist is to be harmed and the kingdom of Christ strengthened. I am of the opinion, of course, that you consider the usual procedure from Kunz Schrötter, the pastor of Regelsbach and his greedy celebrant of mass who is like him to be worthier than this command of God.

On account of my simplicity, as I wrote honestly, I have definitely had more doubts than before about you, who I recognize is gifted with greater intelligence than I am in these theological matters. But understand that it is not that I doubt the Grace of God, but because I think that for someone of your intelligence my faithful letter could be more annoying than pleasing to God. Yet, because of the love which I bear for you and your sisters, who, I know, are in distress, I pondered and both diligently and fervently asked God the true Consoler to strengthen me with His Grace when I despair about the salvation of all of you. With the Lord's Help it got easier for me to bear some burdens dealing with your salvation and your welfare. Finally a thought came to me. I know that you have little knowledge of and even displeasure in all the preachers and teachers of God's Word who are respected as Christians by many here and elsewhere. In truth I cannot make any other conclusion except that it is futile to seek advice from all of them. Now for the last time let God open His Hand with doctor Wenzel Linck.[114] At the time when he

---

113 This is the spirited preacher from St. Laurence who in his many long sermons was unable to "win over" the sisters of St. Clare's who had been forced to listen to him. (See Chapter 37.) When Osiander wanted to marry for the second time (his first wife had died), a controversy began among the Lutherans about whether clergy could marry more than once. After some debate, the wedding was sanctioned and Osiander was married again.

114 Wenzel Linck (1483–1547) came to Nürnberg from Wittenberg in 1517. He had been sent by the vicar general of the Augustinian order, Johann Staupitz, to

held the positions of inspector and provincial he was more experienced in these matters than any other, even a man who lived properly and in accordance with all common decency. I showed him the last letter you sent me. I also revealed to him diligently what I had decided to write to you, even my concern, my humility and my almost complete despair in this matter. I found strength and much consolation from him. He told me in no way to give up. And he moved me to ask him most fervently for the sake of the Honor of God and love of one's neighbor to give me short tracts about the Holy Scriptures. If they enlightened me, I would write again diligently and try to see if God would lift the curtain from my salvation and yours. Despite all your idolatry you never wanted to acknowledge an error and even less did you desire to accept instruction. And yet you like to hear the opposing side in written and oral form and still cling to the old faith. He granted me an answer to my desire and request. I have pored over them and with diligence and some insight I understood some sections.

My insights have filled me with much concern and therefore moved me too zealously so that I did not spare you completely, although it was done out of loyalty. With the best of intentions I have once again decided, as open as I am accustomed to be with you, to avoid the issue and send you the sections of his manuscript which I do now. I have also told him that I did it because I do not know how to help you alone and I have received much comfort from them. May these writings bear fruit, peace and atonement. I earnestly ask God for this. May your supposedly holy rule or, as I hope even more, the Grace of God, grant that you may hear this doctor Wenzel in the future. Again and again I ask for God's sake let me know in whatever way you like best, in my presence or that of others or as a sermon or written or some other way. I will await your answer not without great, indeed the greatest longing. If, however, this does not suit you, then I will open my heart and spirit to you further and in the meantime ask God, if it pleases Him, to grant me the grace to leave you unburdened any further. May He commend you to those with whom you with good conscience have been pleased. Please send Doctor Wenzel's writings back to me when you have finished reading them.

In regard to the young Tetzel girl who undertook the business with her stepsisters and involved me. I am astonished. I do not know her at

head the Augustinian church in the city. A strong supporter of the Reformation, he also assumed the leadership of the Sodalitas Staupitziana. Later chapters (44, 45, 47, 48, 49 and 51) will deal with his "Lutheran" teachings and Caritas's reaction to them as well as his reaction to her.

all. As far as I know I have never spoken to her in my whole life and even less given her an order.

More than one Elector or Prince has decreed that an order be established concerning these teachings according to which no papal priest's sermon or customs be tolerated any more. It goes along well with our local order. What Philip Melanchthon[115] will establish here you will also hear about. He has been commissioned for a good project so that the youth are brought up with a good and useful education and the cursed perversion[116] is exterminated all the better in the future. This is not the case now among the wise people of the world. May God grant us correct, true knowledge! For the struggle is not about the people who want to remain in cloisters and who no longer have fathers or mothers or those to whom God ordered obedience, but instead it is about the knowledge of what one must do and what one must stop doing and what God wants to have freely and without force.

Kaspar Nützel, the Elder.

Chapter 43

To this letter I gave the superintendent the following reply:

The Grace of God be with us all!
Prudent, wise, kind, dear sir,

I have read your letter again and confess that I am too insignificant to answer your honor, much less a learned doctor or to debate with him. I do not consider that necessary. You have read our opinion from my last letter. Let it remain as it is. I am sorry that you find no pleasure in it. What joy could you have, however, if we said yes to everything you wish and yet we did not feel that way in our hearts and our conscience reprimanded us and showed us a different answer? What would it be or whom would we have betrayed? Truly no one but ourselves.

Your honor knows that no one has anything except what is given him by God, without whose Will nothing happens. If both day and night we fervently ask God for the guidance of our spirit and an increase in true

---

115   Philipp Melanchthon (1497–1560) stayed at the home of Willibald Pirckheimer, Caritas's brother, from November 1525 to May 1526 while he was setting up the new Egidien Gymnasium which still exists today as the Melanchthon Gymnasium. In Chapter 50 Caritas describes his visit to her which was arranged by the City Council.
116   That is the Catholic education of the past.

Christian faith, and He gives us no love for the new faith, then we can make ourselves no different than what God has determined for us. If, because of human favor, fear or threat we should appear different from what is in our heart, that would be great hypocrisy which your honor doubtless does not desire of us, for it would be, of course, against God. But since your honor considers it to be true, that we accept the advice of some greedy celebrants of the mass, from the two whom you named or those like them I have honestly sought neither advice nor assistance my whole life. The poor idiots cannot even advise or help themselves.

We do not want to or should not condemn anyone. Everyone stands or falls before his Lord. He will judge him in his time. If someone sells masses or cultivates other evil things, that should not please us. Let us then be told right away what God wants.

If your honor says of me that I am blessed with greater reason than you in these matters, then I know well that I am a poor, simple person, uneducated and inexperienced in everything that is good and that I am worthy of all scorn. I am also well aware that all worldly wisdom is folly before God. In these difficult times it would probably be necessary for God to grant me His Holy Spirit so that I would know what to do and what not to do. I notice that now among the very greatest intellectuals reason is disappearing, not just among the papal ones, but also among those who call themselves evangelical so that many of them no longer want to allow Christ's body and blood in wine and bread. Even that must be the Word of God.

I am sorry that your honor despairs of us. We do not want to doubt God, however. We hope, of course, he will not rob us of his Grace and Mercy because we desire it so earnestly and would like to do what is right. If we left the cloister, we would not be any more blessed, as little as we are certain of salvation in the cloister, for these eternal things neither give salvation nor take it away. We should also be free, as is preached to us daily. However, the holy apostles and the other believers lived together and held everything in common. Why should we not live together too and show one another every sisterly love? Eternal God, the houses of prostitution are tolerated, but we must hear that we are worse than those people. Unfortunately we are bad enough. May God improve us through His Grace! If we knew that it was the Will of God and that we could achieve salvation by leaving, we truly would not delay very long. We are not in the cloister because of the good life. The world knows this and God, in whom all our hope and refuge lie, knows it too.

God also knows that we have no dislike of the Word of God. At the same time, it does not happen that we consider all the scorn, disgrace, vice and dishonor which many look upon as the Word of God to be the

Word of God. We know, however, that the Holy Gospel is the law of love, It does not condemn my neighbor, nor judge him, but punishes him with all modesty. We are, however, not the only ones who doubt the sermons. I do not know what is being preached, but I often hear that many people in this city are despairing and do not go to a sermon any more. They say they are totally confused by the preachers, so that they don't know what they should believe. They would give a great deal not to have heard them.

We have now heard 111 of these sermons and for a while, as you wanted, we listened to Andreas Osiander for up to four hours. A short time ago we also read Doctor Wenzel's work diligently and copied it down. From it we have received sufficient instruction about what the foundation, meaning and goal of all of you are. We are too insignificant to be able to enter into a discussion with such highly learned people. We like to say what we want; we must be wrong. And that is really the reason why we have held back from speaking a great deal with the preachers, so that they would not get upset at our words and would have cause to attack them from the chancel. That did not help at all, however. For even though they have not heard our opinion, they take it upon themselves to present the secret thoughts of our hearts which are know to God alone, even the inner thoughts and opinions which by God have never even occurred to us in such a disgraceful and crude manner as if they were the Lord God Himself. They annoy the listeners and cast harsh judgments on us. We commend this to Eternal God who knows well why He imposes this and other things upon us according to His just and inoffensive Judgment. May he be blessed for all eternity for all the disgrace which he allows to befall us and grant us the power to bear it with patience. At the same time he knows that for us poor, not unfeeling human beings such diverse slander in so many forms and in so many places is difficult, and most difficult because of the great scandal which arises from it. We would much rather suffer that than do it to other people. At the same time we do not console ourselves that the truth will come to light at the proper time. If we ran away from the cloister and occupied ourselves with evil things, then without doubt we would be honored by some good Christians and by all Lutherans and praised by many people. May the Mercy of God protect us from such praise!

Your honor will excuse me. I am perhaps going too far. But since you despair of us so much and yet write that that you want to hear nothing but the truth, then I must also open up my heart to you and be clear about the matter as I have always done with you. We also pray to God, that we might have no idolatry among us, and even less that we do not recognize our error, for that would be against God and reason. No one can justly accuse us of being moved by such a spirit. Saint Paul teaches us to try everything and to keep what is good. We know of no opposing party. We are not in disagreement with anyone. Instead, we are deserted by almost everyone. May God have mercy on us!

We also know that we should not rely on our rule, but on God alone and His only Son Jesus Christ, our Lord. With His Suffering and His Holy Blood he redeemed us and made atonement with His Heavenly Father. May He grant His Divine Grace to you and all of us so that the Agony of His Suffering is not lost on us.

We hope your honor will not be as angry with us poor souls as you threaten to be, but will show us Christian and brotherly love and, in a further uplifting of your heart, act no differently than you would if you were guided by words of the Holy Gospel. Thus, wise gentleman, I who understand little have sent a very short answer to your letter. Truly I am not so clever that I can take responsibility for everything as it would be necessary. Therefore, may your honor pardon me for God's sake if I have gone too far. My lack of understanding is the reason for my leaving out what was necessary. As I noted before, I am, unfortunately, less clever than I would like to be. May your honor judge me as you will!

On behalf of the Tetzel girl we never had any trouble concerning your honor, or else I would not have written you. But I reported her actions to you in the hope that you might help us be freed from the daily burden and the commotion. They hurt us and overrun us and then the people say we sent them away. Everyone wants to teach and show us what we should do. If we had as many helpers as we have guides and teachers, we would be strong enough to oppose an army of peasants. And if we did everything they advise us to do, we would have a stranger regiment than the gypsies. Pardon me once again.

And since your honor wrote to me recently about Herr Osiander and how unpleasant I considered his teaching to be, no teaching is more pleasant to me, on the other hand, than that of Christ and His Apostles. People are people, today as well as a thousand years ago, but the Word of God remains Eternal. Would God, that he[117] had taught us how to prepare for a riot, before so many people had been killed. Nevertheless, it is still good that he teaches how we should prepare for future revolts. God grant that this may happen! I have had everything copied, even the writings of Doctor Wenzel. That is the reason why I kept them so long.

I am glad to hear that Philipp Melanchthon was called here, for I have heard that he is a pious, honest, upright man and a lover of justice. I do

---

[117] Osiander.

not believe he likes everything, especially that they want to compel some people to believe by force and to do things which are against their conscience. May God grant him and all of us His Holy Spirit. I commend your honor to Him forever. He understands everything in the best way.

Chapter 44

This is Dr. Wenzel's instruction which he wrote for me at the request of our superintendent and my answer to it. I sent it to the superintendent along with the letter that had been copied.[118]

Since Christ our Lord in word and deed commanded all his followers to deny nothing to temporal authority, but, for the sake of peace, to give more than was demanded, as St. Paul also emphasizes clearly in Rom. 13, then you can easily judge whether you can consider any privileges which run contrary to it to be Christian or whether you can make use of them in good conscience, let alone encourage someone to protect them. If kings and emperors have granted such things to you and even I and others have assisted in the process, then that occurred doubtless out of ignorance which God will not hold against us and it will be to no one's detriment or disadvantage.

In these things Christ the Lord is to be obeyed, and in the event that you obey the Gospel of Christ and therefore will give up your alleged privileges, then be assured that He will not leave you in the lurch in your poverty, nor shorten your life. Perhaps because of your obedience in this matter He will bring you to greater knowledge and more obedience toward His Word and, as subjects of His Kingdom who in no way make any special claims, He will let you receive sufficient temporal holdings so that you can maintain your standing without having to sell your property. Whoever believes will neither hunger nor be abandoned by God. Nevertheless, if such Christian obedience and general Christian loyalty is found among you and more love of the public good than of selfish privileges can be recognized, then the honorable City Council along with other pious Christians will respond to you in an appropriate manner.

Since you also confess that man's salvation is not based on food and

---

[118] I have omitted the introductory section from MS D which is given in the printed edition in favor of the version from MS A, which is also given and essentially duplicates it.

drink,[119] then I have no doubt you will not disregard Christ's Commandment about such things. Your fellow sisters will strive more to follow Christ and obey His Word than to worry about whether you will suffer hunger or thirst together. My heart aches when I hear of your many concerns about temporal possessions and food and also how you hope for more human privileges, however they may have come about, rather than trusting in God's Word. For if I with good conscience could obtain these or other privileges for you without abusing God's Word, then I would spare no effort and willingly help you. But trust and obedience to the Word of Christ will gain you more in consolation than these or other privileges. God's Grace be with you. Amen,

It is true that every Christian bears the other's burden in order to fulfill Christ's Law with heart felt pity and sympathy. Nevertheless one punishes and criticizes the other also and risks everything in order to lead him to the right truth. For there would be no real sympathy if error or deficiency were not helped whenever possible. He would be no Christian either who would not suffer punishment and correction. The flesh complains only if it is hurt or insulted or troubled, for it always wants to justify itself and does not recognize God's decision. Whoever recognizes himself through God's Spirit will accept punishment and criticism. For love bears all things.

I am not at all surprised that my faith and your faith do not agree for the following reasons:

In accordance with divine doctrine in good times and in bad times I put my whole trust in God alone from whom I expect everything through the only Mediator Jesus Christ, our Lord. But you are not satisfied with Him alone, but set up beside Him like gods who are also supposed to help, or, like mediators and advocates, a Francis and others who not only do not appear in Scripture, but are supposedly saints as is proved by your prayer books and what you consider divine service. For, if you believe in God alone, your prayer books along with your divine services would be destroyed. What kind of Christians those are who have other patrons, helpers in distress and intermediaries in addition to Christ is easy to determine. You will never understand what is not right, even if you subject your reason to the Word of Christ. For you will never understand it through reason, but you will never understand it at all, if you do not believe. No one knows the nature of God, but the Spirit of God Himself. To act against reason and to act against faith is something different, for it is impossible to follow reason and be obedient to faith.

---

[119] See Rom. 14:17.

No one should or can force you to believe or act against your conscience. One must not allow actions from mistaken or false conscience to cause harm or annoyance to other people and one must encourage the external things which support faith such as the fear of God so that willful obstacles are not put in the way of gifts, grace and faith.

One must keep offense away from the Kingdom of God with every effort. Even if you can read the scriptures and have great understanding, you can be deceived since great understanding is an object of deception and temptation for the devil.

If, however, you believe that God alone justifies man through the merit of Jesus Christ, then it follows that you should not attribute so much redemptive power to works or prayers and you should not seek Grace through good works, penance, merit, or intercession of saints, but only in faith through the Grace of Jesus Christ. Why then do you have stations of the cross, rosaries etc. with a specific amount for indulgences? Why do you seek comfort and help from the saints and trust in them rather than in God alone? You certainly cannot say you are performing these works as the fruit by which faith is proved. For faith comes only from love. There are also no Christian works but only those which show the love of God and of one's neighbor. God is not served except by serving one's neighbor, since Christ is both God and Man, who notes what happens to the least of his brethren. If you want to perform works of love, as an example of your faith then you must not cut yourself off from the common people and not choose exceptional paths and life styles, for that love that wants to be open and completely common cannot tolerate that. Therefore Christ will also judge works according to whether or not they have been performed from real faith in true love. I am troubled, therefore, with your private, remote particular works you will show no general Christian love of your neighbor. How many are there among you who could serve the common good of many people by teaching the youth, keeping house, managing servants, raising children and other works by which your neighbor would be served and which on Judgment Day God would claim as the true fruit of righteous faith and of His Word and which instead are prevented by your self-serving invented works and are made impossible like a young tree that is stifled so that it cannot grow and bear useful fruit for people? And so it is apparent, that with your cloistered life you believe you are seeking your own salvation and ignore what is useful to all people and what true love demands.

You also cannot say, we pray, sing and fast for the others. Such things which bring about the death of the old person and the renewal of the inner person should be done, but the works of love should not be omitted. Christ will punish you for it, like the heretics, if you fail to do your duty to your fellow man because you live in a cloister. Thus each is rewarded by God according to his works and judged on how each has served his fellow man from faith, not on how he has sung, prayed and kept the Stations of the Cross.

Ceremonies and external customs are by themselves neither good nor evil. It is not right, however, that one obligates people to perform them and makes unnecessary things into necessary ones. For if that were not case, then one could not punish a sister because of such excess.

Unfortunately many of them cling to these things more firmly than to God's Commandment and often the consciences of the simple people are confused, like a person who walks in an alley. It would be better if one took the usual, correct road of divine commandments and made no special regulations and laws. Then better order would be maintained in a community. Thus many customs, as for example the monks' cowls are more a self-willed deviation from normal Christian life than a proper arrangement. Therefore the orders could be called disorders. Christ and His Apostles taught and determined sufficiently what is useful for a Christian and what is necessary for his salvation, but they have completely forgotten such useless things because the are more harmful than beneficial for Christianity and lead to schisms. Thus St. Paul says, "Among you everything should proceed honorably and orderly."[120] By that he means let nothing happen to confuse common Christianity, but everything should happen in love to build up the community, complete peace in the meetings in the community where one is concerned with God's Word.

It is fitting to keep what one promises to God, but it has not yet been proved and will not be proved that you have renounced your vows in the cloister. For in the whole Gospel or New Testament there is no mention of them. For me it would be frightening, however, if such a great thing which has been held up as being necessary for salvation should not be commanded. For God does not like or dislike what we think He likes or dislikes, but only what He has declared through His Word to be pleasing or displeasing to Him. For no one can indicate God's Will but God alone. Whoever attempts that on his own errs in an unchristian way, just as the people in the religious orders do.

No one knows God's secrets, says St. Paul, "but the Spirit of God."[121]

---

[120] I Cor. 14:40.
[121] I Cor. 2:10.

Therefore, what has been transformed and changed in the name of God without proper knowledge which man cannot have from himself, is nothing but idolatry, forming ideas of God according to one's own opinion and according to human standards, God, as it were, from thoughts about God, who is, after all, unchangeable.

Therefore, where God's Word is not present, there God is not truly recognized. Where God is not properly recognized there exist vain, godless delusion, fantasy and uncertainty before God, as if He liked what we think and choose. All this is godless service by which the true God is not obtained, but in the name of God and in His place the idols and fantasies of the heart i.e. strange gods, even devils that cause such delusion in the heart. From this arise externalized worship service, leadership, doctrine etc.

In this way orders and vows came about from false delusions of the heart, which is an idol beneath which the devil hides and lets himself be worshipped in God's name and in God's place. Above all it was Thomas Aquinas and his companions the scholastics who set this up. Therefore one must look upon the delusion of vows and the cloistered life as a service of idols. For how can I promise something to God or perform a service if I do not know or am uncertain whether He ordered it or taught it or will accept it from me graciously. I must be certain, after all, that I am doing the right thing and that it pleases Him, or else I am doing it without faith and sinfully, for everything that does not happen from faith is sin. I can, however, not receive security from man, but only from God's Word. But since we have no word of God concerning such vows, it remains uncertain and doubtful and this doubt is disbelief. But even if all that did not apply, it is clear that through such vows and binding regulations the cloistered people are prevented from carrying out God's commandments in brotherly love and in service to their neighbors which can be illustrated very clearly. Therefore, above all else you must tear out from your heart this false delusion of vows, if you want to live in a Christian manner. No wonder that your faith and my faith are not the same when you bear such meaningless stuff in your heart and are founded upon false delusion invented by man, something that I detest. My foundation is solely the pure Word of God.

I am also amazed how courageous you have been in allowing your sisters to leave the cloister where, after all, you consider your vow of obedience, poverty etc. so necessary as if it were given to God. In the things that are God's you have no authority to give permission or, where it is appropriate for you to give permission, it must be a question of promises given voluntarily. Either the bond to God has to be nonexistent, or its termination must be unjust. From this you can well recognize that every one of their relatives or the authorities as their sole guardian can and should remove them from the cloister and should try all sorts of methods and ways to lead them onto the correct, true path of salvation, without regard for whether they would, perhaps, like to remain there, and certainly one should wait as long a time and ask whether they want help as one would if one were to see someone threatened by fire or flood. They owe obedience to their parents and the civil authorities since the cloistered life and such a bond by vows without God's Word and Authority is nothing but an invention of man.

Similarly, it is just false delusion and idolatry that they hope they can keep such vows with God's Help, since God has neither promised nor offered them such help. He also bestows no grace and help to sinful things and to such things that He has not ordered or established. Also He helps only in distress for which he has created no other aid or means. And if one appeals to Him nevertheless, then one tempts Him. God does not desire for us to keep an oath if it harms our body or life, even less so if it harms our soul. I could, therefore, just as easily promise to become Roman Emperor. It also does not mean anything that many nuns and monks who have left live badly. We should not consider the examples, but instead the matter as such. Everyone has a judge. We should choose the best, the safest and the most certain of everything by which we can keep God's commandments in the most suitable manner. Faith cannot abide where human delusion is in the heart and God's Word alone does not rule, but instead there is a lifestyle which is beyond the Word.

In short, in the Scriptures all needless worry is forbidden and no difference is made between necessary and unnecessary worry. For whoever does not trust God in important matters will trust Him even less in other matters.

Chapter 45

My answer to doctor Wenzel Linck's letter.

In order that I answer your honor concerning Dr. Wenzel's letter, although I am very clumsy, I will do so very briefly nevertheless as my limited understanding[122] allows, so that your honor might not think we had not read his letter or would despise it.

---

122 Once again Caritas plays the role of the "simple, uneducated woman," a role she plays when it is to her advantage. It is, of course, obvious here as elsewhere, that she is intelligent, well-read, and thus able to discuss serious and complex theological issues clearly and with considerable skill.

First, it is unnecessary to discuss our privileges very much. Your honor heard us earlier and we retain that position. We cannot and will not contradict the honorable City Council in the comforting confidence that God and the honorable City Council will not bother us with the charge that we are too concerned about temporal possessions. God has forbidden unnecessary worry, but it is also not fitting that one should be completely without worry. If we did not cook anything we would have to wait a long time until the food cooked itself. We did not found the cloister and so we do not want to use up its possessions either. If we have to do that, then we do not do it intentionally. If our possessions are all taken away then we must appeal to God. If we can buy no wine we will have to drink water and then we will have all the less tax to pay. We ask that God may be our only hope and take all needless worry from us. Your honor knows well how rich our table is.[123]

It is true that the flesh would always like to complain that it is being hurt and no one loves punishment and criticism. It is also true that "Love bears all things,"[124] although love does not squabble with anyone nor is it violent towards anyone. But God's Word does not tell us at all that a person should give credence to rage and scorn and be obedient in all things, even if they are against his conscience. From the bottom of my heart I grant your honor that you have strong faith, for truly, a true faith is such a rarity that even Christ asked His disciples whether they thought the Son of Man would find faith when He came to the earth. Although faith, as St. Paul says "is nothing without love,"[125] indeed without love there is no true faith. Oh, if only God granted that everyone had true faith, how many difficulties and tremendous burdens would we be freed of, if, in accordance with faith, everyone experienced what he himself wanted to happen.[126] But woe to the person who sets his faith or trust in something other than God the Almighty and His only begotten Son, our Lord Jesus Christ!

We are well aware of what we think of St. Francis or how we should have hope in him. He is no god for us. We worship neither him nor any other saint. Our prayer books will not contain such things either, and if perhaps we mistakenly attribute too much significance to the saints, one should not hold that against us simple women, when, after all, great doctors have done the same and doubtless Dr. Wenzel formerly thought much of St. Augustine. If God has led him to the correct path now, then

---

123 Caritas is being sarcastic. The sisters ate very simple meals.

124 I Cor. 13:7.

125 I Cor. 13:2.

126 See Matt. 7:12.

he should thank Him. The Grace of God has not been denied us either! Who will hold it against us that we poor earthworms honor the servants of God with appropriate respect whom God the Father in heaven honors himself as Christ testified to His servants? Who will blame us also for not believing all at once all that which disturbs the consciences of much greater people, since conscience cannot be forced and the sting of conscience cannot be opposed like some new fantasy?

I also admit that anger cannot be tolerated. But I trust Almighty God. We are not creating anger in anyone, nor do we lead anyone astray. Something like that would be painful to me or then Christ our Lord must have been a deceiver also! If they want to force us to do something or compel us or even drive us out then we must commend that to Almighty God. We know well that nothing happens against His Will, 'not even a hair can be moved."[127] May His Divine Will be done forever.

We are also well aware that all wisdom in this world is folly before God and it is impossible for human understanding to comprehend the Splendor of God. But all that glitters is not gold. I do not know what difference exists between forcing and not allowing, just as the Turk forces no one to give up his faith and lets everyone believe what he wants. I admit that we are not so wise that we cannot be deceived, for no one is so clever that he is not deceived from time to time as we see unfortunately with our own eyes in many places. If the poor peasants had not been so evilly deceived and if they had not believed so quickly, such great bloodshed would not have taken place. However God's Providence sent it.

It is right that we know and firmly believe that justification only happens through the merit of Jesus Christ, as I wrote to your honor earlier. No one knows better than God does how much we rely on indulgences or the merits of the saints. If we have prayed the stations of the cross and the rosary, then we were not alone. Dr. Wenzel and his brothers did that too. If God has freed him of error, why should we not hope that He will let us share His Mercy too? He and no one else can judge us in this, although it is true that we have done away with much and in the course of time much is changed in order to adapt to the times which was alien to us earlier. That we lived cloistered is not something that we began. We also do not consider it wrong. The apostles did it also with the Christians in the early Church, when they held everything in common. As we understand it the separated life is not wrong where it occurs with good intentions and no one is harmed by it. For in this way

---

[127] Luke 21:18.

peace, atonement and order can be maintained all the better among many people.

We also know that we should aid and help our neighbors faithfully. We also hope that we and our sisters do that. If it should be said, however, that we only help our own and no others at all, then we can name many people outside the cloister who could testify differently about that. If we all left the cloister right now, then we could not be of service to anyone because of that. We have, after all, really enough to do in the cloister with our care and service of one another. For we have many old, sick sisters who are in need of every care and attention. They are also members of Christ, Who will accept what is done to them as if it were done to Him. For that reason we see behavior in it[128] which is useful for the common good.

Your honor knows how we run our household, and make our clothes ourselves so that we can clothe others and ourselves. Whether or not we educate young people one can learn from the three daughters who were taken away from us. And so we do not see that if we all left the cloister we could perform more service for our neighbors than now. We cannot be of service to everyone nor do more than we are able. To whom should the old little mothers be of service, as well as many others who are frail and need every bit of care themselves? Therefore we do not seek our salvation alone, but also that of our neighbors. There are too few of us to help all the people. We believe, however, if everyone did for others as we do for ourselves, then all the needy would be helped. We know well that we cannot fast for others, but we can work for others. The Holy Scriptures teach us in many places to pray for one another and woe to us if we forgot our neighbor and sought benefit only for ourselves.

As far as the ceremonies are concerned, we hope we conduct them correctly and confess that that person errs who places more value on the statutes of men than on God's commandments. But dignified, appropriate ceremonies and rituals for maintaining peace and harmony we do not consider improper. Today one can see very well what happens when no order is maintained. It is also true that the Lord Jesus Christ and the Apostles have taught sufficiently. How that is respected, however is also obvious! Impropriety is always impropriety, whether in the area of ceremonies or anywhere else. Let us hope that nothing dishonorable or disorderly occurs among us, or else it would be impossible for peace and unity to prevail among us, something that does not suit many people as we learn every day. If they can only sow many evil seeds among us or

128 The cloistered life.

stir up rebellion and opposition among us then they believe they have performed a service very pleasing to God. Truly not from good motives or brotherly love. But everyone only wants to lead the other to heaven and not strive for that himself. There is nothing easier than punishing other people and seeing their mistakes and nothing more difficult than not being worthy of punishment oneself.

I have shared our opinion about vows with your honor previously. I am too insignificant to be able to enter into a disputation about that. I will leave it to those more knowledgeable than I. Some say if one stays in a cloister, one is damned. Others say if one leaves it, one is damned. Whatever one does is twisted. And yet one sees what benefit and what honor resulted when men and women left the cloisters. What fruits resulted from that we learn from time to time from the great wailing and the tears of such persons. Some of them have almost despaired. They say they were enticed out of the cloister, but it was not their salvation that was sought, but their fortune. Now they are abandoned. No one cares about them and they cannot find their way in this city. When they are outside of the cloister, then their body and their soul are not safe. There is nothing more despised than runaway nuns or monks. When we hear such wailing and despair our heart is touched, but not for the temporal, but for the eternal. Not for the body, but for the soul.

But my dear wise man, I will not let any man on earth, whoever it may be, forbid me what the only begotten Son of God not only allows, but has also commanded. I will not let any creature turn into a sin what the innocent Lamb of God, who takes away the sins of the world, has encouraged me to do, that is to request from the Father in His Name everything I need. He has also promised to hear our prayers. What we request from the Father in His Name He will grant us. Now I am completely in need of grace in order to keep my vows and I hope for the same grace so that I will keep them in the future too. And this is not done against God. I cannot do it with my own power, but in that which can do all things, of which St. Paul says, "I can do everything through Him who strengthens me."[129] I will wait for Him with the help of God. With time we may discover what is best and that we must follow. Our so-called "delusion" will, God willing, not be false or unjust and rely on no other than the crucified Christ. No one can look into our heart, nor can anyone condemn us for having useless things and madness in our heart. Only God, the Lord, the Knower of all hearts, can do that. One recognizes the tree from its fruits. I will let that apply here. If, however,

---

[129] Phil. 4:13.

your honor according to the doctor's letter is amazed that I was so courageous to allow my sisters to leave, and I know not what other things you assume or conclude, then I am not up to such scrutiny. But your honor has forgotten and perhaps the good man knows nothing about the fact that I did not do this of my own volition, but upon the urging and command of the honorable City Council. I have said distinctly and clearly, that if I declare them free of all that they were obligated toward me, I have protested in reference to what they vowed to God. I do not want to get into that, since it is not fitting for a poor creature like me to dissolve what was promised to God the Almighty. The two gentlemen whom the Council appointed for that purpose heard that as well as that we permitted anyone who did not really want to remain with us to go wherever she wanted. That happened with the warning also, that each should keep God in mind as to how she would be responsible in her conscience to Him. Therefore this pointed argument does not hold up. However, absolutely do not believe that any relative has the right to take someone out of the cloister who is of legal age or force her to leave against her will, especially when it is happening for financial gain, as one sees often now. I will not speak of parents who can probably have greater authority than siblings or other relatives. I will let them be responsible for what they do. We cannot prescribe anything to the higher authorities and we cannot defend ourselves against their force either. It promised us it would not allow anyone to be forced to leave except by their parents. We hope they will keep their word also. We are, as God wills, not yet in such danger of fire or flood that we have to be pulled out by our hair. If we were prostitutes this would be appropriate, but they are left alone. But we suffer attacks for we are, as they say, more annoying than they are. We will leave that to God who will judge, not to men. The people cannot speak so much against us that others are not found again who say even worse things and so each judges the other, but not himself. We are not worried whether God will deny us His Help, for no one is abandoned who desires God's help from his heart, especially in matters which are not as bad as many people would like to make them.

If we vow something that we cannot keep, then that would be an impossibility itself. It is correct that everyone has his judge, as you write, who will judge us all.[130] Whoever has done something good will, according to the Words of the Lord, enter into eternal life, but whoever has done evil will enter the eternal fire.[131]

130 See I Pet. 1:17.
131 See Matt. 25:31–46.

Thus I wanted to reply briefly to your honor about Dr. Wenzel's letter. I know that I am too insignificant to be able to answer everything that was necessary. If I seemed a silly woman, please excuse me for God's sake and believe us, we will always do what is right and that our intention is good. We will not accept the idea that we should believe and obey everyone who hurts our conscience in all matters. A while ago your honor praised Zwingli and others to me. If we had followed him, then look where he leads us now with the sacrament.[132] And nevertheless all that is supposed to be God's Word and the pure Gospel. The preachers of Straßburg, as I have been reliably informed, consider Christ no more than another man. If we followed them, we would really have a bad ride. If one says one should follow the truth and the Scriptures, everyone claims to have the truth and be right and everyone uses the Scriptures for his own purpose and no one will give in to another and there is no end in sight. We'll leave that to people cleverer than we are. Meanwhile let us strive for what we consider the least culpable. In other words, let us proceed so that most of all we follow what we know is the most righteous. If we err in something, we are sorry. We know, however, as we do it, we cannot do it correctly, because there is so much confusion now. May God grant us poor people His Grace. Amen.

Chapter 46

Later, around St. Martin's Day,[133] the superintendent requested me to allow him to bring Philipp Melanchthon who was a very learned man from Wittenberg.

Grace and peace from God, our Father!
Honored Lady,

Once again the spirit moved me to write to you. It has happened that I have now eaten twice with Philipp. I am amazed at him. Among other things I have noticed that he is always inclined to mediate. One absolutely cannot write or say enough about the good, virtuous manner by which that happens. As one who does not like to keep his loyalty and love from you, but when possible, is inclined to promote and prove it, I once again did not want to be silent about it. Perhaps God will encourage you to speak with him, either alone if nothing else would be

---

[132] Zwingli declared the bread and wine were only symbolic, not the body and blood of Christ, which was the traditional doctrine.

[133] 11 November.

possible, or however you want. I consider him a treasure of Christianity. He is even loved by his opponents and at least not insulted. Then it would be seen and noted that you have considerable respect for such brave people after all. Blessedness is truly not to be found among the monks and you are really waiting in vain fore the Messiah. The Will of God actually works against such sects. I sense it at work daily, even among the greatest figures. And so many thousand times good night a and blessed times!

Kaspar Nützel, the Elder.

Chapter 47

At the request of the superintendent I wrote to him and told him he could visit me with Philipp whenever he wanted. I desired, however, that he not bring along anyone else. Then he wrote me this letter.

Grace and peace from god, our Father and His only begotten Son, our Lord along with my willing and able service.
Honored and beloved sister in Christ,

With what a happy heart I received your little letter in which you allow me to bring along Philipp Melanchthon to you. I cannot say it often enough. The reason why I have not answered you until now is that I have not been able to get to him. But I have sent a message to him and requested that he visit you with me when it is suitable. His answer was that he considered himself too insignificant for such a visit. Since obedience demands it, he will come and trust in God's Grace. He wants to learn the hour and the day from me.

Now, God knows, I have not been able to find time and yet I do not want to let the devil prevent everything. Today there is a wedding at the city hall and, although I am supposed to be in the city finance chamber at the same time, I have decided to take the day off and, God willing, visit you this afternoon in the confession house. Only he and I will be there and I will gladly leave if that would be best for you. I would be very sorry if something went wrong because of me. If we cannot make it, I will let you know.

I have also received your response to the letter which Doctor Wenzel gave me and could not delay in sending this doctor such a good opinion.[134] He sent me an answer to you again. I have read it and again found it not unpleasant. His offer comes from the depths of his heart, if

---

[134] Nützel seems to have interpreted Caritas's response in a very favorable light,

not understood in an unchristian way. Hence I did not want to delay in sending you his good and loyal opinion. With all my heart I ask God the Almighty to pour out His Spirit in it, so that in addition the praise of God and the betterment of our neighbors may result from it. Amen.

Thus I am bound to you in Christian love and serve you completely with my good will.

Kaspar Nützel, the Elder.

Chapter 48

Wenzel's second letter.

I wish you divine grace through Jesus Christ forever and offer you my services willingly, worthy, dear lady.

Your letter was presented to me that you wrote to the honorable Kaspar Nützel about one of my articles. From that I was induced to give a short reply with few words.[135] I beg you to accept such a friendly, Christian opinion and not to be upset if the words seem too sharp or not sharp enough or the like. May you interpret the whole thing only in the best way. God, who knows all hearts, knows my inner feelings. I have experienced His Grace for which I can never thank Him enough. Would God that I could declare to you and all others such grace for your salvation. With my whole heart I would like to do that. I also know that I am obligated, as I also pointed out to Kaspar Nützel, to see that his intentions for you are completely Christian and faithful. You did not offend me. Likewise, I do not know that I would have been offended by you or other cloisters or orders here in Nürnberg. Even if it had happened, and I knew it, I would not want to offend them in return, but to bring them and me to the best terms. In truth one will never be able to say that of me. I can say this with good conscience before God. Whether one interprets my sermon or other people's as if we were seeking, so to speak, the humiliation and disgrace of others does not bother me. I know, of course, that Satan also twists God's Word. For the honor of Christ and with God's Help we want to wage war and fight against the kingdom of the Antichrist. We do not want to speak out loudly against men, but against the evil of Satan, and, at the same time, love the sinners and hate

judging by his enthusiasm. Most readers would feel that Caritas had "stood her ground" and not given in to Linck at all.

135   Actually, Linck's second letter is longer than his previous one, despite his claim to the contrary.

the sin. Consider also St. Paul and the apostles and how they preached to people amid turmoil and attacks. Love is not suspicious. Therefore I hope you will interpret this and my previous letter in the best light and without suspicion. If I had know that it would be passed on and sent to you, I would have given it a different form, not that of a simple note, for a short letter is not always interpreted the same way everywhere. If several such letters do not satisfy you in all respects, then accept them with the best intentions. It is, of course, impossible to treat such great questions concerning God and consciences in a short letter. I am, however, with God's help, prepared to speak about how the Gospel is to be read. With you I will recognize the Truth of God. We read, to be sure, of the Christians in the early Church who were very willing to take up the Word inwardly and examine the Scriptures daily to see if things really were this way. If you criticize our teachings and consider them unjust, then this will not happen, only if you accept it beforehand and examine and study it diligently. If we criticize the manner of the papist, then we have had sufficient experience and know what it is. We would that other people might recognize that along with us so that everywhere souls would be saved and no one insulted. The people may well say our Gospel is concealed. For those who are lost it is concealed. The god of this world has blinded the unbelievers so that the illumination of the Gospel does not glow brightly from the clarity of Christ. We earnestly want to ask God to remove the curtain from us and let us faithfully in Christian love seek and examine the truth with one another. As far as that is concerned, do not be afraid of me, and I will act the same toward you. It is not a question of own affairs, but of Christ our Lord. We should not doubt that he will assist us as He Himself says, "Where two or three are gathered in my name, then I am in their midst."

You cannot continue your activities except through the divine Scriptures and the Word of Christ . . .[136] If we also do everything from our side daily also, God's Word shall and must be our judge at the same time. This alone must rule our conscience. To it alone we must open our hearts and not plug up our ears as the . . . do who do not want to hear the complainer. It means nothing when the people say they will interpret the Scriptures however they want to. For this reason they even form parties among themselves. This is what we find now in the case of Karlstadt, Zwingli etc. Now it is impossible for simple people to form an opinion about that. Therefore we must wait until the question is decided in a council or by knowledgeable people. For what should the simple people

---

[136] There is a gap in the manuscript here where one or two words are missing.

do if such explanations are delayed? How could they protect themselves from false prophets and listen to no other voice but the voice of Christ? Yet St. Paul teaches we should test everything and accept what is right. In this matter Christ says that the Father will reveal the Gospel to the simple people. For this reason no delay or postponement is possible. Together we will faithfully seek to give honor solely to the Word of God and not persist in our wicked delusion. In this way we will find the truth. May God help us all. Amen.

As far as your own person is concerned, by using all natural reason and your own good sense you should be all the more willing, because you are obligated to other souls to lead them to the knowledge of God and to the true Light. Hence I will answer your letter very briefly with as much as I have considered.

First, do not be bothered by taxes and other burdens. Since Our Lord Jesus Christ through His Word and Example has ordered us to pay such things to the authorities, we should do it obediently with faith that we will lack nothing. His Word is full of such power. He will keep those who believe in His Word and are obedient to Him through pious people. Even if the people did not exist, that would happen in a different way as when he miraculously fed Elijah and a widow by means of a raven. In this point it is very clear how offensive to Christ the papal ecclesiastical style is with its powerful privileges, exemptions and indulgences. On the basis of the Scriptures you will also find that worrying is not permitted. Worry about both superfluous things and about necessary things is forbidden since Christ says you should not worry about what you have to eat, drink or wear or anything else. Likewise as St. Paul says, do not worry about anything, but ask God in all things. We should be concerned only with the Kingdom of God and the salvation of our soul and how we can support one another in that. Temporal things are too small for us to be concerned with them. We should work for them and, according to the grace each has received from God, acquire them appropriately and keep, prepare, share and use them. One should, therefore, cook food, make clothes, build houses, but not be worried about them or be troubled in our hearts. As much as we put our hearts into it, just as much do we take from God and do not give Him room completely. It is right that we ask God to take such cursed evil from us for so long until after this life he also takes away work and the many kinds of evil without which this life cannot exist.

Love bears all things, but not dishonor of God and damage to the soul. Wherever it feels these things, it punishes, criticizes and fights them as much as it can. Thus St. Paul tells every preacher, "Preach the Word, keep it in easy and in hard times, punish, criticize and admonish."

Indeed, he teaches that one should severely punish or rebuke the tempters and the rebellious ones so that they are sound in the faith. Thus God commands the preachers to proclaim the Gospel through the prophet Hosea. Judge your mothers. Judge them because they have broken My Word and clung to their own ideas and the teachings of men. Thus Christ through his actions punished those who besmirched the house of God and the conscience of men, as it was written, "Zeal for your house has consumed me." Indeed, the Holy Spirit, which is, after all, a spirit of love and goodness, punishes the world from the highest down to the lowest, without exception. How should love then criticize no one or tolerate what is unreasonable? Let him preach who wants to and as he is able to, suitably or unsuitably, in a friendly or serious manner. One must not only criticize, but also believe in God's Words alone and follow them and not arbitrarily despise or discard the food because of the container. Let the listener believe and follow, whether it be agreeable or not, whether it help or hurt him, whether it be against his conscience or not. Of course there is no conscience, unless it be based on God's Word. Everything else is error and nothing but ghosts.

I will not deny that you know how you are to behave with Francis and the other saints. Nevertheless, the prayer books show that you look upon them as intercessors and mediators between God and us. That is an obvious error because the Scripture says there is only one mediator between God and man, that is the man Jesus Christ. He who gave himself for the redemption of all is the only mediator of the New Testament because only through Jesus are the promises of God received. The saints are therefore given to us by God as models so that we should see from them how God works in us to console us and to strengthen our faith and to pardon us. When I see how Eternal God has descended to us in Sts. Peter, Paul, Francis, Agnes, Lucia etc., strengthened them in all their sorrow and filled them with all the gifts of Grace, I should praise God and thank Him and put my faith firmly in Jesus. I should have no doubt that he will not leave me or graciously grant me His gifts as he did to them. His arm is not cut short. He can still do everything.

I confess openly that I have gone far astray in holy service. There is a great deal that I would like to announce orally, which I cannot do by writing because of its brevity. I also thank God, my Lord, who has instructed me in this area. It is also fine with me that you do not disdain to take an example from poor me. Without doubt He will not deny you His Grace. Just be certain that your words do not come from a heated temperament. It is true that God respects all servants of Christ. He will honor them eternally on Judgment Day. Even so we should honor the same ones, as it is written in God's Word, our parents and the authorities because we must be subject to them and also all other people because we love them in Christ without harming the love to which Christ alone is entitled. Now we know that the papists in general honor the departed saints as mediators, but despise the living ones whom God will have. Therefore, I speak of this point in general. Now it could well be, worthy, dear lady, that perhaps among you some would be tainted with such an error, although you for your part and others who are within the convent with you are informed. I know how I have erred, when I put more trust or just as much in Barbara, Katharina, Nicolaus of Tolentino and other saints as in Christ when in times of distress diseases and afflictions came. And so I know well in what an unchristian manner the people were directed to them. Therefore, be careful. There will be no pardon for your faith, whether or not many great people still believe what is right. Your reason, your will and your conscience must be subject to the Word of God, be captured by it, even if people do not force you. Then the ache in your conscience will stop, but never until then.

I would be sorry if some force or extraordinary burden were placed upon you. Without doubt the honorable City Council will not permit anything like that, even less drive you out by force. You need not worry about that. Arm yourself, so that you base your faith on divine Scripture and your conscience is firm, so that the Word of God does not struggle against you, as the Lord so faithfully warns, "Let your adversary have his way[137] . . . as long as you are still on the path with him." This is what one struggles for. I will also hope that you do what is proper in this regard. If, on the basis of Scripture, it should be found that perhaps your external customs are not useful, it would be useful or Christian to improve if you should follow other people and basically follow the truth, even if you do not recognize it or find it in your conscience. You should not worry, if possible. For if you can maintain it with a certain foundation of divine Word, then, God willing, no one will oppose you and force you to leave. So long as you confess, no one would be so clever that he was never deceived, you should faithfully desire to search for the truth with us.

That you do not consider your separation unjust is really not right and is an error, for the Scriptures punish those who separate themselves from the general Christian community. About this Christ says, that we should not believe, if people say Christ is in the desert or in the chamber, for this is the first way by which even saints have been deceived by an apparently good faith. A Christian life is not restrained, but proceeds

---

137   There is a gap in the manuscript.

freely, so that one goes out into the world, confesses Christ publicly and brings people to Christ. He Himself says, you do not light a lamp to hide it under a bushel. The apostles and other believers did not separate themselves from the Christians either, but only from the non-believers. In this way, they created neither barriers nor confusion, but went out openly in order to preach God's Word and to listen and console the people in other ways. If separation were right, then one would hardly find better people than the Beghards who base their activity on the example mentioned of the apostles. Be that as it may, even if one lived properly and very wisely, one has to consider many consequences. Naturally, from a fear of danger and disgrace, people think the cloistered life is better than a normal Christian life. For this reason even the clerics call their life a state of completeness. Yet because one is prevented from practicing Christian love or the divine commandments, what results are not just entanglements of the body, but also of the conscience.

Vows cannot be left up to other people. Each person in his own conscience must be certain and sure, for each will bear his own burden. Therefore, my worthy, dear lady, you will not be able to shove that off onto the highly educated; it is on your conscience. Even if the scope of this letter does not allow me to write enough about this, I really want to discuss it with you in written form or orally. In summary, if it is proved to me that the cloister vows are made by God, then I will accept that and take my punishment for it. One does not do anything to God. Let one have the basis of his conscience in His Divine Word or Command. How can I then do anything in faith or how can I know that something is pleasing to God or is acceptable to His Honor and to Him if I do not have His Word through which alone God's Will is revealed to us. Now I would like to see the person who can prove to me that these vows come from the Word of God, when the entire Gospel and the New Testament know nothing at all about vows. If I base my conscience on merit or sin in a matter for which I have no basis in the divine Scriptures or in the Word of God, but only by my simple opinion or human delusion I soothe or comfort my conscience, then I am letting someone besides God alone and His Holy Word rule and remain in my conscience. That means putting Lucifer next to God or the Antichrist in Christ's place, the horror of the desert into the holy city. I admonish all good hearts and faithful people for God's sake not to burden their conscience for life and limb with anything special or weighty, be it that God will count that as sin or a heavy burden. They should be certain of this from the Word of God. This alone should sit on the throne of David and rule your conscience. Oh, this is the great wailing and death of the soul which the

Antichrist carries on with the people of Christ. Would God that the consciences were free and no one were subject to anything but the Word of God, then food, clothing and other external things would not matter. The example of the renegade monks and nuns has nothing at all to do with this matter. Good and evil people are found next to one another everywhere. This matter concerns God alone and is no joke.

It is not acceptable that you are also cautious about permission to leave the cloister and maintain you want to consider your obligation to yourselves void but not that toward God. This matter does not concern the people, as even the scholastics confess that a vow is a work of reverence of God which is fitting for God. A prelate is, however, no more than a servant who carries this out for his master and not at all for himself. Therefore, it is a terrible mistake if people say, "I vow to the Mother of God, Saint Francis and you Mother or Father." Here they are imparting to a creature what is suitable for God according to their own teaching. In summary, as little as the baptized person in the font is bound to the priest or servant who baptizes him, but to God alone, likewise, just as little does the monk who makes vows bind himself to the prelate of the cloister, but to God alone. He cannot negotiate with him in matters of conscience any further than God commands. But since they often go too far, why should not the authorities or relatives bring the appropriate release to their relatives?

You should ask God and not let that be forbidden to you, as you write. But may that happen so that you ask in Christ's name, that is for the honor of Christ, on the command of Christ, and according to the teaching of Christ. Otherwise he will say, you do not know what you are asking for. Now consider whether God has commanded you to renounce such vows or not. If you want to rely on the crucified Christ, you must remain in His Word and not let yourself be driven above or below it even with no appearance of what is good. He will say yes, if you remain in My Word, you will recognize the Truth. On the other hand, if you let yourself be driven off this path, you will be deceived and misled.

Thus I hope to have refuted your letter briefly, although it would be good to write much more about such high, vital things. Please accept this for God's sake in a friendly manner and pray to God for me. At the same time I am not pleading my own cause. I would also not want anyone to be offended, but rather that everyone be saved. You must not believe me or anyone else, but only the Word of God. If the Holy Scriptures keep you from this, then inform us and listen to what we bring forth for the Scriptures. Discuss and compare this in your hearts with one another as Mother Mary did, with humble prayer and heart-felt desire and without being seen by anybody seeking the Truth of God.

Certainly God will also do his part. If, however, you appeal to the highly learned and, in the meantime, you want to live according to what you like, then make sure that the door is not closed. It is not sufficient that you are sorry, if you err in something, for if you are sorry, you will try to get rid of it. If you cannot find peace with men, then you certainly can find peace with God through His Grace. May He grant you and us this Grace to His Honor and Praise. Amen.

Chapter 49

My answer to Dr. Wenzel.

Prudent, wise, dear sir,

Recently your honor again sent me a long letter from Doctor Wenzel. I informed your honor earlier, that I am too insignificant to hold a disputation with such highly educated people. I find that does not bear any special fruit. Also, as many errors as there are, the people insist on their opinion and, if they did not do that, they would be contradicting themselves. Since we also persist in our plan and cannot accept everything they say with good conscience, then we must be as stubborn and godless and more angry than anyone else. Should we then act against our conscience? We cannot bear that either. If the dispute is concerned with temporal matters, then, as far as we are concerned, it should be settled soon, even if should mean that we lose all that we have. But to act against our conscience, when no one can give an answer but us ourselves, then nobody can be angry at us, if we proceed slowly, So many highly educated people are in opposition to each other in many matters. Each claims to be right and yet nobody knows how he stand, not just against those who call themselves evangelical[138] and the papists, but also the evangelicals among themselves.[139] And we poor females are supposed to follow what every single one of them is saying. We should not recall that St. Paul taught us that we should test the spirits and accept the best. In my opinion in many hundreds of years it has never been more necessary to be cautious in accordance with Christ's warning, "Be as clever as the serpents and simple as the doves." There are so many errors about. I am informed that those from Straßburg, Puczer, Capito and elsewhere are now saying Christ was not God, but only a pious man

---

[138] The Lutherans.

[139] She notes that there is no unity among the Lutherans; that is among the various Protestant sects that are springing up, either.

and therefore He is called a son of God. And some people get baptized again.[140] There are so many claims that if we followed them all we would not know where we would end up. Yes, it is said, follow those who speak the truth. But they all claim to be right and each maintains he is telling the truth. And thus we are too lowly to decide the controversy. God knows our heart. He knows we are not so stubborn that we really would not want to believe correctly, but to believe everything is folly. Therefore, wise, dear man, it is not necessary to answer the long letter. If the good man is doing it with the best of intentions, then God will thank him. He must not hold it against us if we do not believe everything that he says immediately. Without doubt he also occupied himself with it for a long time until he arrived at his present opinion and who knows whether he is still free in his conscience. I hope he will conduct himself toward us as St. Paul teaches his Timothy. A servant of the Lord should not argue, but should be gentle toward everyone, a clever and patient teacher who corrects with kindness those who stubbornly oppose him so that with time God will give them the realization of truth. But now everyone wants to force the other person to believe and do what he wants. If that does not happen, he gets angry and criticizes and ascribes guilt to the other person and harms the people. Is this the correct evangelical way? I will leave that up to God.

It is really true, as he writes, that we cannot continue our activity any longer than God wants. But it also cannot be destroyed unless God wills it, because even the hairs on our head are counted. His will be done on earth as it is in heaven. He also writes of the false prophets. I really know that no one can know who the false prophets are but God also. Karlstadt, Zwingli, Puczer, Capito, Icolampadius and others do not consider themselves false prophets, but true ones. I was also informed that Karlstadt has not yet recanted. Luther, he says, did not understand him correctly. At the same time, however, they reviled one another in the coarsest manner.

The good gentleman teaches us very clearly that we should not be worried about the temporal, nor be troubled about taxes. He is not bothered that previously we brought everything to the attention of the honorable City Council. In this way he wants to teach us about what we did earlier. Unfortunately it is as clear as day who is worried about the temporal and who is not. If the Gospel and the handing over of the cloisters are mentioned together, then that must mean merit and justice, but if we move forward, we stick to the temporal. I have no doubt God will not

---

140 The Anabaptists.

desert us. If, however, we are asleep, then we will experience what Solomon says of the lazy man.

I admit that we should punish, criticize and threaten the leaders and the rebels, just as he writes. But, God willing, we are not such unreasonable people as is said. People also say that we want to start a rebellion. God protect us from that! How could we poor ones lead anyone or start a rebellion since we ourselves have been abandoned by almost everyone? To whom do we preach? Whom do we want to follow us? Of course, they say, you do not want to accept the Word of God. Oh yes we do, as God wills it. If, however, we were to accept everything that is called God's Word, then we would, perhaps, fall from one sect into another, as has happened to some people. Look, they say, no one should be forced or permitted to do things either. What difference is there? Does your honor think the matter is settled when we are not permitted to do some things, but forced to do others that are against our consciences? Indeed, that only works when the conscience struggles with itself and recognizes that it has made the wrong decision. Then it easy to understand if some one despairs and thinks everything will be all right if only he leaves the cloister. That is really far from being right. Your honor knows what Philipp said about using pressure. I will leave it at that. Forced joy is never right.

I have also written to your honor previously about what we believe concerning the saints. I will leave it at that. I do not deny that there has been abuse in many matters. We have done away with much of it where we felt it in us. But to drop everything all at once goes against our conscience. It will not permit it either. Your honor knows that the children of Israel could not drive out the unbelievers all at once and we should not be expected to drop what has been rooted in us for so many years. It may well be true that time does not make something wrong right, but something is not wrong just because people say it is wrong. How many people have written against Luther and condemned him? Not just papists, but also members of his own sect have called him evil, self-seeking and a heretic. If he were therefore considered a heretic, that would not please everybody. He could thus be the victim of injustice too. I know well and all my sisters know that between God and men there is no other mediator than the man Christ. I also do not consider it right that we should not honor the dear saints as they should be honored, for Augustine, Hieronymus, Cyprion and others teach me otherwise. If people say these were men and may have erred, then they themselves are not gods either and may err also. Yet these great people, some of whom have poured out their blood for the Christian faith, are more to be believed than the iconoclasts and saint haters of today. Whoever thinks more of Francis than Christ will answer for it. Wrong is always wrong.

Your honor will have to excuse me, for the good man desires for us to take an example from him. If I should follow him, then I would also have to take a husband. Perhaps I could not find one because I am old and ugly. How am I supposed to do it then? If I should keep running to your honor for answers then you would have much to do. Jesus Christ should be our example and not a mortal man. May He grant us His Grace that we may act correctly, not incorrectly. Are Sts. Augustine, Hieronymus and similar great people who have long since died to be rejected? I believe those who are still alive cannot be recognized as models because even a new born child is not without sin. Let us ask God to grant Grace to us miserable, sinful people, so that our words and works do not come from heated spirits. Above all may he protect us from all words and works which come from a false, evil conscience and which others may accuse us of. We know that we should follow the truth, but not every spirit that pretends to be the truth. For all that glitters is not gold, nor is everything the truth that it pretends to be. Unfortunately we can see now in many ways where the black angel can also change himself into an angel of light. He can probably also make himself glitter. Therefore it is really necessary for us to follow the message of St. Paul that we should be careful and only accept what is good.

It is not our fault that we should not have complained that they did not let us freely have what should be free for everyone. Now they want to charge us with not confessing and not going to Holy Communion and will not let us receive the sacraments from whom we want to. We will leave to God whether that is distress or not. In that area where everyone is free, we are to be restricted and not have the power to accept whomever we want. May it be lamented to God that in this way we are deprived of His Holy Corpus Christi or are forced to accept a court of damnation. We confess again that we are human and can be deceived. But other people can also be deceived since they are human just like us.

We have already answered your honor earlier concerning isolation and I will let it remain that way. In this we have a model not only from the apostles, but also from saints, Hieronymus and Augustine whom we should believe as much as the others. We know that the cloister does not bring us salvation. It also cannot remove salvation from us if we have the correct attitude. Whoever thinks he gets salvation from the cloister is just as wrong as the one who thinks if he just leaves the cloister he will obtain salvation. There is more to it than that. Inside the cloister and outside the cloister there are abuses and yet they are not the fault of the cloister or of the state, but of people who commit abuses. In isolation, however, much can happen in a more orderly fashion than when there are many distractions. Therefore even the most holy man born of a woman, John the Baptist, was isolated from his childhood on. And the apostles not only separated themselves from the non-believers, but also from those who did not share everything in common with them. The city gives and takes nothing and therefore it should be free. It is better, however, for one to stay in his house and cloister than to run through the entire city and want to rule everyone but himself. One must show works of mercy in the cloister as well as outside of it, although one can fail to perform them in the world too. But if only the cloisters are destroyed, then everywhere things would be fine. It is amazing that God forbade the common houses, since one sins openly there and no one has pity for those poor people or considers how they could be taken away from their sinful life. Yet everyone wants to pull us to heaven by our hair. We confess that maintaining chastity is not given to everyone by God; it is also not denied to everyone. If one could not maintain it, then all the wives whose husbands are often away for a long time would not be pious. God did not want this, however. Christ made it clear enough to us which state is the better one. Likewise the words of St. Paul are also clear that the one who has his daughter marry is not wrong, but would do better if he did not have her marry. He also immediately gave the reason why he wishes that all men were like him. If marriage were such a good thing, then Christ could well have taken a wife, since man can decide to marry or not.

As far as oaths are concerned, your honor got our answer earlier. It is true that each person must bear his burden himself. But how is it possible for someone to be certain in everything? We often hear nowadays that no one is more uncertain or restless in his conscience than those who leave the cloisters. Without doubt that would also happen if we followed them. We would not only encounter the temporal, but would also have no more clear conscience. If, however, we are forced or compelled by evil means and pressure in such a way that we cannot ever stay, then we must do as God wills. May he protect us graciously from such things. I do not consider it bad to vow to do good things. To do evil things even without an oath cannot be good. If taking vows is wrong, then the vow at baptism must also be wrong, especially for young and innocent children. We will leave it up to everyone to keep or not keep what he has vowed. At the same time we also want very much to be allowed to still do what we hope to achieve with God's Help. We also do not doubt that we could continue to exist if we had judges who were not caught up in the matter themselves. Luther himself has not yet destroyed a cloister or forced people to leave. In Wittenberg the church's hourly prayers are still sung and read. It is said that there is also still a Franciscan cloister there. Yet here everything is looked upon as being improper. May God grant that this happens for a good reason. We could also say, would God that our consciences were all free. But through such a wish we believe few become free. Instead they are troubled if they do not keep what they vowed and this is not serious. Now some people are not attacking vows. A time could come in which they are attacked too much. If, however, some one leaves the cloister, then he is not thinking that someone can leave, either in accord with or against his conscience. He does not care.

But when the good gentleman again comes to me with a harsh argument as if I would need a warning to leave, he does me an injustice. He does not consider that I was directed by the Council and I have been forced to free each one from her oath. I had to do this and I have freed them of the obligation they vowed to me. More I did not have to do. The good gentleman catches himself when he says this matter does not concern men, but God, which is the truth. How could I then free anyone, who was not obligated to me and do something reserved for God alone? Therefore I also understand how very naturally they demanded of me that I release the sisters from all their vows, even those they made to God. I did not have to do that. I have enough personal sins to bear. Let each person decide to do it or not as he pleases. At his time he will be held responsible. How did he think I was supposed to do it? If I had refused to release them from their vows, then I would have acted against the will of the honorable City Council. Since, however, I freed them from the vow they made to me, this does not apply. I am no more than a servant. How could I free them from something belonging to God? If I do not get involved in what is vowed to God, then they say I need a warning. These are truly sophistic arguments with which they like to catch the people. They should act, speak or do, as those people would like. If no one is bound to me, then I cannot free anyone. If, however, he has bound himself to God, what advice do they have?

It is not necessary for the authorities or the relatives to save their people, for I will not hold anyone by force. Like Herr Philipp Melanchthon[141] I do not consider it right that someone who is of legal age is forced to leave against her will, especially when the father and mother are not present. This has also been promised us by the honorable

---

141 It is obvious that Caritas is familiar with Melanchthon's writings. It is no wonder that she looked forward to speaking with him.

City Council, although almost every day we are overrun because of it and are subjected to insults. Whoever can criticize, mock, rebuke and bother us the most thinks he has done something especially pleasing to God. There is no love, no pity, and no mercy, only storming the cloister and pulling the nuns out by their hair. If that is the fruit of Christian love, then it is truly a bitter fruit, because it is the reason why so many fervent tears have been shed and so much sorrow, trouble, misery and distress have been caused. Truly, if we did not rely on the crucified Christ, we would despair of the whole world. We have probably deserved this distress from God, but we would not want to be responsible for it because of these people or act differently from what we would want to happen to us.[142] We pray to God that we remain in the Words and in the Grace of Christ, even though people condemn us. For not they, but Christ will be our judge and He will judge us righteously.

If one remains in the cloister, then it is not right. If one leaves, then he does not know where to go. The distress of the old, feeble women is not considered. The danger facing a young person is not taken to heart. If only the cloisters are destroyed, then everything will be just fine. For a long time the peasants have been storming the cloisters and destroying them. Unfortunately it is clear what good has come of this. I am not so learned that I can argue from the opposite side. Yet I hope by the Lord God we will remain in His words and not be dissuaded. Let anyone interpret them as he will.

And so once again and for the last time I have answered the long letter of Doctor Wenzel. Although it could have been done in a cleverer manner, I cannot do any better. I am very worried that nothing will help, even if I say what I want. May the Lord God grant us the Holy Spirit and His Grace so that we can all be delivered from all error. Men cannot deliver us from that, however. Everyone claims he is right and the person you don't follow says you are acting against the Word of God. It is all the fault of our sins. May God grant that we act correctly in everything and that even your honor does say sometime, "I did not mean that." For God's sake forgive me, if I have written too much. The doctor's letter brought about this reply. From now on I will refrain from answering and commend myself to the Grace of God. If he wants me to be different, then he can make me different without the help of all men, for man's handiwork is always in vain. His Blessed Will be done to us all for ever and ever! Amen.

142 Caritas is trying to apply the "Golden Rule" here.

Chapter 50

After a few days the superintendent came to the confessional house with Philipp. The latter said a great deal about the new doctrine. However, when he heard that we relied on God's Grace and not on our own works, he said we could attain salvation just as well within the cloister as in the world outside, if we did not put faith in our vows. On both sides we agreed in all points. Only in the matter of vows we could not agree. He felt, of course, they were not binding and we were not obligated to keep them. I, on the other hand, felt that what we had promised to God we were obligated to keep with His Help. He was more moderate in his speech than any Lutheran I had ever heard.[143] He was deeply offended that our people were being subjected to force. He left us on friendly terms.

Afterwards he spoke emphatically to the superintendent and the other men about many things, especially concerning their having forbidden the Franciscans from holding divine service and having removed the children from the cloister by force. He told them openly and frankly what a great sin they had committed by doing this.

I hope that God brought this Lutheran man here at the right time. For at the same time it had again been decided that we were to be driven from the cloister. The cloisters were to be torn down or the old nuns who would not accept the new faith were to be brought together into one cloister and the young ones were to be forced out into the world. There were many very angry attacks against us, but Melanchthon rejected them all. He said it was extremely contrary to God to compel people with such force. Among other things he said the both the father and mother would answer to God in their conscience for having taken their children from the cloister by force and against their will. Some people asked what should be done with the cloisters and if they were not to be destroyed. He answered no. They should let them remain. If they did not want to give them anything, then they should not take anything from them either. In Wittenberg and in other Lutheran areas no cloister had been destroyed yet.[144]

And so he brought it about that the people calmed a little and did not attack us so violently any more. He had a serious conversation with the

---

[143] Coming right after the correspondence with Linck, this meeting must have been a refreshing change for her. In Chapter 52 she writes more of her favorable impressions of Melanchthon.

[144] Caritas made the same point in her response to Linck's second letter.

superintendent so that he would not cease taking care of us as he had
threatened to do so eagerly at that time. Therefore the superintendent
wrote me the following letter.

Chapter 51

Grace and peace, dear lady, mother and sister in Christ,
    I received your last letter along with the answer to Doctor Wenzel's
previous letter and brought it to his attention. He answered me after his
good ideas had not only proved fruitless for you, but he noted that you,
who are more than dear to him, had been driven to make spiteful
remarks. After all this he wants to let the matter rest just as you do and
not bother with you anymore and let God prevail. Similarly, I wish you
and others would understand no differently than God does, that it was
with a lack of understanding and yet with the best of intentions that
sometimes I made you endure some preachers and other things.[145] He
knows this. At the same time I have gone further than is appropriate for
my duty and my office. Therefore I have decided not to burden you and
your sisters with such things any more. The past actions should suffice.
I do not regret them, nor do they bother me either, but I am grateful to
God for them as is fitting. In order to conclude these spiritual questions
in a friendly way I cannot refrain from sending you another copy now. It
is sent from the Landgrave William of Hesse as an answer to his
father-in-law Duke Jörg of Saxony. From this you can see that Nürnberg
is not alone in this opinion, nor is there as much criticism than among
those who are reluctant to hear the truth spoken. Elsewhere people also
do not doubt that God's Will will be done without regard for the innocent blood that is shed every day and it is supported, indeed carried out
by those who belong to the anti-Christian party and are sinners. They
threaten both me and people like me and are not unknown to you. They
understand better than I. I am also worried that they know very well that
they should stop for the sake of justice. Please send the letter back to me
when you have read it as I requested.
    You know my weakness. Thanks be to God every day for seven years
I have wandered about in the mayor's office and at the city hall and have
not missed one session of the council. That will go on as long as God
wants. If you want to put up with me even longer (don't flatter me in this
matter), then I willingly offer you my service in all temporal affairs. I

[145] It sounds as if Melanchthon's views have had a moderating effect on Nützel too.

will apply myself even more than I have up to know. The right to terminate this position should remain with you, however. Even Philipp Melanchthon advised me not to give it up. It has truly never been difficult for me to serve you, but on the contrary, I have always enjoyed it. I must confess, however, that I would not have given up this happiness for anything. Now I know, however, that I have been guilty of being zealous because the temporal authority established by God[146] obligated me and I could not refuse. Wenzel Linck was upset that I sent you his letter which was only meant for instruction. He wants me to send it back to him. Please send it back to me if you will. I warned him that he could lose in this matter. He doesn't think so. He can do nothing more than commend the matter to the Justice of God. If I knew which side would lose, then I would have good reason to wish that he would give up his plan without justification.

If you send me back the document as I suggested and as I already promised, then you will see with time that those people are wrong who believe that Philipp did not come here for the sake of the education of our youth, but was called by me to destroy you. They will find the opposite is true. They are the destroyers and I, God willing and with His Grace, am a protector of order more than they are. Indeed, to the extent it is possible for the general welfare, I should be recognized for protecting your cloistered life as much as I could.

May you be commended to God.

Kasper Nützel the Elder.

Chapter 52

The Grace of God be with us all. Prudent, wise, dear superintendent, I, along with the whole convent, have read your faithful letter with pleasure. As far as your friendly offer is concerned, we hope Almighty God has caused your honor to have pity on us poor, miserable, abandoned souls and that you will show mercy toward us.[147] You also desire that God be gracious and merciful at the time of His strictest judgment. For that we thank your honor as heartily as we can. We know that we can do nothing to merit it, but we will ask God to hear us poor sinners and grant to your honor whatever you may need.

---

[146] The City Council.
[147] This letter can be looked upon as a successful attempt at "fence mending." Once again Caritas shows her ability to be charming and humble at the same time. The tension and testiness of the past have vanished.

If your honor only knew how deeply it struck our hearts when you threatened to lay down your office as superintendent and the like, you would truly pity us. We know well that your honor has done his best and that since we are all human, there is no one living on earth who can do everything right and never make a mistake. We do not accuse your honor, but pour out to you our fear and distress which oppress us most grievously and from which we may well be freed. May God be praised eternally. He can lead us to the depths of hell and then turn all sorrow into joy according to His Mercy. We really deserved this and even more because of our sins. But, be that as it may, we beg your honor for God's sake and in accordance with your request remain our superintendent, protector and guardian, for we desire no change. We also do not want to have a role in the process of termination, but commend that to God, our Faithful Father. In His eternal wisdom He will recognize whomever he should bring together each time. May he hold us together on both sides through His Mercy in the bonds of divine and fraternal love, so that neither here nor there we are divided in His Praise. As far as we are concerned, you will never receive a termination notice your whole life long. May you receive the reward from Christ our Lord who promised, "What you have done to the least of these my brethren, you have done unto me."[148]

In the matter of Philipp Melanchthon, we truly never heard, nor did it ever occur to us in our hearts, that your honor brought him here to destroy us. We do not believe it either. If we had been afraid of him I would not have spoken with him in the least way. Would God that everyone had Philipp's modesty, for then we might hope that much would not have happened which did not turn out for the best. If the good man had done nothing here but advise your honor not to give up our care, then God might well have sent him here. May he be praised for eternity.

I have not only read the letter which the Landgrave sent to Duke Jörgen, but also had a copy made in the hope that your honor would not be opposed to that, for I like to read all sorts of things very much. That is also the reason why I drew out the answer so much. Nowhere in the letter mentioned is it written that one should force someone to do this or that and especially that everyone should be free to marry or not. The abuses have always been wrong, but they cannot be eradicated root and branch all at once. Let us ask Almighty God to grant us all a real, true faith and release us from all error and keep us in His Grace.

148 Matt. 25:45.

A short time ago we sent your honor some letters in a box. They concern the purchase of Zolner's meadow. If the man who opposes us has received an answer from your honor please send them back to us. May you and yours be commended to God's Grace eternally. Please convey our warmest greetings to our pious little Clara[149] and tell her that by God's Grace we have a new superintendent.[150]

Chapter 53

On Tuesday after New Year's in the 26th year a clerk from the chancellery visited us. He reported from the City Council that since St. Martin's Day we had brewed some batches of beer. It was the opinion and command of the honorable City Council that in the future we should cease brewing beer, or, if wanted to make beer, we should have an authorized beer inspector present. He would perform measurements from the vat as was customary for other brewers.

And so it began. We always had to inform the clerk who was appointed for this purpose in advance whenever we wanted to brew beer. He then sends us a beer inspector. Each time he comes we have to give him 14 pennies and a meal.[151]

Chapter 54

On All Saints' Day anno domini 1527 Sigmund Fürer and Andreas Imhof came and brought along Doctor Jugler and a court clerk by the name of Karl Ortel. We had to let them into the convent through the cloister.

The doctor spoke first and said approximately the following: The honorable City Council had assigned them to us out of its great, paternal love for us after some cloisters had complained that they were poor, abandoned and oppressed children. As a result the honorable City

---

149 Kaspar Nützel's daughter who was forced to leave the convent. See Chapter 34.
150 Obviously she does not mean "new" literally, since Kaspar Nützel has kept his position as superintendent. It may be that she means only that Clara's father has been reaffirmed in that position.
151 Although she does not mention it here the major "issue" at hand is the tax levied on all beer that was brewed in the convent. From this point on taxes due from the convent become a greater and greater concern as the City Council exerts more and more pressure on it.

Council had discussed with its experts that they were obligated to take care of us as the authority instituted by God. They had also been advised to visit us. Moreover they had heard credible accounts that we were suffering shortages and afflictions to such a degree that they had to be attended to. Therefore they were charged by the honorable City Council to visit us in the name of the City Council itself. For that reason we should speak to them freely and unashamedly about all our shortages and afflictions. They wanted to listen to each sister alone.[152] Without any fear the sisters were to tell them all the troubles they had in spiritual and temporal matters and everything that bothered their conscience and what scruples they had in their conscience. They would write this down faithfully and bring it before the honorable City Council. The latter would then pass it on to its advisors who would faithfully offer suggestions so that everything could be improved or at least some of the difficulties would be taken from us. All this was said with much flattery.

I gave them this answer among other things. We did not imagine that they would take this office upon themselves. Hence I did not know the answer of my convent. First I wanted to speak with my sisters. They agreed to that. Then they left the room for a while.

When they came back, I gave them this answer. The convent is deeply grateful to the gentlemen for their paternal intentions. We hope they are doing this for no other reason than from true concern. The sisters empowered me to answer for all of them, for no sister wanted to speak with them alone. I received support for this commission from two old, two middle-aged and two young sisters. They all stood up and testified that this was the opinion of the convent.

When the men heard that the sisters did not want to speak with them alone, they were hardly content. They said the honorable City Council had ordered something else. The conflicts of conscience could not be revealed if they could not speak alone. Each one would be afraid of the other and then nothing would get any better.

The sisters all defended themselves a great deal and would not speak with them alone. They added that a number of the sisters had been in the convent for 50 years and had never spoken alone with someone from outside. Some could not hear and some could not walk plus many other reasons we also had. They rejected all of them, however.

They said that if the provincial head sat there then we would not be

---

[152] Up until this point it appeared that the representatives were acting in good faith. By desiring to speak with each sister alone, however, they show their lack of respect for the traditions of the order and hint at the possibility of an "ulterior motive" behind their visit.

afraid of him. We should be just as little afraid of them. They knew in advance, however, what we would say.

Herr Fürer told me I should release the sisters from their vows so that they could speak all the more freely.

I replied that they had made a vow not to me, but to God. I cannot release them from what binds them to God. As far As my person is concerned, however, I will allow each one to say whatever she wants to in good conscience. When the sisters did not want to proceed, the gentlemen left a second time and conversed with one another for a long time. When they came back they said they had not carried out their commission, for they had been ordered to hear us individually, not all together. The gentlemen were doing this for no other reason than out of a sense of duty. They considered it their duty to provide for our souls so that they could purify their conscience and know how to answer God, and even the Emperor and the Confederation and where ever else it might become public knowledge. If, however, we disobeyed the honorable City Council in this matter, then they would have no further orders for dealing with us this time. We should consider what a poor attitude we were assuming and how angry both we and the sisters of St. Katharine's would make the honorable City Council which was so faithfully concerned about us. In the future they would probably ignore our other affairs and just not be bothered with them. They also made many other threats.

Then, among other things, I said the following: "My dear gentlemen. You are severe father confessors. Oral confession, which was carried out alone with one other person and was to be kept silent forever, was recently done away with. And now you want us to confess to all four of you and bring to light the flaws in our consciences. At the same time, however, you told us earlier that you did not intend to keep that private, but bring it before the honorable City Council and its advisors. That seems very strange to us."

They all said it was not supposed to be anything like confession. They only wanted to learn the flaws of our consciences so that we could be helped in these matters.

Thereupon the one-eyed clerk began argue a great deal about how difficult and dangerous oral confession had been up to now, communion in both forms and a lot of other heretical issues. Afterwards I said, "Dear Herr Ortel. We are not here for a debate."

And so the gentlemen stood up and were about to leave, so that we could hardly tell that they wanted to hear from me what the convent had agreed on for me to say.

When they had sat down again, I spoke. "Dear, wise gentlemen.

Since you are asking about our problems and afflictions, the whole convent has ordered me to announce to your honors our suffering is a suffering which we all share. The most pressing thing on our consciences is that we are poor, sinful people who sin constantly. Every day we bewail these sins to Our Lord in the bitterness of our soul. Although we do not consider ourselves better than other people who sin very frequently, we do not, however, feel in our conscience that we are such special cases that ought to be brought before the council's advisors or would need special treatment. If you know of such items as you have just mentioned, then please point them out to us. We would like to furnish you with information about them and, with God's Help, reform as much as our conscience will allow."

Then the doctor spoke. "We are here to learn about them."

Then I spoke. "No, doctor, you said at first that the honorable City Council had heard about them and you are here so that you can find out precisely what flaws exist among us which need improvement. We would also very much like to know what they are. For three years we have crawled and wriggled like poor worms. If we could have hidden under a stone, we would have been happy to do so. If we have offended anyone, however, please point it out to us."

The doctor spoke to Fürer. "What else should I say? I do not understand the matter. Therefore let Fürer speak to it so that this point does not remain unanswered."

After this I spoke. "It is deplorable and the source of much sorrow for us all that for almost three years we have been living in the midst of Christians without any Christian sacrament. This is miserable especially in the case of death when we must die like cattle. From this many problems and burdens for our conscience arise, which, perhaps, no one will believe who has not experienced it. In addition without any justification our worthy fathers, who had faithfully served our convent for 250 years, were taken away from us by force. This whole time no evil rumor or trouble or problem arose which led to any inappropriate or improper behavior which would have justified their being taken from us. Even the gentlemen who removed them said they had no charges against the Franciscans, or us nor had they ever heard anything bad about them. But, since they were doing it at other cloisters where they had much justification, they would not serve the peace, if they left us alone. If they were taken from us without cause and because of other people, then we have had enough of it and it is time to return them to us, for we did not want to be separated from this holy order. Thus we did not want to and could not take away anything from the rights the authorities had over us. It is true, that at first they wanted to give us other fathers whom we did want to accept. We also would not have the right to accept any from the new sect. If we had followed these fathers, we would have long since left the cloister and would have had to take husbands as quickly as possible. You will recognize them by their fruits.

"Every day we asked God to share the new doctrine with us if it were a Grace of God. If it was a plague then he should protect us from it. The longer it lasted the less it appealed to us from what we heard every day about what fruits it had produced. We were poor, simple, unlearned females and therefore did not want to get involved in this conflict. We preferred to have the educated ones fight it out. We were well informed about how they argued and wrote against one another and the most educated fell one after the other, such as Ocolampadius and Zwingli and others. If we followed these people we would probably even deny the Holy Sacrament and get baptized again.[153] Therefore we finally decided to stay with the old Christian faith until a council was called or God granted unity to Christianity. We do not want to rebel against what the general Christian Church accepts."

I also spoke about the preachers. "You sent us a Carthusian who was supposed to preach to us the Word of God clearly and simply. I have read a great deal in my life, but I have never read a stranger Gospel with so much criticism, abuse and chasing after the devil. But I do not want to complain about him, for I listened to his sermon with particular diligence. It was also useful for me, for he strengthened me more in the old faith than a Franciscan could have done who would have preached at this time. From his sermon, you see, in which he contradicts himself about six or eight times, we noticed what an adventure lies in the Lutheran teachings, so that will protect myself from these Lutheran teachings for the rest of my life. I say this not to put down the good father. He speaks from the spirit which he possesses."

Afterwards I spoke to them briefly about our burdens with temporal things, that now we had been ordered to pay 300 gulden. We asked that they be lenient with us in this matter. These, I said, are the problems and concerns which burden all of us in spiritual and temporal matters. If only they would remove them from me, as if each sister had spoken to them individually. Then the whole convent stood up as a sign that this was the general opinion of all of them.

Then the gentlemen spoke. They would present this opinion to the

---

153 The nature of the Eucharist and the need to be baptized a second time were, of course, issues which were the subject of considerable debate, much of it among the various Protestant sects themselves.

honorable City Council, but did not think that anything fruitful would come of it. Since we had not wanted to follow the honorable City Council and had disparaged it, none of this was valid without the sisters having been heard individually. Perhaps there was a single, confused little lamb who was troubled in her conscience and who might be helped by such a private conference.

Then I spoke and said that whatever sister wanted to should go to the gentlemen alone and not be afraid.

Fürer then spoke. Each one must be worried that she would not have a single good day with us any more, if she singled herself out. I should request the sisters to obey me when I told each of them to go to the gentlemen alone.

Then I spoke. "First you told me to release the sisters from their vows and now you want me to force them to obey me. How should I do that? I have released the sisters from their vows to me. You can see perfectly well that no one wants to go with you alone. You are making my sisters disobey me."

Then Fürer spoke. "I did not tell you to be disobedient. I would like, however, for the sisters to have a release in this hour, so that each might say what is on her heart and afterwards be obedient to you again." Still no sister wanted to stand up.

While they were speaking to the sisters in this way and the sisters gave their answer very openly, although none of it counted since it did not go on in secret, the doctor came over to me. He said he would have liked to see us satisfy the order of the council, for he wished us all the best. He wanted to assure me that there was no deception involved. They did not desire to know anything secret either and did not want to interrogate us under oath. They would also be satisfied if one sister said nothing except for being satisfied with what had been said previously.

Fürer came over too and said, "I would like to have seen you be a little more obedient than those sisters at St. Katherine's." He also wished it on my behalf. He even told me that I judged very severely by the advisors in the honorable City Council. They were all of the opinion that all my sisters had to believe whatever I wanted them to. None of them was allowed to speak against me. Therefore I should consider speaking with the sisters so that they would give in to the wish of the council. They would then come back on another day.

When I heard that they wanted to come back again and that it had to be that way, then I was afraid the next time there would be an even bigger argument. I told the gentlemen to leave the room and told the sisters what I had heard and that they wanted to come back another time. I asked the sisters to give in for God's sake and say a few words. Then the sisters agreed, but only if each could take along another sister whom she trusted.

The gentlemen, however, would not allow that. They sat down in the workroom and wished for all the sisters to be sent out. One was to go in after the other. We told them we would do that only if the provincial were there. Then they ran out of the room and sat down in the cloister and one after the other went to them. Then they asked each one her name and what concerns she had in spiritual and temporal affairs and how the abbess and the preacher behaved and whether there was discord in the convent. The sisters all remained firm in the opinion that they desired the Holy Sacrament from our fathers and in those things which I had reported earlier. They left it at that.

When they had heard 16 sisters then all the others came together and wanted to give opinion with one another since it was nearing time for vespers. The men were startled, however, and were got ready to leave. None of that would count since some of the young ones did not give their opinion alone. Once again I did what I could and brought more sisters to them. When they had heard 39, I went to them and had the names read aloud of those who had spoken to them. I positioned myself as if I were about to send the others to them also, for there were 13[154] more outside who simply did not want to go to them.[155]

Then the gentlemen said, no, that would not be necessary. The sisters were all whistling the same little song. Since they had heard the entire convent and our problems had been reported sufficiently, I implored them to defend us diligently before the honorable City Council so that we would be helped. They promised to do this with all due effort. And so they went away again during complet.

May God protect us from such visitors with broad brimmed hats, patched trousers, low-cut shoes and long swords at the sides.[156] They

---

[154] Using the figures given here, there were 53 sisters in the convent, including Caritas.

[155] Here we see how Caritas was able to make the best of a "bad" situation. She was counting on the men being tired of listening to the sisters and was obviously pretending that there were 13 more who wished to be heard. In truth, these final 13 had no intention of speaking with the representatives of the City Council. As we see in the next paragraph, her scheme worked. What would have happened if they had wanted to hear the last 13 sisters can only have been detrimental to the convent and to its relationship with the City Council.

[156] Caritas paints an amusing picture of her guests here. Considering the gravity of the situation and the pressure she was under, we can perhaps excuse her lack of "charity" in this instance. Although she does not mention it, we might even assume that she and her sisters broke into laughter shortly after the door was closed.

bring us no consolation and nothing suitable for our prayers. Of course Kaspar Nützel had visited me a few days before this and had said that our monks had visited us every year. What harm would it do if these gentlemen visited us too after three years?[157] May God protect us from this plague!

Of course the sisters told them enough in the manner in which they spoke with them, not, however, as if it were a visitation, but rather as good friends. There was much conversation back and forth during this worldly visitation which cannot all be written down. Whoever was present during this circus has no doubt withstood such fear and trembling that she would have no desire to go through it again.

Chapter 55

The day after this I wrote the following letter to Sigmund Fürer:

Wise, kind dear sir,

My sisters have requested me to ask your honor as our kind, dear lord, from whom we hope for support and kindness, that for God's sake you prevent yesterday's events from being brought before the advisors of the City Council and the preachers. As your honor himself knows, these people are not well disposed towards us. If the whole matter were in their hands, these gentlemen would destroy us. Therefore, we implore you not to inform them. We would rather wait for the gracious decision of our wise, dear lords who, without doubt, are more concerned for us than those other people. Without the latter's advice they know how to think paternally for us poor, miserable, imprisoned women in our affairs so that they do not burden their own conscience by restraining our simple consciences which God wants to be free.

I can also not believe that it pleases Almighty God if one Christian wants to oppress the other in matters that concern the soul, especially in the anguish of death. We confess here freely that we do not yet have the completeness of Karl Ortel, so that we want to receive the Holy Sacrament without confession. We would rather follow St. Paul who admonishes us that man should test himself before he eats of this bread. Therefore we should not be annoyed that we want to have special people

---

[157] As Caritas mentioned earlier, they had been without the spiritual guidance of the Franciscans for three years. It seems possible that Caritas is continuing in her humorous vein. Kaspar Nützel was probably unaware of the impression that Fürer, Imhof, Jugler (and possibly Ortel too) would make.

for that. It is, of course, human that one person trusts one person more than the other, according to whether he has experienced more good things from the one than from the other. Therefore, dear sir, we all beg your honor that you be our good messenger to the honorable City Council so that our problems get somewhat smaller or at least that something even more difficult does not happen to us with the appointment of a person whom the convent would not accept.

We hope, of course, you will not allow anything bad to happen to us and that no more force is applied to us so that the great fear that we all had yesterday was for nothing. We also humbly beg you to forgive us for having behaved so inappropriately. We were not used to something like that. Act as we faithfully expect of you, for you are a good nun-father after all. May you be commended to God eternally.

Chapter 56

The next day old Frau Schwarz came and demanded her daughter Anna Schwarz. She said, "Dear child, what did you say? How did you behave before the gentlemen? The whole city is talking about it. Even in the chancery they are talking about you."

We received the news that she had spoken to the gentlemen about Holy Communion in both forms. Although the gentlemen did not let us notice anything, they had, nevertheless, told other people, "They have a weed among them. It would be best to remove her from them."

Much could be written about this person. For the best of reasons, however, we will skip that and only write a little bit. She began to live as a Lutheran. She went eagerly to the sermons, used Lutheran freedom, accepted no discipline from her superiors or her fellow-sisters. She said she did not want to be a sheep, but a shepherdess. By that she meant she could perform the office of abbess too since she was so learned and clever. Whoever advised her against such an unreasonable plan became her enemy. Nobody wanted to have anything to do with her. Nobody wanted to live with her either. She set herself up in opposition to the sisters and made disputations on the Lutheran teachings to such an extent that no one ever left her without feeling sad. She went eagerly to the sermons[158] and lived as an opposition order. When the convent sat at table, she slept. When they were in the choir, she ate. She was uninhibited and did whatever she wanted to. Her relatives often came to the

---

158 These were probably the sermons by Osiander which Caritas found so tedious.

speaking-window for her. She let it be known that she could stay in the cloister. Her brother said, "Dear sister, if you can stay, then stay. In our father's house things are no longer the way they were when you left. Everyone is going his own way."

The life of such a person became burdensome and troubling for the worthy mother and the entire convent.[159] Often she was ordered to come alone, even to the advisors and finally before the entire convent. In a kind and friendly manner they urged her to give up this manner of living. They spoke to her in serious words and told her the convent had decided that it could not burden its conscience that such things were being instituted in our time. Not that they wanted to cause her to leave the convent by this or drive her away from us. No, it was every sister's wish not to drive her away. However, her free life, her big words along with other things she was accused of, these were all great sins and adversely affected the salvation of her soul. If they punished her for these things and assigned penance to her for them, they hoped to thus remove them from her. Every sister addressed her conscience and asked her to consider these things carefully and how she would be responsible for them before the Living God.

Some sisters stood up in the convent and said that on Judgment Day they could not testify to God the Almighty that she had kept what she had vowed to do. They demanded that her mother be sent for and the matter presented to her. The worthy mother told her she did not need her mother. She would have to do better. But she was stubborn. Afterwards it was just like before.

On the seventh Sunday before Easter, her mother, old Frau Schwarz, came and demanded that her daughter come to the speaking-window. She had to speak with her alone. She was with her longer than two hours. When she left the window, she acted as if she wanted to stay with us and gave no sign of the things that had been discussed this time. However, we received word that the mother had begged her daughter to remain, if she could and might. There was a lot of unpleasantness between the children and siblings even with the relatives and everybody was keeping to himself.

The daughter said she could not and did not want to remain in the cloister. She could not obtain salvation here. We did not observe the Gospel. She demanded that her mother have her taken away in a coach

---

159 From here on the narrative takes on a third person perspective which makes it sound as if the passages were dictated or composed by someone other than Caritas.

and that they drag her out and force her just as had been done to the other three sisters.[160] Her mother replied, "I shall bring the coach, but I cannot drag you or force you very much. Walk out by yourself."

Our venerable mother admonished her the next day to gather up all the things she had lent. She was afraid that if it were done for her later, she might not be satisfied although she had long since brought everything together herself. She said, "I don't want to leave. You really want to be rid of me, but I want to torment you even more." She said many other things too. On the Monday, it was the eve of St. Matthew's Day,[161] her mother came after dinner with her daughter-in-law Frau Hans Schwarz along with a coach and demanded her daughter, although she would have preferred to have her stay with us. Later on she often confessed that since she took both her daughters from St. Katherine's and from us she had nothing but misfortune. Her wealth decreased more and more so that she had to move away because of debts and became pitifully impoverished and finally died in misery and half-deaf at the home of her son-in-law the abbot of St. Giles.[162] Then our worthy mother suggested she go into the choir and commend her soul to God. To all appearances, however, there was no sign of devotion present. Then she went to the door. When the door was opened, she embraced her mother and climbed into the coach without any sign of sadness in leaving.

As far as her soul is concerned, however, our hearts were moved to no small degree, although a great burden had been taken from us and she was a very small loss for the cloister.

After a few days a clerk from the chancery came and reported from the mayor, whom Hans Schwarz[163] had constantly been bothering, that

---

160 All of these histrionics were, of course, unnecessary. Like all the sisters, Anna Schwarz was free to leave whenever she so desired. Asking her mother to make a "show" of using force shows that she wanted the convent to be put in the worst possible light. To the "outside world" it would be another example of a daughter not following her parents' wishes and of the convent interfering with the rights of parents. This charade would also make Anna Schwarz the center of attention, something she would, no doubt, enjoy. If she could not become abbess, she could at least get this revenge on the convent and its abbess. Ironically, her mother did not want her to leave and her refusal to go along with her daughter's scheme effectively dashed all her hopes for revenge.

161 24 February.

162 This historical footnote of sorts is interpolated here, before Anna Schwarz has left the convent. It would be more effective if it appeared at the end of the chapter.

163 Anna's brother.

he had an order to transact with us. We were to grant Anna Schwarz 100 florins that her late father had paid to the convent in addition to some jewelry too. Then our venerable mother said that her late father had paid the 100 florins as room and board for her and during the 12 years she had been with us, it had been used up. Then the clerk said the gentlemen of the council had ordered it so that we would not withhold it from her. Thus we had to give it to her. They gave us the following receipt:

I, maid Anna, the lawful daughter of the late Jörgen Schwarz, fisherman, citizen of Nürnberg and the widow of said late Jörgen Schwarz, attest with the agreement, knowledge and will of my dear mother and also of Hans Schwarz, my dear brother, for me and all my heirs and descendants. I had formerly entered the cloister of St. Clare of the Franciscan order here in Nürnberg. For my upkeep my parents sent 100 Rhenish gulden to the aforenamed cloister along with personal effects and jewelry in the value of 8 florins, 3 ort which have since been sold. Now, however, I have decided to leave the cloister. The worthy, spiritual mother, Caritas, Abbess and the convent of the aforementioned cloister of St. Clare have returned, sent back and transferred possession the 100 florins which I brought along to the convent together with 8 florins, 3 ort which was received for my personal effects or jewelry to my complete gratitude and satisfaction. Therefore, I declare for my heirs and descendants the abbess named and the convent and all its successors to be completely free, independent and not responsible for these items. I give them my promise never to make or carry out a complaint or demand upon them, their successors and the convent. As a sign of this document, I have requested the honorable, wise Anton Tetzel and Meichsner – both from the great Council in Nürnberg – to put their own seals at the end of this document. Tetzel and Meichsner named above affirm that this has happened by their request, but without harm for our heirs and us. Given on the 10th day of March 1528.

Postscript. She gave the reason for the receipt that she was driven out of the cloister. Such a cloistered life was against the Holy Word of God and the Gospel. In this she was wrong, but did not know it. We did not want to have this paragraph in the receipt and so she had to make another one as mentioned above.

Anna Schwarz also spread the story that she never used the 100 florin for her own benefit. Her brother Hans Schwarz set her up here in a house in the Carthusian garden. Before the house was finished he had to leave because of debts.

Chapter 57

In this year a letter in Latin was sent to us from the Bishop of Bamberg which is given here in German.

Wigandus, by the Grace of God Bishop of Bamberg.

Honored, spiritual, devout and dearly beloved,

For some very serious reasons which concern not just our church in Bamberg and us, but also your status and your office we have called to the great hall of our bishop's court all abbots, priors, provosts, deacons and abbesses who live anywhere in our city and in the bishopric of Bamberg on Wednesday after the feast of Peter's enchainment, next Wednesday 5 August. We call you also on the aforementioned day and urge you earnestly and with all due effort to appear in the person of a wise and honest procurator equipped with full powers to hear the reasons brought forth and to accept our thoughts about them. Given in our city of Bamberg an Monday

Wolfgang Balckmacher the State Notary signed it.

As an answer the worthy mother wrote the following letter in Latin which is given in German.

Most worthy prince and lord, highest Lord,

We have most humbly received the letter of your most honored reverence in which, among other things, we were called on the 5th day of the month of August to the hall of the Bishop. We would be prepared to be obedient to you, most worthy person, in all appropriate and honorable matters. But since we poor creatures are no longer permitted to decide our actions and are also oppressed by all manner of misery, it is not within our power to appear. Therefore we beg your most worthy person to most kindly accept our distress as a reasonable excuse. We commend ourselves most humbly as the wretched ones who are almost completely without human assistance.

Written in Nürnberg on 1 August in the year of salvation 1528.

[A note written by the same hand is loosely inserted here.]

Concerning what happened from this year up to the year 1541 we have written a documentation. With time that is to be written into this book also.

Chapter 58

The following deals with facts concerning taxes and how they were first introduced to us. First, that we had to pay them regardless of all our freedoms and privileges which we have from popes, emperors and kings and then what transpired from year to year.

In the year of Our Lord 1525, on the eve of Christ's Ascension Day, the lords sent an inspector to us so that he could inspect all the wine in our wine cellar.

And so, on the evening after St. Laurence Day, an inspector came and announced three items from the council. The first, that we should allow our wine and beer to be inspected. The honorable abbess Caritas Pirckheimer, who held office at that time, answered that the wine had already been inspected and that we brewed the beer ourselves. They were to let us know what we should do.

Then he said, whenever we buy wine, we should always send for a note from the tax collector and inform him how many barrels it is. The third item, that we should let the certified wine deliverymen deliver the wine.

Through our superintendent we demanded to know from the councilors if they would allow our servants to place the barrels in the cellar. That was still permitted if we gave the certified deliverymen their established pay. This was to be paid into the general fund, one penny per barrel. The inspector is given the same amount.

In the year of Our Lord 1526, on the Tuesday after New Year's, Willibald Kromer visited us. He said that the opinion of the honorable City Council was that after Martini we had brewed some beer. In the future we should no longer do that or have a certified measuring clerk present as the other brewers did. Therefore we hired a measuring clerk.

Not long afterwards the tax collector sent us a note. The worthy mother wrote our superintendent a letter about it as follows: [the letter already appears in Chapter 38].

[At the conclusion of the letter the greeting "to our pious little Clare" is missing. Instead it reads: Your wise honor's well-intentioned daughter Caritas Pirckheimer, abbess of St. Clare's.]

Chapter 59

Such a letter did not receive much of an answer.

Since they were silent, we were silent too. But on St. Ursula's Day, the tax collector sent us a note again. Then the worthy mother composed a petition to the older councilors. She sent it to the superintendent. She asked him to read it aloud to the older ones and make our distress known, since he knew how things stood with us. He said, however, it would have to go through the whole council.

A petition to the honorable City Council.

Prudent, honorable, worthy, dear gentlemen,

Yesterday your honor's tax collector sent us a notice indicating a tax due of 8 gulden 4 shillings 2 pennies for 18 kegs, 3 vats minus 6 quarters of wine, plus 16 kegs of beer. He requests a tax of 159 gulden 4 shillings 5 pennies. If we were so well off that we had a surplus left over from what we use every day, we would naturally present no special problem to your honors and the city. As is well known to your honors yourselves, our income is not so high that we can live off it completely. Can your honors consider how difficult it would be for us, if you maintained your plan and we therefore had to suffer a shortage even in the little nourishment which we made use of up to now?

Therefore, it is our humble request to your honors that in this case you be gracious and merciful to us and consider the matter in such a way that we nevertheless receive sufficient food. If this decision is not made we know very well that we should not and cannot oppose your honors in this matter. We must, therefore, let happen what your honors decide. Thus, to a certain extent, your honors have our health or our ruin in your hands and can profit from it. Although such a breaking up is very difficult for us, as mentioned above, it is, however, more tolerable for us to suffer physical want, than to burden our conscience in another way. If the body is too fragile, then the present time is short too. We can survive on water. The burden of conscience, however, goes further and touches our future life too.

Therefore we will ask God to grant to your honors what is most useful for you and for us. We commend ourselves as poor, miserable women, who are deserted by everyone but God.

This time our superintendent did not answer the petition. We received no news either. We put off the matter until we bought wine. Then a note from the tax collector was sent to us again. We sent a message to the superintendent and asked for his advice. On 3 January 1527 he wrote us the following letter.

Chapter 60

This is the letter the superintendent wrote to our worthy mother.

The Peace of God be with you, worthy woman and in Christ, Our Lord, beloved sister.

I intended to take your written request concerning the tax to my lords yesterday as I promised your administrator and will do it very soon. The reason I hesitated is that I was reminded by one of your good friends and my attention was drawn to the fact that you sent a petition to the older council last year. In it you reported your distress and your situation because you felt you could get advice and perhaps in order to avoid these problems after I was separated from you. No exact answer was forthcoming for this petition, however. Then you were referred to the Council with this request. I do not know whether they listened to you or not or what kind of answer resulted. To ask me about it was very difficult for me because I did not have the time. It seems to me, however, that you allowed it to reach the honorable City Council. I ask you to inform me about it as you remember it since you surely have a copy of it. I would be troubled if it was said later, that I had kept your petition and not reported your distress to the council.

As soon as I have a report and knowledge of what you want, I will immediately have your request brought to the lords again. I do not doubt at all that I will time desired by Walpurgis Day. You are, of course, not going to make my lords rich with this money. For them not so much is at stake as your giving in. Certainly after that the German lords will follow who need a lot here, the group of all abbots and prelates, and the lay priests, of which there are many here. Up to now they have all paid willingly. They would want to be free of it unjustifiably. It would be more just, if they released those who devote themselves with all piety to the common welfare in providing for the poor as in this case the pastors and others. I would not like to learn that you were the ones who caused all the difficulties that resulted.

I beg you most heartily for the sake of the honor of God to consider what is more appropriate for the divine command and word, to rely on a false plan and avoid the common good, or to suffer and bear it, just as many poorer than you must endure it. Also, consider whether you should trust in God to help you, especially on account of the very difficult times. If I went too far against my previous promise not to get involved in these things any more, then please have the instigator come before I've gone to the sermon and not find me guilty. If, of course, my agreement did not exist, I would have had a reason to deal with you more in an oral or written manner. That would have troubled you as coming from someone uninformed. But know one thing, I will not cease appealing to God for you and yours as well as for myself. May He lead us eternally to His Praise and according to His Will.

Kaspar Nützel, the Elder.

Chapter 61

The worthy mother wrote this letter in answer to the superintendent's letter.

Prudent, wise, kind, dear superintendent,

I send your honor a copy of a petition we sent your honor on St. Ursula's Day in order that it be presented to the older councilors, but if it should be necessary, to the whole council. No other answer has been given to us. When we bought wine again afterwards, we asked for permission to store it. They told the servant orally that we should store it. The tax collector would be informed.

Up until now it has remained this way, until a few weeks ago, when the tax collector sent us this little note which I am sending to your honor also. I do not know whether he did it on orders of the honorable City Council or on his own. Because of the immediate payment demanded we wrote a petition yesterday and asked your honor to help us obtain a longer delay. We have no lack of faith in God, Our Lord, but perhaps we are just worried. Please know that in truth we trust God with our hearts. If it were not so, we would have long since despaired. We have also not refused to do what was asked of us and was possible. But your honor is well aware that payment of the tax is impossible for us. If my lords would only be gracious to us, poor children in this matter, we would accept it with great gratitude. If not, we know full well that we should not and cannot take a stand against the honorable City Council. We must let it be done in the certain hope that God will preserve us after all. If it does not turn out as we want, then it will happen according to the divine will of Him who is our greatest desire in heaven and earth.

I commend this matter to your honor in all loyalty, so that you will act in the manner best suited for it. Our most devoted gratitude to your honor for interceding with God for us. Know also that no night passes without my doing that for you. May God, Who knows all hearts, direct our affairs in all ways according to His Will which we love beyond anything else. Thus may you be commended to God's Eternal Grace.

When the worthy mother noticed that the superintendent had kept the petition sent to him as prescribed for so long, she wrote her petition on the note from the tax collector and sent it to the mayor so that he would answer the council. She asked the superintendent to see to it that they would wait until Walpurgis Day,[164] as mentioned above. We sent him a copy of the petition as he desired.

The tax collector's note.

From the nuns of St. Katharine's and St. Clare's a quarter of the tax due which they owe should be paid now. They should be allowed to lay in wine until Easter. Up to that time they should have a period of time for paying the amount which is left from the debt.

3 January 1527.

Chapter 62

This is the second petition we sent to the Council through the mayor.

Prudent, honorable, wise, dear sirs,

After your honors' tax collector has sent us a note and demanded that we should pay one fourth of the tax due that we owe up to today, please be informed that this is no time for payment and we have no money at all. Even grain won't count if your honors do not grant us an extension in the payment of the tax. We have absolutely nothing to pay the debt with and must make do with the smallest portions of food for our body. And so we ask your honors for God's sake to delay this payment until the next Walpurgis Day in view of the fact that your honors have the security in your hands and can pay it yourselves if we would not pay. We want to merit this from God with our poor deserving prayer for your honors.

The superintendent's letter.

Honorable woman and beloved sister in Christ,

Yesterday I read your petition with your request before the honorable City Council and reported orally what seemed useful. I noticed an addition on the note sent you by the tax collector. For the remaining ¾ of the tax due you are to be granted an extension until Easter. At the time of reading it before the council I noted that now from you, Saint Katharine's and those others which are included in God's nourishment one quarter of the amount due has been taken and you are to be permitted to

[164]   1 May.

lay in wine until Easter. Then it shall be up to the further deliberations of the council to weigh what is to be allowed and what is to be stopped. For reasons easily understood, they went no further than this. Since you lack any cash, you also request that the fourth part appear on your account at the city hall. The answer was given that you and the people mentioned above be granted your request in this matter. That the councilors themselves should guarantee the amount was not acceptable to them, however. They would rather extend your Walpurgis interest without restrictions and let it suffice that you allow the quarter due now be paid to their representative, the tax collector. Half will be in gold and the other half in coin at 8 hellers 12 pennies or 15 piles, however they prefer. Who knows what the councilors will decide about further debt and what will accrue? I also told the councilors that you yourself would not reply, but that with time you hope for mercy and goodwill in future affairs. I did not want to neglect to report that to you. It seems unnecessary, therefore, to the council that you institute a change in what you eat and drink for your fellow sisters. They ordered me forestall that with appropriate pressure. With this letter I have done that. I truly believe if they really knew the extent of your poverty, they would look for means and ways to remedy it. May God protect us all and grant that we act according to His Will.

Kaspar Nützel, the Elder.

Chapter 63

The worthy mother's letter in answer to the superintendent's letter.

Prudent, wise, kind, dear superintendent,

I note from your letter that you presented our case before the honorable City Council in the best way possible and obtained an extension until Walpurgis. For this the entire convent and I thank your honor most graciously. I can well imagine that in this as in other matters we have the benefit of your wisdom. May God reward you for eternity. Your honor also reports that the honorable City Council will not guarantee our debt until Walpurgis themselves. We must accept in God's Name whatever you and the honorable City Council decide at that time. I have written your honor previously more than once, that we will not oppose whatever burden is imposed upon us. I sense your mild spirit when you demand that we remove nothing from the convent.[165] I would like to do that too.

---

[165] Probably with the intention of selling them.

Yet with the burden of taxes things cannot go on without particular debts which I have incurred anyway in the last two accounts. By the Grace of God grain is selling at a good price.[166] I have also considered how we could better afford the taxes as far as the domestic affairs, the servants and the convent are concerned. In all my searching I cannot find anything that we could curtail or do without because it was superfluous, as dear Anton Tucher of blessed memory often advised me. Thus we commend ourselves to your faithfulness and your honor to the protection of God.

Chapter 64

After Easter 1527 the tax collector sent us a little note. He reminded us.
    Then the honorable mother sent the superintendent this letter.

Prudent, wise, kind, dear superintendent,
    After the tax collector admonished us a few days ago to pay the tax and, specifically, as the note states, one fourth of it, I, as one who is inexperienced in such things, could not figure it out. I asked him to make it clear from the note, which I am sending you herewith, and to designate how much is to be given for every beer or the wine which he has not tabulated yet. Now I am worried that your honor along with the other councilors might consider this disobedience on our part. Therefore I am sending your honor herewith the fourth part of the tax. If we have not calculated it correctly, then we will have to make up what they do not want to give up. Enclosed also a small petition to the honorable City Council with the humble request that your honor, who essentially knows our income and household expenses, will do his best so that we are granted a further extension. In the event that that is impossible, we offer to do even more for the welfare of the community. We do not desire to gather treasure on earth. I commend the matter to your paternal loyalty completely, which we have experienced so often, and commend your honor to the Grace of God.

The third petition to the Council that we sent to the superintendent.

---

166 This is another example of Caritas humbly accepting "God's will" even though it has an adverse effect on the convent. The high cost of grain means there will be even less money available to pay the taxes. In the next chapter she is a bit more specific about this.

After your honors' tax collector admonished us again that according to the note he sent us we should pay one fourth of the tax, we determined that such a payment would exceed our means. In any case, as frugally as we live, we cannot get by with our income, especially now, since grain is so expensive. So that we are not considered punishable however, or are suspected of acting counter to your honors' command, we are sending your honors the required money herewith. In addition, we beg your honors for God's sake not to be so harsh against us poor, miserable people, but to be merciful and patient with us as before, so that we are not forced to just drink water. If not, we will have to give in to your honors' will in this matter. May God's will be done. Herewith we humbly commend ourselves to your honors.

Chapter 65

The letter of the superintendent.

Honorable woman,

I have received your letter along with the petition to the honorable City Council and have also handed over the money to the tax collector.

He said that it was very much more than the quarter that he had been ordered to collect.[167] When I was about to deliver your petition at this hour, I remembered a decree that was published about it by the Council last week. I wanted to bring this to your attention before I acted, because I do not think it was rescinded in the meantime and perhaps an unnecessary dispute could result from it. Please understand I did this for you with the best intentions. The decree which was also delivered in written form to the tax collector goes as follows: The cloisters which are provided with meals from general alms, even the other cloisters besides St. Clare's and St. Katharine's such as the German Order and all the other spiritual and secular inhabitants and citizens shall pay their tax completely, without any reduction. But both women's cloisters shall, as St. Katharine's has already done, pay and it shall be calculated from the taxes, how much they owe up to the day of reduction. On the next St. Martin's Day the women shall again pay one fourth of the same amount. They are permitted to lay in what they need after the supply time. Then the honorable City Council will again decide how it shall be done in the future.

---

167 Caritas obviously was right when she stated in Chapter 64 that she was "inexperienced" in such matters. She had paid too much.

If you desire that your petition be submitted as it was written or shortened or lengthened, then I will, as best I can, submit it as you send it to me again. Thus I will have commended all of us to the Grace of the Most High. In haste at the city hall.

Kaspar Nützel, the Elder.

Then nothing was done until St. Francis Day. Then the tax collector sent us a note. Then the worthy mother sent the superintendent this letter.

Prudent, wise, kind, dear superintendent,

I am informing your honor that a few days ago the tax collector sent us the bill for the last two years along with that for the present year 1527. I am terribly shocked, for it contains a considerable sum, namely 301 florins IIII lb XII den. When at Walpurgis we were ordered to pay one fourth of the tax due, we did this and had hoped that the three quarters were forgiven. I implore your honor most earnestly for the Love of God, to draw a line through the old debt and be gracious and merciful with the new one. Your honor knows very well that it is impossible for us to pay such a large sum. In addition, we are worried that the frost has caused such damage that wine will be much more expensive than in other years. If I should then, contrary to your order and prohibition, withhold much that they need from my sisters, that would make me very sad and depressed, especially for the old ones whose hearts look forward to a little drink.

Therefore I earnestly ask you once again to act like a true gentleman and father and help us find grace and mercy from our kind councilors. Herewith I send your honor a petition and leave it up to you, whether your honor will consider it better to read it to the older councilors alone or to the entire Council or whether your honor can present it orally better and more effectively. You will proceed in this matter like a loyal father with his poor children and will receive the reward for it from Our Faithful Lord. He said, of course, what you do to the least of these my brethren, you have done unto me.[168] I commend your honor to His Eternal Grace.

The fourth petition to the Council.

Prudent, wise, kind, dear Councilors,

Recently your honors' tax collector sent us a note that contains 301 gulden 4lb XIII den taxes for the quarter that we paid last Walpurgis day as ordered by your honors. It is obvious if we were well-to-do and had a

---

[168] Matthew 25:45, one of Caritas's favorite passages in the New Testament.

surplus from our daily use, then we would not be sending a complaint to your honors and the city in general. Of course your honors know from the bill itself that our income is not so great that we can even pay for our body's nourishment with it, when price of grain is high and wine will probably be more expensive because of the frost. Therefore, we earnestly ask your prudent honors, as our kind, councilors and loyal fathers, for God's sake be gracious and merciful to us in the case. Let it speak to your heart, that we are poor, simple women and have old and weak ones among us whose hearts are very attached to a little glass of wine. Without doubt they would get very ill if they had to make do with just water. We therefore ask most humbly that you be gracious to us. We will ask God to be gracious and merciful to your prudent honors and also to reward you a hundredfold for what you are excusing us from.

Herewith we commend ourselves to your prudent honors as our kind, dear lords and fathers.

We sent both this letter and the petition to the superintendent's house. Five days later we read from the superintendent's letter when the next pronouncement day was to be in the Council. Soon the superintendent was written. Had he received no answer to the petition since he had kept quiet? He replied that he what the next decision was. He did not want to bring it up before St. Martin's Day. Therefore, no petition was written this time. He sent it back to us. Then we were happy.

Chapter 67

The tax collector delivered this note on the Monday after Epiphany 1528.

On 8 January it was decided in a full Council meeting to accept now from the cloisters, that is St. Clare's, St. Katharine's and the Dominicans half of both old and new taxes due on St. Michael's Day and, until further payment, to allow them to lay in wine up until next Walpurgis Day. As long as they do not pay this half, however, they should refrain from laying in wine. An exception should be made for the Franciscans. They are to be allowed to lay in wine until Walpurgis also.

The worthy mother wrote this letter to the superintendent.

The Grace of God be with us forever.
Prudent, wise, kind, dear superintendent and loyal father,

The tax collector visited me recently and reported to me the decision of the councilors concerning the tax. We are to pay half now and borrow the rest by Walpurgis Day. Half the amount comes to more than 150 gulden. We would like to be as obedient as we can. But truly we cannot pay this great sum now, except by giving up everything that we need for our daily nourishment without which we cannot live, since we do, of course, have to eat and drink. Your honor forbade us to discontinue anything. But this clashes with everything that is happening, since we have a debt of 153 gulden according to the last account and we do not yet have a supply of wine and have no other sources of income anywhere. I earnestly implore your honor for God's sake have pity on our poverty, since we wish no more than the bare necessities. Please help us poor, miserable women to find favor from the honorable City Council so that a longer extension is given until we can get advice and sell some of our possessions during Lent. Without this we cannot pay. I am ashamed now that we must beg for more mercy beyond that which has already been shown to us. But, as I hope your honor can well observe yourself, misery knows no laws. I am fully aware that if your honor yourself desired, you could serve us better orally than if we wrote a lot of petitions. If you are of the same opinion and believe you can attain something in this way, we will do it too. Your honor said we should wait without petition until after St. Michael's Day when they notify us again. We will do whatever you advise us to do in this matter. I know if you knew how much we must save you would take pity on us and help us and advise us in every way. Therefore we commend this matter completely to your loyal honor in the hope that you will do your best and receive a reward from God. To Him I commend your honor and your family forever.

Note. In the previous letter we sought an extension. Then a warning came to us by no means to ask for mercy and or send a petition. Another letter was written omitting the request for mercy and asking for only an extension. The superintendent did not answer this letter. It got too long for us not to have to buy something. The cellar was empty too. Wilhelm[169] was sent to the superintendent to tell him that we had collected 50 fl. Did he think it a good idea to send it to the tax collector until we had collected the rest and would we be permitted to lay in some wine in the meantime? He said he did not have the authority to decide that. He had also forgotten how the remission was worded exactly. We were to find out how much the whole outstanding amount was and then he would bring it before the Council tomorrow. They quickly told him the amount. The sum was 301 gulden, IIII lb, XIII den. The next day he

---

[169] A servant.

brought it before the honorable City Council. The answer was what was contained in the superintendent's letter that he wrote the same day. It was on Wednesday after morning mass 1528. We had not asked for it to be brought up, nor could we have assumed it. And so we were all that much more surprised at the answer. We had not expected it.

Chapter 68

The superintendent's letter.

Grace and peace, worthy mother and beloved sister in Christ,

I offer you and your sisters my willing service. It is also appropriate that you learn that at your request I have negotiated with my friends, the honorable City Council, concerning the extension for payment of the tax. Although I know that they entertain all Christian feelings and intentions toward you, for good reasons things did not turn out favorably for you. The solution arrived at is that you are to send the tax collector the 50 gulden, half in gold. In regard to the 100 gulden still outstanding, I have offered to lend them to you. I was glad to do this and gave half in gold to the tax collector. You are to repay me between now and Walpurgis. In the meantime you should brew beer and lay in wine when you can. It will remain this way at Walpurgis in regard to the 150 gulden outstanding and whatever is laid in as it has been determined for you and others. I write this in haste because I did not want you to remain ignorant of how you were to behave. I wish you a blessed time. It is certainly granted to those whom God grants His manifold Grace after so much rain and thawing. May almighty God grant that to us. Amen.

Kaspar Nützel, the Elder.

The worthy mother's response to the superintendent's letter.

Prudent, wise, kind, dear superintendent and loyal father,

From your honor's letter I have seen the good will of the honorable City Council and also of your honor. I, along with my convent, am grateful for that, as is fitting. In no way would I have dared to request such a great loan from your honor, since you are already burdened with daily demands from us. If you have shown us this great goodness from your free, good will, then we ask of the gentle Giver of all that is good, who leaves nothing unrewarded that is done in His Name to the least of His Brethren, that He grant you the eternal for the temporal. But, wise, dear man. I will, nevertheless, need your faithful counsel, for Saint Walpurgis Day is not far off. On that day I will have much to pay. In the meantime I must buy wine and have some beer brewed, all of which takes a lot of money. I do not know where I shall get it. I would like to discuss with your honor what we could see for money. Perhaps we could see some parcels of land, if we could only find buyers who would pay in cash. Even if we begin selling soon, Saint Walpurgis Day will probably arrive before the payment does. I hope your honor will help us in this matter and, as a faithful advisor, advise us and receive a reward for it from God, to whom I commend your honor eternally.

Note. The new tax collector N. Held came on Corpus Christi 1528 and admonished us about payment of the tax as ordered by his lords, but did it in a pleasant way. He did not, however, bring along a note and advised us to write a petition. He had to act in accordance with his orders. Then we sent the superintendent a little letter and a petition in addition. After five days we received the answer, that we first had to find out from the tax collector how much old and new taxes we owed. Nevertheless, we were to buy some things and lay in 1 barrel, or 3, 4, or 5 and should buy some supplies.

Chapter 69

The worthy mother's letter to the superintendent.

The Grace of our merciful Father be with us all.
Prudent, wise, kind, dear superintendent,

The tax collector visited me yesterday and reminded us of the tax. I am unable to forget about it, although unfortunately I am unable to pay it despite all my activity. I ask humbly that your honor have more patience with the 100 gulden that you lent us out of your sense of loyalty. I hope if efforts are made to get money from those people from Erfurt[170] that then we will be able to settle with your honor and others. I humbly ask your honor to talk with Schlüsselfelder so that someone is sent to Erfurt who will have authority from us to act at your request. Otherwise nothing will happen if your honor does not order it. The longer it drags on, the less it will happen.

I have composed a petition to the honorable City Council which I enclose. Would you please look it over and see if we could obtain some mercy or an extension. We rely first on God Our Lord completely and then on your honor, that you would help and advise us so that grace and

---

[170] Perhaps to sell some property.

mercy are shown to us and perhaps a line is drawn through the old tax. For God's sake excuse me, if I ask too much. I know very well that your honor overlooks nothing and I thank you for all the effort you have shown with our affairs on behalf of us poor people who bother you almost every day. May God, the Almighty be your reward in eternity. I commend you and yours to His Grace forever.

The fifth petition to the honorable City Council.

Prudent, honorable, wise, dear sirs,

After your honors' tax collector again reminded us that we were to pay the outstanding tax and, in the meantime, not lay in any more wine, we would have been completely ready to obey him, if we could have. However, since things are not going well for us and this year is especially harsh, we cannot pay this tax without selling our holdings and dividing them up. The people from Erfurt have not paid and owe us 200 fl. We also had to give 100 fl. to the Schwarz woman who left us. In addition to that there remains the tax your honors levied on us. We still owe our wise superintendent the 100 fl. with which he faithfully helped us out. We have, therefore, not only a considerable lack of money, but also debts. We must save in such a way that we are interfering with the nourishment of our own bodies. Therefore, it is our most humble wish that your honors would, for God's sake, lessen this burden or at least grant us a later date and an extension. Perhaps God will grant us His Grace that we need so much, so that we can accumulate enough so that we can fulfill your honors' demands. And so with our accounts we can also provide a convincing report on how we manage our household. Of course we know that your honors' messengers could not be kept with so little food. We do not wish to kive lavishly. If we could have our simple, very humble nourishment for our bodies we would not desire anything else. We earnestly hope your honors will think of us with mercy and have pity on us. As much as we can we will endeavor to deserve this.

Note. Afterwards, on Saint Margaret's Day, the tax collector sent us a notice of 412 gulden, IIs, XVIII den. No other response was given. Afterwards, three days after St. Margaret's Day, the sisters of Saint Katharine's composed a petition that they be allowed to lay in wine. Then the superintendent appeared and had our petitions read first. He had kept all of them until that time.

Afterwards, on Saint Barbara's Day, we sent the sixth petition to the Council.

Prudent, wise, kind, dear gentlemen,

We hereby inform your honors that in accordance with your prohibition since before Saint Margaret's Day, we have refrained from laying in wine. The reason was that we could not pay the tax and were always hoping for our money from Erfurt. If that appeared, we would show our obedience. But since this money is still outstanding and we can do nothing further, we beg your prudent honors humbly, for God's sake, to allow us to lay in wine. We cannot do without it. There is great distress among us. May merciful God show your prudent honors mercy too. We will faithfully ask for His Mercy.

After this the tax collector brought us the following note:

The sisters of Saint Clare shall be allowed to lay in as much wine as they want. Whenever the money arrives from Erfurt, they should pay all taxes.

Friday, 4 December 1528.

Interpretive Essay:
The Rebellion of the Abbess of St. Clare's

The advent of the year 2000 was cause for celebration in the Franconian city of Nürnberg. The first documented mention of the city had occurred 950 years earlier on 16 July 1050, when Kaiser Heinrich III granted personal freedom to a young female surf by the name of Sigena. Thus, the history of the city was forever linked to the concept of personal freedom in general, and to that of the woman who symbolized that freedom in particular.

On the eve of the Reformation, Tetzel was promoting the sale of indulgences, a practice that had long been an acceptable activity. Indeed, Nürnberg's churches and monasteries had applied for and been granted indulgences many times. Just as the question of the validity of the Church's granting indulgences would occupy Luther and eventually lead to the Reformation, the larger theological issues such as that of faith versus good works, a concept championed by St. Paul and also taken up by Luther, as well as the right of an individual to follow the dictates of his or her conscience in matters of faith, would occupy Caritas Pirckheimer. Sigena was a simple, peasant girl. Caritas Pirckheimer, however, was educated, a member of one of Nürnberg's most respected patrician families, and, more important, held the responsible position of abbess of St. Clare's. What became of Sigena after she had obtained her freedom? There is no mention of her in any documents after this date. She disappears only to be used as a symbol whenever the need arises.

Caritas Pirckheimer might well have become another victim of historical neglect had she not shown the foresight to record in her *Journal* her "finest hour," when she alone defended her right and that of the other members of St. Clare's to maintain a system of beliefs and a way of life whose very validity and legitimacy had been openly challenged.

Why is Caritas Pirckheimer important and in what way is her *Journal* significant? Thanks to her *Journal* we can conclude that Caritas Pirckheimer deserves our respect for her courageous stand for the right of a woman to freely choose her position in society. If a woman had chosen the cloistered life as a nun at St. Clare's, she had a God-given right to obey her conscience. Whether she decided to continue her life as a cloistered nun or opted to leave the convent and live with her family, or even to marry and perhaps have children, it was her decision alone. The City Council's efforts to persuade the nuns of St. Clare's to renounce their vows and abandon the convent remained ineffective. Caritas insisted each nun should decide for herself, despite the threats, harassment, and abuse with which many of the Lutheran preachers punctuated their sermons when they addressed the sisters of St. Clare's. Caritas and her sisters were subjected to considerable harassment. Osiander, the popular and dynamic preacher at the St. Lorenz church (previously Catholic, but now Lutheran), even went so far in one of his 100 fiery sermons at St. Clare's to likening the sisters to the prostitutes of Nürnberg, one of the most extreme and most ridiculous claims he was to make.[1]

Is she "relevant" today? Caritas Pirckheimer is as relevant today as the idea of "equal rights" or the freedom of the individual to choose his or her lifestyle or career. What begins as an attempt to link the political and religious chaos unleashed by the Reformation to an earlier prediction of a deluge (*Sintflut*) for the year 1524, an example of hyperbole to say the least, turns into a documentation of the attempt of the Nürnberg City Council to force its will on the cloister of St. Clare's, and the efforts of Caritas Pirckheimer, the abbess of St. Clare's, to defend its right to exist and its members' right to follow their conscience and maintain the "old faith," including the vows which formed the basis of monastic life. Caritas's defense of her cloister flies in the face of what was expected of her both as a woman and as a loyal citizen of Nürnberg. Neither Kaspar Nützel, the superintendent of St. Clare's, nor the City Council itself could have anticipated the resistance which its decisions would evoke from this learned and highly respected daughter of one of Nürnberg's most significant patrician families.[2]

In compiling her journal from letters she wrote to or received from

---

[1] Osiander's reputation was not lily-white, however. In addition to being criticized for his preference for "fancy" clothes, his three marriages to wealthy women did not escape the critical eye and tongue of many Nürnbergers.

[2] The City Council may have shown a far more "paternal," or less draconian, attitude toward St. Clare's than it did in dealing with other issues. St. Clare's enjoyed a special position, as a convent for citizens of Nürnberg who were also women of rank in that city's social structure. It would have been possible for the City Council to close St. Clare's by force and arrange for all members to return home. As much as they may have believed the whole idea of oaths and the cloistered life was not supported by the Bible and might well be classified as heresy, they opted for a "gentler" method which tended to make compliance rather drawn out and especially tedious for St. Clare's.

Kaspar Nützel, the City Council, and others, Caritas assumes the role of a historian. From time to time she interpolates her own interpretation of events so that the journal is far from being an impartial account. There is, however, no attempt by Caritas to sum up the final events, something which a true historian might be expected to attempt. Thus, the journal seems to end on a rather anticlimactic note, the issue of taxes. It may well be that Caritas began to lose interest in the journal when it became obvious that the pressure from the City Council would be unrelenting. She may have honestly believed that she would succeed in persuading the City Council to allow her convent to continue as it had before the Reformation. After all, she had known little but success up to this time. Although Caritas presents, for the most part, a vivid picture of the cloister's problems during the four years from 1524 to 1528, as well as her personal views, the journal tends to lack a sense of direction, since Caritas chose not to impose one.

Her description of the "agony" the sisters of St. Clare's had to endure when listening to sermons from "guest preachers" such as Osiander (who gave over 100) reflects her willingness to obey the wishes of the City Council, as well as her sense of humor. The truth of the matter is that these sermons did not "win over" the sisters to the Reformation as the City Council had hoped. Instead, they were bored to tears and could hardly wait for them to be over. If anything, they strengthened Caritas's and her sisters' resolve to stay with the "old faith." Although Osiander served as an ambassador of the city many times at various conferences and became one of the leading forces of the Reformation in Nürnberg, he was a complete "failure" in his efforts to persuade the sisters of St. Clare's to renounce their vows, leave the convent and accept the "new teachings" of the reformers. He certainly did not win their favor when he likened them to the city's prostitutes, an especially nasty claim which Caritas never forgot. At the end of the journal, there is also no real sense of closure. The reader comes away wishing Caritas had taken the time to either write or dictate her final thoughts on what had transpired, or perhaps her thoughts about what the future might hold for her and her convent.

Recently there has been a great effort by women-historians to search for the women whose contribution to Nürnberg's history has previously been mostly ignored. Historians such as Nadja Bennewitz, for example, have shown the important contribution women made from the medieval period to the present. Caritas Pirckheimer and other women played a significant role in late medieval Nürnberg's growth and prosperity.[3]

---

3   Perhaps the best study of the position of women in late medieval Nürnberg is by the Nürnberg historian Nadja Bennewitz, *Sigenas Schwestern im mittlel-*

The most dramatic part of the journal is Chapter 34, in which Caritas paints a vivid, if not apocalyptic picture of the forced removal of three members of the cloister, Margaret Tetzel, Katharina Ebner and Clara Nützel, the latter the daughter of the superintendent Kaspar Nützel, on Corpus Christi Day 1525.[4] This represents the "high water mark" of open opposition to the convent as an institution of the "old beliefs." An unruly crowd which was not above throwing stones and breaking windows gathered outside, possibly also preparing to enter the convent itself and attack its inhabitants and destroy the building. Mothers were determined to use physical force, if necessary, to literally drag their daughters out of the convent, despite their pleas to be allowed to remain. Surely, Caritas and her sisters never imagined they would be compelled to witness such an ugly perversion of filial piety and Christian freedom. Was this a manifestation of the end times which Caritas had referred to at the beginning of her journal? No other contemporary account of Nürnberg offers such a picture of violence, hatred, and mob rule.

Chapter 56 offers a sharp contrast to this emotionally charged scene. Here Anna Schwarz voluntarily leaves the convent on 10 March 1528. Caritas is very open and honest in her description of Anna Schwarz's reasons for wishing to leave St. Clare's. Her departure was further proof that Caritas respected each member's right to follow the dictates of her own conscience. This was, of course, the very essence of Caritas's defense of her cloister and her faith. If the sisters of St. Clare's desired to follow their conscience and remain in the cloister, they should be allowed to. This was what the concept of Christian freedom meant.

Anna Schwarz was outspoken, confident that she was cut out for

alterlichen Nürnberg: Frauen in der spätmittelalterlichen Stadt (Nürnberg: Eigenverlag, 2000). In addition to excellent documentation and a select bibliography, the numerous illustrations, woodcuts, paintings and photographs of religious art complement the text very well. A second work by the same author must be mentioned also: *Meinten sie vielleicht, wir sollten einen Mann nehmen? Davor behüt uns Gott!* (Nürnberg: Eigenverlag, 1999). This study is invaluable for its coverage of the rise of the Reformation in Nürnberg and its effect on women, ranging from Ursula Tetzel, Argula von Grumbach and Caritas Pirckheimer to the Anabaptists. A third book, *Sigennas "Schwestern" im mittelalterlichen Nürnberg* (Nürnberg: Eigenverlag, 2000), documents the various "occupations" of women, including Hausfrauen, midwives, prostitutes, nuns, and Jewish women. The illustrations, which range from woodcuts and photographs of paintings to excellent color reproductions of manuscripts, make the work a rich source of valuable and fascinating information.

4   These three women did marry. The City Council had promised to offer "support" to the nuns who left the convent and married. Unfortunately, we lack the documentation concerning these three after they married.

greater things than being a mere nun, and unwilling to listen to reason, even when her mother strongly begged her not to leave. She was the only member of St. Clare's to leave of her own accord. One is tempted to assume that no one at St. Clare's was very sorry to see her go. Her overall attitude and outspoken self-promotion must have been difficult for the other nuns to bear. She even demanded that the 100 gulden "dowry" she had brought with her when she took her final vows be returned. Caritas's claim that Anna had long since "used up" the amount was, however, not accepted by Anna. Also, her brother Hans managed to get his hands on the 100 gulden and used it to build himself a house. Anna never saw a penny of it again. Her tale does have a "happy ending," however. She married the former abbot of the St. Giles cloister, Friedrich Pistorius. Their epitaph can be seen in the St. John's cemetery.[5]

Many chapters describe Caritas's futile efforts to persuade the City Council to alter its decisions following its formal acceptance of the Reformation in the spring of 1525. One of the most valuable sections of the journal is that dealing with Philipp Melanchthon's visit to Nürnberg, in Chapter 50. While he was in Nürnberg, Melanchthon stayed at Caritas's brother Willibald's home on the marketplace. Ostensibly in the city in order to open a new school, Melanchthon proved to be a "peace maker" rather than the dogmatic and cold theologian that some might have expected. The meeting between Caritas and Melanchthon proved especially fruitful. Having just completed a very detailed theological discussion with Wenzel Linck, Caritas must have been relieved to find Melanchthon such a congenial and sympathetic person. In her written responses to Linck's dogmatic, sometimes condescending "sermons," Caritas had proved herself to be more than capable of defending herself and her faith. According to Caritas, she and Melanchthon agreed on all issues except that of oaths, where they seem to have agreed to disagree. Caritas defended their oaths, while Melanchthon felt they were not binding. Caritas notes, however, that they parted "in good friendship." Melanchthon's report to the City Council reflected the warmth with which Caritas described him.

It is perhaps ironic that the author of the *Augsburg Confession* should have made such a lasting and positive impression on Caritas. Recent studies of Caritas have seen in this meeting a possible source of ecumenism. Obviously, the two found they had more theological issues on which they agreed than those which divided them, certainly an essential

---

5   See Bennewitz, *Meinten Sie vielleicht*, p. 19.

element for any effort at ecumenism.[6] Unfortunately, the chapter dealing with this important meeting is very short. As mentioned before, Caritas had just finished a rather long and detailed exposition of her own theological positions in her letters to Wenzel Linck, a colleague of Melanchthon's. She may have preferred to give a very general, but very favorable report of her discussion with Melanchthon, rather than repeating much of what she had said earlier. Had she met with Melanchthon before Linck, we might have had a better, more detailed description instead of the short, rather general one she has given us.

Caritas Pirckheimer was the product of a rarefied atmosphere resulting from her patrician background, her education, and her isolation from society. She entered the convent as a student at twelve and became a novice only a few years later. How well did she "know" Nürnberg? For example, did she ever see any of the great works of art that Nürnberg was famous for? Probably not. She knew Dürer, who was also her brother Willibald's best friend, but there are no signs that Caritas was especially interested in art. Her strong humanistic education was restricted to the writings of the Church Fathers, classical authors, and, of course, a solid background in theology and the Scriptures. She seems to have had access to many contemporary works, including those by supporters of the Reformation. Nevertheless, she remained a faithful daughter of the Church, having dedicated her life to her convent and her Church. She was familiar with enough of the "new teachings" to recognize that they often contradicted one another or offered not one but several "alternatives" to her faith. It appears as if she preferred to remain within the familiar loving embrace of the "old" Church, since the reformers offered chaos and uncertainty.

Although the journal shows her to be a sincere "defender of the faith," she was, of course, no Thomas More. Nürnberg was no London, and the City Council was no Henry VIII. Caritas was not executed because she refused to abandon "the old faith," i.e. Catholicism. Caritas's journal records more than her defense of her faith. Unlike More, who was executed for his beliefs, she lived to see her world turned upside down. Since the Franciscans had been denied access to the convent, there had been no mass, no confession, and no communion.[7] With no more novices permitted, it was only a matter of time until the convent would "die out." The pressure from the City Council

---

6   An example is the pamphlet *Caritas Pirckheimer und die Reformation in Nürnberg: Impulse für die Ökumene heute* (Erlangen: Caritas-Pirckheimer-Haus, 1991).

7   There were rumors that a Franciscan priest managed to enter the convent secretly

proved unrelenting, despite the unselfish efforts of Kaspar Nützel to act as mitigator. Ironically, what had begun as a rather formal relationship between the superintendent and the abbess of St. Clare's, gradually developed into a warm, sympathetic relationship of mutual respect and even friendship. When the "business" affairs of the convent grew more and more complex and the debts and taxes seemed out of control, it was Kaspar Nützel who came to the convent's aid, even though he was a strong supporter of the Reformation.[8] His daughter was one of the three nuns who had been removed from the convent against her will. This might have made his communication with Caritas difficult or awkward, but there are no signs of bitterness or coldnes in the *Journal*.

Again and again this *Journal* shows Caritas Pirckheimer defending her faith and her cloister against the charges of the City Council and others, such as Linck, and, at the beginning, Kaspar Nützel himself. Many times Caritas shows her indebtedness to the teachings of St. Paul and cites his words of justification by faith alone,[9] the same source Luther used in his important work "On the Freedom of a Christian" (1520). Ironically, only Melanchthon, the major theologian of the Lutherans, recognized that, theologically speaking, Caritas was very close to Luther's position. In her conversation with Melanchthon and in her writings to Linck she stated clearly that faith, not "good works" was what justified her existence. In some cities, what had once been Catholic convents became Lutheran convents, a sign that it was possible to find a "common ground" between the Catholic and Protestant positions. In Nürnberg, however, the failure to recognize this common ground resulted in a standoff. After numerous efforts by the City Council to persuade Caritas Pirckheimer to "give up" had proved futile, both sides ended up playing a waiting game. When the last member of St. Clare's died in 1596 (Caritas died in 1532), the cloister was closed forever.

How should we judge Caritas Pirckheimer? Is her *Journal* a testament of success or failure? Caritas Pirckheimer should be ranked as the most significant Nürnberg woman of the late fifteenth century through the Reformation era. No other woman showed such independence, idealism and willingness to defend women's (in this case nuns') right to choose their place within society. Despite pressure from Nürnberg's City Council, Caritas did succeed in keeping St. Clare's "open." Unfor-

and offer the offices and services. Nevertheless, there is absolutely no documentation to support such a claim.

8   He had translated Luther's famous *95 Theses* into German and had them published in Nürnberg.

9   Rom. 3:28.

tunately its members no longer enjoyed such basic religious elements as confession, mass, and communion. Yet if one takes the long view, the nuns were able to spend the rest of their lives in the convent. Certainly their life and customs had suffered a degree of "compromise," but thanks to Caritas they could continue enjoying the fellowship of "like-minded" women, the excellent library, as well as other activities such as copying manuscripts, and in some instances, weaving, sewing, and a few other "typical" activities. Caritas's *Journal* remains as a testament of faith as well as a unique document of one woman's opposition to the Reformation in Nürnberg, and her defense of the God-given right of women to choose their own "profession" or role in society.

Annotated Bibliography

Primary sources

Caritas Pirckheimer – Quellensammlung. Vol. 1. *Das Gebetbuch der Caritas Pirckheimer*. Ed. Josef Pfanner. Landshut: Solanus Druck, 1962. Despite the title, this is not by Caritas Pirckheimer. Instead it is a collection of prayers written by members of the convent of St. Clare's during the period when Caritas was abbess.

———. Vol. 2. *Die Denkwürdigkeiten der Caritas Pirckheimer*. Ed. Josef Pfanner. Landshut: Solanus Druck, 1962. This is the most recent critical edition of Caritas's major work.

———. Vol. 3. *Briefe von, an und über Caritas Pirckheimer aus den Jahren 1498–1530*. Ed. Josef Pfanner. Landshut: Solanus Druck, 1966. The correspondence of Caritas Pirckheimer, as well as letters to her and those in which she is mentioned by name. The letters are in Latin and German and those in Latin are accompanied by a German translation. The collection is especially valuable for the correspondence with her brother Willibald.

———. Vol. 4. *Das Grab der Caritas Pirckheimer*. Ed. Augustus Syndikus. Landshut: Solanus Druck, 1961. This short work details the discovery of Caritas's grave and the disinterment and removal of her remains to the right of the altar in St. Clare's.

Briefe der Äbtissin Caritas Pirckheimer des St.-Klara-Klosters. Ed. P. George Deichstetter. Trans. Benedicta Schrott. St. Ottilien: EOS Verlag, 1984. A modern German translation of letters by Caritas Pirckheimer. Valuable for scholars whose knowledge of sixteenth century German is limited.

An Heroic Abbess of Reformation Days: The Memoirs of Mother Caritas Pirckheimer, Poor Clare of Nuremberg. Trans. Francis Mannhardt. St. Louis: Catholic Verein of America, 1930. An incomplete translation of the *Denkwürdigkeiten*. The selection and notes reflect a strongly Roman Catholic viewpoint. For today's reader the language seems stilted and "dated."

Die Denkwürdigkeiten der Äbtissin Caritas Pirckheimer. Ed. Frumentius Renner. St. Ottilien: EOS Verlag, 1982. A more recent edition with some critical apparatus including examples of the manuscripts.

Die Denkwürdigkeiten der Äbtissin Caritas Pirckheinmer des St.-Klara-Klosters zu Nürnberg. Ed. Georg Deichstetter.Trans. Benedicta Schrott. St. Ottliien: EOS Verlag, 1983. A modern German translation of the *Denkwürdigkeiten*. Both this work and the previous one were published to commemorate the 450th anniversary of the death of Caritas Pirckheimer. It is a very helpful translation for those who can read German, but are not familiar with the language of the sixteenth century.

Secondary sources

Anzelewsky, Fedja. *Dürer: His Art and Life*. Trans. Heide Grieve. New York: Alpine Fine Arts Collections, Ltd., 1980. The standard work on Dürer.

Datsko Barker, Paula S. "A Mirror of Piety and Learning: Caritas Pirckheimer Against the Reformation." Ph.D. dissertation. University of Chicago Divinity School, 1990. The best recent examination of Caritas Pirckheimer. It enjoys all the advantages of the latest scholarship. In addition, it is very well-written and presents the most convincing argument of Caritas Pirckheimer as a representative of both humanistic and religious idealism.

————. "Caritas Pirckheimer: A Female Humanist Confronts the Reformation." *The Sixteenth Century Journal*, 26 (1995), 259–272. A study of Caritas Pirckheimer's humanistic background. The author presents an image of Caritas Pirckheimer as a sixteenth century proto-feminist who was forced to assume a major leadership role in a male-dominated society.

Deichstetter, George, ed. *Caritas Pirckheimer: Ordensfrau und Humanistin, ein Vorbild für die Ökumene. Festschrift zum 450. Todestag*. Cologne: Weinand Verlag, 1982. One of several studies written in 1982 to commemorate the 450th anniversary of Caritas Pirckheimer's death. An attempt to use the idealism of her life and works as a symbol to promote ecumenism.

Grafe, Joanne King. "Caritas Pirckheimer: Sixteenth Century Chronicler." Fordham University. 1997. A doctoral dissertation which examines Caritas Pirckheimer's *Chronicle* and relates it to her later activity as abbess when she compiled her *Denkwürdigkeiten* and defended her "reformed" cloister during the era of the Reformation.

Hutchison, Jane Campbell. *Albrecht Dürer: A Biography*. Princeton: Princeton University Press, 1990. A biography by a major Dürer scholar. Well-written and valuable to the specialist as well as the general reader.

Kist, Johannes. *Caritas Pirckheimer: Ein Frauenleben im Zeitalter des Humanismus und der Reformation*. Bamberg: Bamberg Verlagshaus Meisenbach & Co., 1948. The "standard" biography which has become very "dated" due to the considerable research of the last 50 years.

Krabbel, Gerta. *Caritas Pirckheimer. Ein Lebensbild aus der Zeit der Reformation* 5th ed. Münster: Aschendorff, 1982. A rather dated (originally published in 1940) but very detailed appreciation of Caritas Pirckheimer's life and works with a strong emphasis on her defense of her Roman Catholic faith.

Loewenich, Walter v. "Charitas Pirckheimer." *Jahrbuch für fränksiche Landesforschung*, Vol. 31 (1971), 35–51. A rather old, but well-written treatment of Caritas Pirckheimer's life and works.

MacKenzie, Paul A. "Piety and Patronage: Aspects of Nürnberg Cultural and Religious Life 1477–1526. Anton (II) Tucher and Veit Stoss." *Forum for Modern Language Studies*, 29 (1993), 41–61. An examination of the role of patronage as seen in the relationship of Anton (II.) Tucher and Veit Stoss whose "Englischer Gruß" was one of the last great examples of artistic patronage in sixteenth century Nürnberg.

Moeller, Bernd. *Imperial Cities and the Reformation*. Philadelphia: Fortress Press, 1972. A standard historical work which remains unsurpassed.

O'Collins, Gerald. " 'A Woman For All Seasons:' The Last Abbess of the Poor Clares of Nuremberg 450 Years after her Death." *America*, 147 (1982), 121–13. A short, rather partisan appreciation of Caritas Pirckheimer written to commemorate the 450th anniversary of her death. She was, of course, not the last abbess, but was succeeded by her niece.

Pfanner, Josef. "Caritas Pirckheimer." *Fränkische Lebensbilder*. Neue Folge der Lebensläufe aus Franken. Vol. 2. Würzburg: Kommisionsverlag Ferdinand Schöningh, 1968. pp. 193–215. A detailed, but largely uncritical biographical essay.

Pfeiffer, Gerhard. *Nürnberg – Geschichte einer europäischen Stadt*. Munich: Verlag C.H. Beck, 1971. An extensive (over 600 pages), collaborative work covering the earliest period to the post-war era. It has become the standard study of Nürnberg. Topics covered range from political, social, and economic history to cultural areas such as art, music, literature and theater. The list of authors reads like a veritable "Who's who" of Nürnberg scholars.

———, ed. *Geschichte Nürnbergs in Bilddokumenten*. 4th ed. Munich: Verlag C.H. Beck, 1996. A "picture book" originally published to complement Pfeiffer's *Nürnberg – Geschichte einer europäischen Stadt*. The text accompanying the illustrations is in German, English and French, although it should be noted that the English text is considerably shorter than the German. A useful work, but hardly on a scale to match Pfeiffer's earlier work.

Schlemmer, Karl. *Die frommen Nürnberger und die Äbtissin von St. Klara. (Nürnberg als religiöse Stadt in der Lebenszeit der Caritas Pirckheimer)*.A brief, sympathetic and thorough examination of sixteenth century Nürnberg and Caritas Pirckheimer by one of the most respected historians of that era.

Seebass, Gottfried. "The Reformation in Nuremberg" in *The Social History of the Reformation*. Ed. Lawrence Buck and Jonathan Zophy. Columbus: Ohio University Press, 1970. An excellent examination of the social background of the Reformation in sixteenth century Nürnberg by one of Germany's most respected scholars of that period.

Smith, Jeffrey Chipps. *Nuremberg: A Renaissance City, 1500 –1618*. Austin: University of Texas Press, 1983. Without question the most comprehensive study of sixteenth century Nürnberg in English. The introductory essays are supported by representative illustrations a well as extensive footnotes. The volume presents the works of many artists (only in black and white, however) ranging from Wolgemut to Dürer and Grien. Highly recommended for the general reader as well as the specialist.

Spitz, Lewis. *Conrad Celtis, the German Arch-Humanist*. Cambridge: Harvard University Press, 1957. The best study of Conrad Celtis in English by one of the foremost scholars of the period.

Strauss, Gerald. *Nuremberg in the Sixteenth Century*. Bloomington and London: Indiana University Press, 1976. Strauss's treatment of Nuremberg remains one of the best reference works in English. He treats history, politics, religion, the Reformation, daily life and learning and the arts. An indispensable work for layman and expert alike.

Ullmann, Ernst, ed. *Albrecht Dürer. Schriften und Briefe*. Leipzig, Reclam Verlag, 1993. A useful volume which contains Dürer's letters from Venice to Willibald Pirckheimer as well as letters to other prominent friends. Also included are Dürer's theoretical writings plus several illustrations (color, and black and white). Certainly no subsitute for Rupprich's three-volume critical edition, but a valuable reference tool.

Wailes, Stephen L. "The Literary Relationship of Conrad Celtis and Caritas Pirckheimer." *Daphnis*, 17 (1988), 423–40. A brief, but detailed critical study of Caritas Pirckheimer's relationship with the Poet Laureate Conrad Celtis.

Caritas Pirckheimer und die Reformation in Nürnberg. Impulse für die Ökumene heute. Erlangen: Druckerei Lengenfelder, 1991. A 62–page booklet distributed by the Caritas-Pirckheimer-Haus (in Nürnberg) containing the text of three lectures given on 17 March 1990. The first treats the history of the Reformation in Nürnberg 1520–1533. The other two discuss Melanchthon. A useful collection. The idea of using Caritas Pirckheimer's life and works as a catalyst for promoting ecumenism is well-taken, but does not appear to have born fruit.

Caritas Pirckheimer 1467–1532. Eine Ausstellung der Katholischen Stadtkirche Nürnberg. Kaiserburg Nürnberg 26 Juni – 8 August 1982. Munich: Prestel Verlag, 1982. Catalog of the most complete exhibition ever dedicated to Caritas Pirckheimer, on the 450th anniversary of her death. Essential for any serious study of Caritas Pirckheimer and her age.

Reformation in Nürnberg – Umbruch und Bewahrung. Ausstellung im Germanischen Nationalmuseum Nürnberg 12. Juni bis 2. September 1979 zu 18. Deutschen Evangelischen Kirchentag 1979. Nürnberg: Verlag Medien & Kultur, 1979. Exhibition catalog of a 1979 exhibit covering all aspects of the Reformation. Useful for the excellent essays as well as for the many paintings, woodcuts and documents included.

Martin Luther und die Reformation in Deutschland. Frankfurt am Main: Insel Verlag, 1983. Exhibition catalog of an exhibit in the Germanisches Nationalmuseum from 25 June to 25 September 1983 commemorating Luther's 500th birthday. An invaluable collection of documents, paintings, woodcuts etc. along with detailed analyses of the major figures and historical events of the period.

Gothic and Renaissance Art in Nuremberg 1300–1550. Munich: Prestel-Verlag, 1986. Exhibition catalog. Outstanding selection of art works of this period. Thoughtful essays on the imperial city of Nuremberg and its art.

Studies on women in the Reformation era

Bryant, Gwendolyn. "The Nuremberg Abbess Caritas Pirckheimer" in Katharine M. Wilson, *Women Writers of the Renaissance and Reformation.* Athens: University of Georgia Press, 1987, pp. 287–303. Following a short biographical sketch, the author presents a translation of a letter by Caritas Pirckheimer to Conrad Celtis. The study ends with a translation of one of the most dramatic passages in the whole journal, the forced removal of three nuns from the convent. An outstanding introduction to Caritas Pirckheimer's life and works.

Harris, Barbara J. "A New Look at the Reformation: Aristocratic Women and Nunneries, 1450–1540," *Journal of British Studies*, 32 (1993), 89–113. An important study of the impact the closing of the monasteries had on the spirituality of women.

Wiesner, Merry. *Women and Gender in Early Modern Europe*. New York: Cambridge University Press, 1996. A significant historical study by one of the leading figures in women's studies. Among other things the author shows how the Reformation brought about "new roles" for women. She shows that many more convents than male monasteries survived in Germany.

———. "Ideology Meets the Empire: Reformed Convents and the Reformation," in *Germania Illustrata. Essays on Early Modern Germany Presented to Gerald Strauss*. Ed. Andrew C. Fix and Susan C. Kerant-Nunn. Sixteenth Century Essays and Studies 18 (Lirksville: Sixteenth Century Journal, 1992), 181–196. An examination of seventeen German abbeys and their powerful abbesses who managed to overcome traditional limits of gender and religious ideology. Caritas Pirckheimer is not included in this study, however.

Index

Library of Medieval Women

Already published